# Parallel MATLAB

## for Multicore and Multinode Computers

# SOFTWARE • ENVIRONMENTS • TOOLS

The SIAM series on Software, Environments, and Tools focuses on the practical implementation of computational methods and the high performance aspects of scientific computation by emphasizing in-demand software, computing environments, and tools for computing. Software technology development issues such as current status, applications and algorithms, mathematical software, software tools, languages and compilers, computing environments, and visualization are presented.

## Software, Environments, and Tools

Jeremy Kepner, *Parallel MATLAB for Multicore and Multinode Computers*

Michael A. Heroux, Padma Raghavan, and Horst D. Simon, editors, *Parallel Processing for Scientific Computing*

Gérard Meurant, *The Lanczos and Conjugate Gradient Algorithms: From Theory to Finite Precision Computations*

Bo Einarsson, editor, *Accuracy and Reliability in Scientific Computing*

Michael W. Berry and Murray Browne, *Understanding Search Engines: Mathematical Modeling and Text Retrieval, Second Edition*

Craig C. Douglas, Gundolf Haase, and Ulrich Langer, *A Tutorial on Elliptic PDE Solvers and Their Parallelization*

Louis Komzsik, *The Lanczos Method: Evolution and Application*

Bard Ermentrout, *Simulating, Analyzing, and Animating Dynamical Systems: A Guide to XPPAUT for Researchers and Students*

V. A. Barker, L. S. Blackford, J. Dongarra, J. Du Croz, S. Hammarling, M. Marinova, J. Waśniewski, and P. Yalamov, *LAPACK95 Users' Guide*

Stefan Goedecker and Adolfy Hoisie, *Performance Optimization of Numerically Intensive Codes*

Zhaojun Bai, James Demmel, Jack Dongarra, Axel Ruhe, and Henk van der Vorst, *Templates for the Solution of Algebraic Eigenvalue Problems: A Practical Guide*

Lloyd N. Trefethen, *Spectral Methods in MATLAB*

E. Anderson, Z. Bai, C. Bischof, S. Blackford, J. Demmel, J. Dongarra, J. Du Croz, A. Greenbaum, S. Hammarling, A. McKenney, and D. Sorensen, *LAPACK Users' Guide, Third Edition*

Michael W. Berry and Murray Browne, *Understanding Search Engines: Mathematical Modeling and Text Retrieval*

Jack J. Dongarra, Iain S. Duff, Danny C. Sorensen, and Henk A. van der Vorst, *Numerical Linear Algebra for High-Performance Computers*

R. B. Lehoucq, D. C. Sorensen, and C. Yang, *ARPACK Users' Guide: Solution of Large-Scale Eigenvalue Problems with Implicitly Restarted Arnoldi Methods*

Randolph E. Bank, *PLTMG: A Software Package for Solving Elliptic Partial Differential Equations, Users' Guide 8.0*

L. S. Blackford, J. Choi, A. Cleary, E. D'Azevedo, J. Demmel, I. Dhillon, J. Dongarra, S. Hammarling, G. Henry, A. Petitet, K. Stanley, D. Walker, and R. C. Whaley, *ScaLAPACK Users' Guide*

Greg Astfalk, editor, *Applications on Advanced Architecture Computers*

Roger W. Hockney, *The Science of Computer Benchmarking*

Françoise Chaitin-Chatelin and Valérie Frayssé, *Lectures on Finite Precision Computations*

# Parallel MATLAB

## for Multicore and Multinode Computers

Jeremy Kepner

Massachusetts Institute of Technology
Lexington, Massachusetts

Society for Industrial and Applied Mathematics
Philadelphia

Chapters 5 and 7 are based on work previously published as "pMATLAB Parallel MATLAB Library." The final, definitive version of this paper has been published in the *International Journal of High Performance Computing Applications*, Special Issue on High Productivity Languages and Models, J. Kepner and H. Zima, eds., Volume 21, Issue 3, pages 336–359 (August 2007) by SAGE Publications, Ltd. All rights reserved. © SAGE Publications. The article is available from SAGE Journals Online at *http://hpc.sagepub.com/cgi/content/abstract/21/3/336*.

Chapter 6 is based on work previously published as "Performance Metrics and Software Architecture," by J. Kepner, T. Meuse, and G. Schrader, in *High Performance Embedded Computing Handbook*, D. R. Martinez, R. A. Bond, and M. M. Vai, eds., CRC Press, 2008. © Taylor & Francis Group LLC.

Figure 6.12 is based on Figure 4.4 on page 109 from *High Performance Computing: Challenges for Future Systems* by David Kuck (1996). It is used by permission of Oxford University Press. Visit *http://www.oup.com*.

This work is sponsored by the Department of the Air Force under Air Force Contract FA8721-05-C-0002. Opinions, interpretations, conclusions, and recommendations are those of the author and are not necessarily endorsed by the United States Government.

**Library of Congress Cataloging-in-Publication Data**

Kepner, Jeremy.
  Parallel MATLAB for multicore and multinode computers / Jeremy Kepner.
      p. cm. — (Software, environments, and tools ; 21)
  Includes index.
  ISBN 978-0-898716-73-3
  1. Parallel processing (Electronic computers)  2. MATLAB.  3. Multiprocessors.  I. Title.
  QA76.58.K46 2009
  004'.35—dc22
                                                                                        2009013013

 is a registered trademark.

For
Jemma
Alix
Clay
Diane
and
Gordon

# Contents

# List of Figures

# List of Tables

# List of Algorithms

# Preface

MATLAB® is currently the dominant language of technical computing with approximately one million users worldwide, many of whom can benefit from the increased power offered by widely available multicore processors and multinode computing clusters. MATLAB is also an ideal environment for learning about parallel computing, allowing the user to focus on parallel algorithms instead of the details of the implementation. The succinctness of MATLAB allows many specific examples to be presented to illustrate parallel programming concepts.

The subject of this book is parallel programming in MATLAB and is hopefully the first of many books on this topic, as there are now a wide variety of parallel MATLAB libraries [Choy 2004] for users to choose from. I am fortunate to have been involved in the development of two of these libraries [Kepner 2004, Kepner 2003]. The most widely used of these libraries include pMatlab (developed by MIT Lincoln Laboratory), the Parallel Computing Toolbox (developed by The MathWorks, Inc.), and StarP (developed at MIT, UCSB, and Interactive Supercomputing, Inc.). All of these libraries provide direct support for parallel computing using distributed arrays and other parallel programming models. The specific examples in this book are written using the freely available pMatlab library. pMatlab has the advantage of running either standalone or on top of the aforementioned parallel MATLAB libraries. So all the examples in the book can be run in any of the parallel MATLAB environments. Fortunately, the concepts illustrated in the book are independent of the underlying implementation and valid for any particular parallel programming syntax the user may prefer to use. The software along with installation instructions can be found at the book website:

http://www.siam.org/KepnerBook

The expressive power of MATLAB allows us to concentrate on the techniques for creating parallel programs that run well (as opposed to the syntactic mechanics of writing parallel programs). Our primary focus is on the designing, coding, debugging, and testing techniques required to quickly produce well-performing parallel programs in a matter of hours instead of weeks or months (see Figure 1). These techniques have been developed over the years through thousands of one-on-one interactions with hundreds of parallel MATLAB users.

A general familiarity with MATLAB is assumed (see [Higham & Higham 2005] and [Moler 2004] for an introduction to MATLAB). The target audience of the book

xix

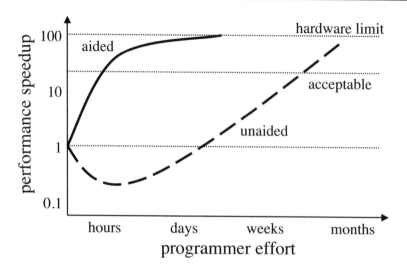

**Figure 1. Performance versus effort.**
Depiction of the performance achieved versus the user effort invested for
a typical parallel MATLAB program. The bottom curve shows the effort
required for an unaided user. The top curve shows the effort required
for a user aided with expert assistance.

is anyone who needs to adapt their serial MATLAB program to a parallel environment. In addition, this book is suitable as either the primary book in a parallel computing class or as a supplementary text in a numerical computing class or a computer science algorithms class. Ideas are presented using a "hands-on" approach with numerous example programs. Wherever possible, the examples are drawn from widely known and well-documented parallel benchmark codes that have already been identified as representing many applications (although the connection to any particular application may require examining the references). For historical reasons, most of the examples are drawn from the technical computing domain, but an understanding of numerical methods is *not* required in order to use the examples. They are simply convenient and well-documented examples of different types of parallel programming.

The book is organized around two central concepts: the core programming process (i.e., design, code, debug, and test) and the core parallel programming models (i.e., distributed arrays, manager/worker, and message passing) [Lusk 2004]. The distributed array programming model will be the baseline programming model used throughout the book. Distributed arrays are easiest to understand, require the least amount of code to use, and are well-matched to the array nature of MATLAB. Distributed arrays allow very complicated communication patterns to be illustrated far more simply than with a message passing approach and perform well on both multicore and multinode parallel computers. In addition, distributed arrays naturally illustrate the core parallel design concepts of concurrency and locality. Distributed arrays are sufficient for 90% of parallel applications, but there are instances where other programming models are optimal and these are discussed where appropriate. The ultimate goal of this book is teach the reader to "think [distributed] matrices, not messages" [Moler 2005].

Throughout the book the approach is to first present concrete examples and then discuss in detail the more general parallel programming concepts these examples illustrate. The book aims to bring these ideas to bear on the specific challenge of writing parallel programs in MATLAB.

To accommodate the different types of readers, the book is organized into three parts. Part I (Chapters 1–3) provides a general conceptual overview of the key programming concepts illustrated by specific examples. Part II (Chapters 4–6) focuses on the analysis techniques of effective parallel programming. Part III (Chapters 7–11) consists of specific case studies. Parts I, II, and III can be treated independently and may be used as modules in a larger course. Finally, in recognition of the severe time constraints of professional users, each chapter is mostly self-contained and key terms are redefined as needed. Each chapter has a short summary and references within that chapter are listed at the end of the chapter. This arrangement allows the professional user to pick up and use any particular chapter as needed.

Chapter 1 begins by introducing some notation and the basic parallel programming interfaces used throughout the rest of the book. Chapter 2 provides a rapid introduction to creating and running simple parallel programs. Chapter 2 is meant to give readers a taste of the ease of use that parallel MATLAB provides. Chapter 3 focuses on a more complex example and highlights interacting with distributed arrays. Chapter 4 is a broad overview of the field of parallel programming, exposing the key principles that will be covered in more detail in the rest of the book. Chapter 4 uses a more sophisticated example than that used in Chapter 3, exposing the boundaries of the different parallel programming models. In addition, Chapter 4 introduces several key questions that must be dealt with in parallel programming:

Design: when to use parallel processing, concurrency versus locality, how to predict parallel performance, which parallel programming model to use: distributed arrays, client/server, or message passing.

Code: how and where to use parallel code, how to write scalable code (e.g., scalable file I/O), good coding style.

Debug: what the techniques are for going from a serial to a fully parallel execution, what kind of errors to check for at each stage along the way.

Test: how to measure performance achieved and compare with what is predicted.

Chapter 5 introduces the theory, algorithmic notation, and an "under the hood" view of distributed array programming. Chapter 6 discusses metrics for evaluating performance and coding of a parallel program. Chapter 7 is a selected survey of parallel application analysis techniques, with a particular emphasis on how the examples used in the book relate to many wider application domains. Chapters 8–11 use a set of well-studied examples drawn from the HPC Challenge benchmark suite (see http://www.hpcchallenge.org) to show detailed solutions to the challenges raised by parallel design, coding, debugging, and testing.

Throughout this book we draw upon numerous classical parallel programming examples that have been well studied and characterized in the literature. It is my hope that in seeing these examples worked out the reader will come to appreciate the elegance of parallel programming in MATLAB as much as I have.

# References

[Choy 2004] Ron Choy, Parallel Matlab survey, 2004, http://supertech.lcs.mit.edu/~cly/survey.html

[Higham & Higham 2005] Desmond J. Higham and Nicholas J. Higham, MATLAB Guide, Second Edition, SIAM, Philadelphia, 2005.

[Kepner 2004] Jeremy Kepner and Stan Ahalt, MatlabMPI, Journal of Parallel and Distributed Computing, Vol. 64, No. 8, pp. 997–1005, 2004.

[Kepner 2003] Jeremy Kepner and Nadya Travinin, Parallel Matlab: The Next Generation, Seventh Annual High Performance Embedded Computing Workshop (HPEC 2003), September 23–25, 2003, MIT Lincoln Laboratory, Lexington, MA, http://www.ll.mit.edu/HPEC/agenda03.htm

[Lusk 2004] Ewing Lusk and Marc Snir, Parallel Programming Models, DARPA HPCS Productivity Team Workshop, January 13–14, 2004, Marina Del Ray, CA.

[Moler 2004] Cleve Moler, Numerical Computing with MATLAB, SIAM, Philadelphia, 2004.

[Moler 2005] Cleve Moler, Householder Meeting on Numerical Linear Algebra, Champion, PA, May 23–27, 2005.

# Acknowledgments

There are many individuals to whom I am indebted for making parallel MATLAB and this book a reality. It is not possible to mention them all, and I would like to apologize in advance to those I may not have mentioned here due to accidental oversight on my part.

The development of parallel MATLAB has been a journey that has involved many colleagues who have made important contributions along the way. This book marks an important milestone in that journey: the broad availability and acceptance of parallel MATLAB. At a more technical level, this milestone signifies the broad availability and acceptance of the merger of the distributed array parallel programming model with high level languages such as MATLAB.

My own part in this journey has been aided by numerous individuals along the way who have directly influenced the content of this book. My introduction to numerical computing began at Pomona College in a freshman seminar taught by Prof. Wayne Steinmetz and was further encouraged by my undergraduate advisors Profs. Catalin Mitescu and Robert Chambers.

In the summer of 1990 I worked at the Aerospace Corporation, where I was introduced to high-level array languages by Dr. John Hackwell. This was followed by my first experience with parallel computation in the fall of 1990 provided by Prof. Alexandre Chorin at UC Berkeley [Kepner 1990]. Since that time I have worked to bring these two capabilities together. My first opportunity to do so occurred in 1997 when I worked with Dr. Maya Gokhale and Mr. Ron Minnich [Kepner et al. 1998]. This work was encouraged at Princeton University by my Ph.D. advisor Prof. David Spergel.

In 1998 I joined MIT Lincoln Laboratory, where Mr. Robert Bond was leading a team developing one of the first distributed array libraries in C++ [Rutledge & Kepner 1999]. In the spring of 2001, at the encouragement of Prof. Stan Ahalt, I wrote MatlabMPI in one week [Kepner 2001]. It's first user was Dr. Gil Raz. MatlabMPI, although difficult to use, developed a following at Lincoln and Ohio State (thanks to the efforts of Prof. Ashok Krishnamurthy and Dr. John Nehrbass).

In the summer of 2001 I was first exposed to the StarP work of Profs. Alan Edelman and John Gilbert and their students Dr. Perry Husbands, Mr. Ron Choy, and Dr. Viral Shaw [Husbands 1999]. At this point I realized the distributed array concepts developed in C++ libraries could be brought to MATLAB with MatlabMPI underneath. From this concept Ms. Nadya Bliss created the pMatlab

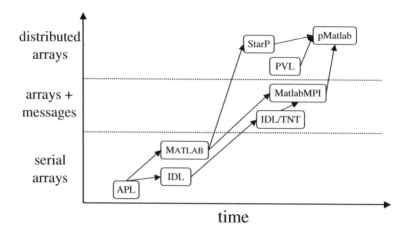

**Figure 2. Development of parallel MATLAB.**
A selected view of the evolution of some of the technologies that led to
the development of pMatlab beginning with the first interactive array
based language APL and ending with the current pMatlab library.

library [Kepner & Bliss 2003], which when coupled with the interactive LLGrid concept developed with Dr. Albert Reuther and Mr. Andrew McCabe became very popular at Lincoln [Reuther et al. 2004]. This early parallel MATLAB work was supported internally by Mr. David Martinez and externally by Mr. John Grosh.

Over the next few years I had the opportunity to interact closely with Dr. Cleve Moler and many others at The MathWorks as they brought parallel MATLAB out of the laboratory and made it into a product.

At the same time, I was also involved in the development of a suite of new parallel benchmarks designed to test new parallel architectures and parallel languages. The HPC Challenge benchmark suite was developed with Prof. Jack Dongarra, Dr. Piotr Luszczek, and Dr. Bob Lucas [Luszczek et al. 2006]. Mr. Andrew Funk, Mr. Ryan Haney, Mr. Hahn Kim, Dr. Julia Mullin, Mr. Charlie Rader, as well as many of the aforementioned individuals contributed to the parallel MATLAB implementations of these benchmarks. This later parallel MATLAB work was supported internally by Dr. Ken Senne and externally by Mr. Robert Graybil.

A visual depiction of this particular technology thread leading to pMatlab is shown in Figure 2.

In addition to those folks who have helped with the development of the technology, many additional folks have helped with the development of this book. Among these are my editor at SIAM, Ms. Elizabeth Greenspan, my copy editor at Lincoln, Ms. Dorothy Ryan, and the students in the spring 2008 MIT Applied Parallel Computing course. Finally, I would like to thank several anonymous reviewers whose comments enhanced this book.

# References

[Husbands 1999] Parry Husbands, Interactive Supercomputing, 1999, Ph.D. Thesis, MIT, Cambridge, MA.

[Kepner 1990] Jeremy Kepner, Comparison of Canonical and Micro-Canonical Sampling Methods in a 2D Ising Model, 1990, Lawrence Berkeley Lab report LBL-30056.

[Kepner et al. 1998] J. Kepner, M. Gokhale, R. Minnich, A. Marks & J. DeGood, Interfacing Interpreted and Compiled Languages for Computing on a Massively Parallel Network of Workstations (MP-NOW), HPEC98, September 23–24, 1998, MIT Lincoln Laboratory, Lexington, MA.

[Kepner 2001] J. Kepner, Parallel Programing with MatlabMPI, HPEC 2001, September 25–27, 2001, MIT Lincoln Laboratory, Lexington, MA.

[Kepner & Bliss 2003] Jeremy Kepner & Nadya Travinin Bliss, Parallel Matlab: The Next Generation, 7th High Performance Embedded Computing Workshop (HPEC 2003), September 23–25, 2003, MIT Lincoln Laboratory, Lexington, MA.

[Luszczek et al. 2006] P. Luszczek, J. Dongarra & J. Kepner, Design and Implementation of the HPC Challenge Benchmark Suite, CT Watch, Vol. 2, Number 4A, November 2006.

[Reuther et al. 2004] A. Reuther, T. Currie, J. Kepner, H. Kim, A. McCabe, M. Moore & N. Travinin Bliss, On Demand Grid Computing with Grid Matlab and pMatlab, DOD HPCMP User's Group Conference 2004, June 8, Williamsburg, VA.

[Rutledge & Kepner 1999] Eddie Rutledge & Jeremy Kepner, PVL: An Object Oriented Software Library for Parallel Signal Processing, Cluster 2001, October 9, 2001, Newport Beach, CA.

# Part I

# Fundamentals

# Chapter 1

# Primer: Notation and Interfaces

**Summary**

The mathematical notation for describing parallel algorithms is introduced, and a corresponding set of parallel functions found in the pMatlab library are also described. The map-based parallel programming style using these functions is presented, and a simple example is given using the parallel notation and these functions.

This book deals with parallel programming and requires a way to succinctly describe parallel algorithms. The language used to describe these algorithms will be that of mathematics. This chapter gives a brief introduction to some of the core mathematical notation used to describe parallel algorithms in the rest of the book. This notation will be augmented (as necessary) over the course of the book (see the appendix for a more exhaustive description of this notation).

Implementing these algorithms in MATLAB requires a set of parallel functions that corresponds to the parallel algorithms. While it is assumed the reader is familiar with MATLAB, the functions used to write parallel MATLAB programs are new. This book is written using a restricted subset of the pMatlab interface. This chapter gives a brief introduction to some of the core functions used to write parallel algorithms in the rest of the book. These functions will be expanded (as necessary) through the course of the book.

## 1.1 Algorithm notation

Numbers are the fundamental units that will be manipulated by the algorithms presented in this book. These numbers can be of a variety of types: boolean, integer, real, complex, .... The notation used to specify these types is as follows:

| Type | Name | Examples |
|------|------|----------|
| Boolean | $\mathbb{B}$ | true (1), false (0) |
| Integer | $\mathbb{Z}$ | $-5, 0, 1, 3$ |
| Real | $\mathbb{R}$ | $5, 6.2, -3.8, 0.37$ |
| Complex | $\mathbb{C}$ | $5 + 6.2\sqrt{-1}$ |

MATLAB is an array language, and much of its power is derived from its ability to work on collections of numbers in various dimensions. In particular, it is convenient to work with scalars, vectors, matrices, and tensors. These will be denoted as the following:

| Dim | Name | Notation | Example |
|-----|------|----------|---------|
| 0 | Scalar | lowercase | $a : \mathbb{R}$ |
| 1 | Vector | boldface lowercase | $\mathbf{a} : \mathbb{R}^N$ |
| 2 | Matrix | boldface capital | $\mathbf{A} : \mathbb{R}^{N \times N}$ |
| 3 | Tensor | boldface capital script | $\mathcal{A} : \mathbb{R}^{N \times N \times N}$ |

To denote subarrays, standard MATLAB notation will be used. For example,

$$a = \mathbf{a}(i), \quad \mathbf{a} = \mathbf{A}(i, :), \quad \mathbf{A} = \mathcal{A}(i, :, :)$$

Likewise, the standard MATLAB notation for element-wise addition ($+$), subtraction ($-$), multiplication ($.*$), and division ($./$) will be used. Using this notation, a simple algorithm for adding one to a matrix can be written as Algorithm 1.1.

**Algorithm 1.1.  Add one serial.**

$\mathbf{Y} : \mathbb{R}^{N \times N} = \textsc{AddOneSerial}(\mathbf{X} : \mathbb{R}^{N \times N})$
1   $\mathbf{Y} = \mathbf{X} + 1$

## 1.1.1   Distributed array notation

Describing parallel algorithms requires some additional notation. In particular, the number of copies or instances of the program running is given by $N_P$. When an algorithm is run in parallel, the same algorithm (or code) is run by every instance of the program. This is referred to as the Single-Program Multiple-Data (SPMD) computation model [Flynn 1972, Darema 1984]. To differentiate the $N_P$ programs, each program is assigned a unique processor ID denoted $P_{ID}$, which ranges from 0 to $N_P - 1$. These $P_{ID}$s could have been launched onto a wide variety of computing systems. For example, suppose the $N_P$ instances of the program are run on a multinode parallel computer containing $N_P$ nodes, so that each node is running one $P_{ID}$. This type of execution will be denoted by $N_P*1$. Another common situation is to run all the $P_{ID}$s on just one node. This type of execution will be denoted using the notation $1*N_P$. If the node is a multicore node, there is potential for the program to be accelerated. If the node has just one core, the program is unlikely to be accelerated, but this is still a very useful scenario for parallel debugging and testing purposes. Note: $N_P$ denotes how many $P_{ID}$s are created independent of how many physical nodes or cores there are. Finally, $(N_P/4)*4$ can be used to indicate the hybrid situation where $N_P/4$ nodes are each running four $P_{ID}$s. Throughout the course of the book the multicore performance $(1*N_P)$ and the multinode performance $(N_P*1)$ will be explored. Fortunately, the distributed arrays model can work as well as the underlying hardware will allow in both cases, and the same programming model can be used for both multicore and multinode systems. This is one of the main benefits of distributed array programming.

In distributed array programming, it is necessary to map the elements of an array onto a set of $P_{ID}$s. This mapping process describes the indices of a distributed array each $P_{ID}$ "owns." "P notation" provides a convenient shorthand for describing this mapping [Choy & Edelman 1999]. A matrix that is mapped such that each $P_{ID}$ has a block of rows is denoted

$$\mathbf{A} : \mathbb{R}^{P(N) \times N}$$

Likewise, a matrix that is mapped such that each $P_{ID}$ has a block of columns is given by

$$\mathbf{A} : \mathbb{R}^{N \times P(N)}$$

Decomposing along both rows and columns can be written as

$$\mathbf{A} : \mathbb{R}^{P(N) \times P(N)} \quad \text{or} \quad \mathbf{A} : \mathbb{R}^{P(N \times N)}$$

In this instance, it is also necessary to specify a $P_{ID}$ grid (e.g., $N_P/4 \times 4$). These different distributions are illustrated in Figure 1.1.

### 1.1.2 Distributed data access

Accessing a particular data element in a distributed array is given by the usual subarray notation. If $\mathbf{A} : \mathbb{R}^{P(N) \times N}$, then $\mathbf{A}(i,j)$ will cause the $P_{ID}$ that owns the $i, j$ element of $\mathbf{A}$ to send this value to all the other $P_{ID}$s. Similarly, given two matrices with different mappings $\mathbf{A} : \mathbb{R}^{P(N) \times N}$ and $\mathbf{B} : \mathbb{R}^{N \times P(N)}$, the statement

$$\mathbf{B} = \mathbf{A}$$

will cause the data to be remapped from $\mathbf{A}$ into the new mapping of $\mathbf{B}$.

Access to just the local part of a distributed array is denoted by the .loc appendage. For $\mathbf{A} : \mathbb{R}^{P(N) \times N}$ the local part is $\mathbf{A}.loc : \mathbb{R}^{(N/N_P) \times N}$. This notation is very useful when specifying operations that are entirely local to each $P_{ID}$ and require no communication. Using this notation, a simple parallel algorithm for adding one to a matrix can be written as Algorithm 1.2.

**Algorithm 1.2. Add one parallel.**
$\mathbf{Y} : \mathbb{R}^{P(N) \times N} = \text{ADDONEPARALLEL}(\mathbf{X} : \mathbb{R}^{P(N) \times N})$
1   $\mathbf{Y}.loc = \mathbf{X}.loc + 1$

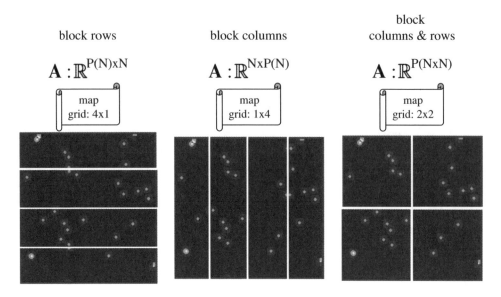

**Figure 1.1. Parallel maps.**
A selection of maps that are typically supported in a distributed array
programming environment.

## 1.2   Parallel function interfaces

The previous section described some of the parallel algorithm operations that are
necessary to write parallel programs. To actually implement these requires corresponding parallel functions. This book is written using a subset of pMatlab functions. This list of pMatlab functions will be expanded upon over the course of the
book. The functions can be broken up into a few groups.

**Parallel run time parameters**. These functions provide information about
the overall parallel environment running the program.

Np  A function returning the total number of MATLAB instances currently running
the program (i.e., $N_P$). Usage:
Np;

Pid  A function returning the identity of each MATLAB currently running the program (i.e., $P_{ID}$). Takes on a value of 0 on the first MATLAB instance and
increases to Np-1 on the last MATLAB instance. Usage:
pID;

**Distributed array construction**. These functions allow distributed arrays
to be constructed and used. When used correctly, none of these functions should
ever incur any communication between each MATLAB instance.

`map([Np 1],{},0:Np-1)` Construct a one-dimensional map that will map an array along the 1st dimension. Usage:
`Amap = map([Np 1],{},0:Np-1));`

`map([1 Np],{},0:Np-1)` Construct a one-dimensional map that will map an array along the 2nd dimension. Usage:
`Amap = map([Np 1],{},0:Np-1));`

`zeros(N1,...,map)` Overloaded `zeros` function that constructs a distributed array with a distribution specified by `map`. Usage:
`A = zeros(200,100,Amap);`

`local(A)` Returns the local part of a distributed array as a regular MATLAB numeric array. Usage:
`Aloc = local(A);`

`global_ind(A,dim)` Returns a list of global indices that are local to `Pid` along the specified `dim`. Usage:
`myI = global_ind(A,1);`

`put_local(A,Aloc)` Copies a regular MATLAB numeric array into the local part of a distributed array. Usage:
`A = put_local(A,Aloc);`

**Distributed array remapping**. These functions allow the mapping of a distributed array to be changed. These functions almost always incur communication between $P_{ID}$s.

`=` Assign data from one distributed array to another. Usage:
`B(:,:) = A;`

`agg(A)` Copy the entire contents of a distributed array to a regular MATLAB numeric array on the "leader" $P_{ID}$ (i.e., `Pid == 0`). Usage:
`Aagg = agg(A);`

**Point-to-point communication**. Underlying all of the above functions are the functions that provide point-to-point communication between MATLAB instances. These functions should be used only when absolutely necessary since they result in programs that are difficult to debug.

`SendMsg(dest,tag,var1,var2,...)` Sends the specified variables `var1`, `var2`, ... to the MATLAB instance designated by `Pid == dest`. The message is tagged with `tag`, which is typically a numeric value from 1 to 256. Usage:
`SendMsg(2,9,pi,i);`

`RecvMsg(source,tag)` Receives the variables sent by MATLAB with `Pid == source` with corresponding `tag`. Usage:
`[pi i] = RecvMsg(1,9);`

## 1.2.1   Map-based programming

The above relatively short list of functions is all that is necessary to implement a wide variety of parallel programs. The challenge is to implement parallel programs that are easy to code, debug, and test and give high performance. This book uses "map-based" programming [Lebak et al. 2005], which adopts a separation-of-concerns approach that seeks to make the algorithm and how it is mapped to the parallel processor orthogonal.

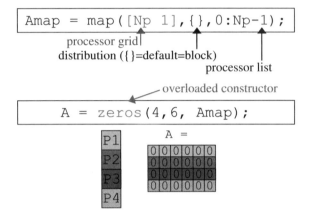

**Figure 1.2. Anatomy of a map.**
A map for a numerical array creates an assignment of array indices to processors. It consists of a processor grid, a distribution description, and a list of processor IDs. An overloaded constructor uses a map to create a distributed array.

Parallel maps contain only information about how an array is broken up onto multiple $P_{ID}$s, and the addition of a map should not change the functional correctness of a program. A map (see Figure 1.2) contains a description of how array indices are mapped to a set of $P_{ID}$s. In addition, it requires corresponding array constructors that use the map to create distributed arrays. An example of this style of programming is shown for the simple AddOne program in Code Listing 1.1 (see also Examples/AddOne/pAddOne.m).

Listing ID: 0830M86GYCX
Order-Item ID: 55662750872803
Condition: New
Comments: Brand new in perfect condition. All items sent by Royal Mail or DPD courier depending on weight and destination.

**Thanks for buying on Amazon Marketplace.** To provide feedback for the seller please visit www.amazon.co.uk/feedback. To contact the seller, please visit Amazon.co.uk and click on "Your Account" at the top of any page. In Your Account, go to the "Orders" section and click on the link "Leave seller feedback". Select the order or click on the "View Order" button. Click on the "seller profile" under the appropriate product. On the lower right side of the page under "Seller Help", click on "Contact this seller".

Dispatch to:

**Samantha Simons**
**61 Molewood Close**
**CAMBRIDGE**
**Cambs**
**CB4 3SR**
**United Kingdom**

**Order ID: 026-5638479-9894724**

Thank you for buying from academicbookshopuk on Amazon Marketplace.

**Delivery address:**
Samantha Simons
61 Molewood Close
CAMBRIDGE
Cambs
CB4 3SR
United Kingdom

| | |
|---|---|
| Order Date: | 17 Sep 2012 |
| Shipping Service: | Standard |
| Buyer Name: | Samantha Simons |
| Seller Name: | academicbookshopuk |

| Quantity | Product Details |
|---|---|

**Code Listing 1.1. Add one parallel MATLAB program.**

```
1  N = 100;                    % Set matrix size.
2  XYmap = map([Np 1],{},0:Np-1);   % Create parallel map.
3  X = zeros(N,N,XYmap);       % Create distributed X.
4  Y = zeros(N,N,XYmap);       % Create distributed Y.
5  Xloc = local(X);            % Get local part of X.
6  Yloc = local(Y);            % Get local part of Y.
7  Yloc = Xloc + 1;            % Add one to local part.
8  Y = put_local(Y,Yloc);      % Put back into Y.
```

In the above program, line 2 creates a map to decompose an array in the first dimension. Lines 3 and 4 use this map to create corresponding distributed arrays. Lines 5 and 6 get the local parts of these distributed arrays. Line 7 performs the computation on the local parts. Line 8 puts the local result back into the distributed array. This style of programming will be applied to most of the examples throughout the rest of the book. The primary advantage of this style of programming is that it lends itself to a very well-defined code-debug-test process that allows well-performing parallel programs to be written quickly.

## 1.2.2 Parallel execution

Once the mathematical notation and parallel functions necessary to specify and implement a parallel MATLAB program have been defined, it is time to run the program. The pRUN utility program accompanying the software in this book is used to execute a MATLAB script on multiple instances of MATLAB (see installation instructions at the book website: http://www.siam.org/KepnerBook). For example, go to the Examples/AddOne directory (e.g., cd Examples/AddOne), start MATLAB, and type

```
eval(pRUN('pAddOne',2,{}))
```

This will run the pAddOne program by starting two instances of MATLAB on the local node. This execution would be denoted by 1*2 in the aforementioned notation. What happens during this execution is shown in Figure 1.3. When a parallel program is run, it creates $N_P$ (or Np) copies of the same program. Each copy has a unique $P_{ID}$ (or Pid). Distributed arrays implicitly use the $P_{ID}$ to determine which parts belong to which processors. Finally, when the program completes all the MATLAB instances shut down and exit.

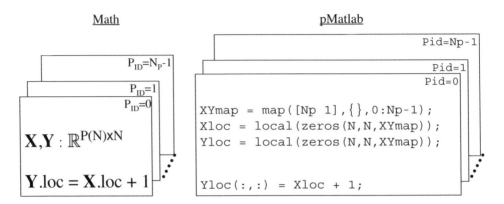

**Figure 1.3. Parallel execution.**
Math and MATLAB code running in parallel create $N_P$ (or Np) copies
of the same program. Each copy has a unique $P_{ID}$ (or Pid).

# References

[Choy & Edelman 1999] Ron Choy and Alan Edelman, Parallel MATLAB: Doing
it right, Proceedings of the IEEE (Feb. 2005), Vol. 93, No. 2, pp. 331–341.

[Darema 1984] Francis Darema, IBM Memo, 1984.

[Flynn 1972] Michael Flynn, Some computer organizations and their effectiveness,
IEEE Trans. Comput., Vol. C-21, p. 948, 1972.

[Lebak et al. 2005] James Lebak, Jeremy Kepner, Henry Hoffmann, and Edward
Rutledge, Parallel VSIPL++: An open standard software library for high-
performance parallel signal processing, Proceedings of the IEEE (Feb. 2005),
Vol. 93, No. 2, pp. 313–330.

# Chapter 2

# Introduction to pMatlab

**Summary**

Several example parallel MATLAB programs are presented and run. The map-based programming approach and its corresponding design-code-debug-test process is employed in each of these example applications. A Mandelbrot set calculation is used to demonstrate a fine-grained embarrassingly parallel application. The ZoomImage application is used to show a coarse-grained embarrassingly parallel program. The ParallelIO program shows how to read and write files from multiple processors.

Welcome to parallel programming in MATLAB. By the end of this chapter, you will have successfully run and demonstrated the performance benefits of several parallel MATLAB programs. This chapter quickly walks through several programs that give a feel for writing and running a variety of parallel programs. Each example is self-contained and can be explored independently. [**Note**: to run these examples requires that the example programs and the underlying parallel software be installed. Please see the book website (http://www.siam.org/KepnerBook) for installation instructions.] The subsequent sections are presented in a similar manner. Each section begins with a "getting started" subsection in which the program is run on a number of different processors, the output is examined, and the execution time is recorded. In the second subsection, the mathematics of the problem are presented along with a basic parallel design. The third subsection is a look at how the parallel MATLAB program was written. The fourth subsection is a walk through the process of debugging the program. Finally, the timing results are examined in context and the overall performance is assessed. This chapter concludes with a discussion of why these programs worked and showed good performance results.

# 2.1   Program: Mandelbrot (fine-grained embarrassingly parallel)

A very common application of parallel computing is running the same program over and over again but with slightly different input parameters. The programs are usually referred to as "embarrassingly parallel" (or "pleasingly parallel") because the programs can be run independently and don't require that the programs interact while they run [Moler 1985]. Of course, there is nothing embarrassing about these programs at all. The term refers to the fact that it is so easy to make these programs run well on a parallel computer. In general, in choosing among parallel designs, the embarrassingly parallel one will almost always be the best.

This first program takes an embarrassingly parallel approach to compute the Mandelbrot set [Mandelbrot 1982], which is among the most popular to implement in parallel because it is easy to get good performance and is representative of a wide variety of simple, but computationally intensive problems. The output of the program is the characteristic "Horseshoe Crab" image of the Mandelbrot set, which adorns the covers of many science books and is a popular screen saver.

## 2.1.1   Getting started

To run the program, start MATLAB and go to the Examples/Mandelbrot directory (i.e., type `cd Examples/Mandelbrot`). At the prompt, type

```
pMandelbrot
```

This runs the program on your local processor and will produce an image (see Figure 2.1) and timing data similar to

```
Compute Time (sec)                  = 29.396
Launch+Comm Time (sec)              = 0.003034
```

Record these times for later analysis. Repeat this for each of the following commands:

```
eval(pRUN('pMandelbrot',1,{}))
eval(pRUN('pMandelbrot',2,{}))
eval(pRUN('pMandelbrot',4,{}))
```

These commands run the Mandelbrot program using one, two, and four $P_{ID}$s. Running on a parallel computer will produce timing values that look similar to Table 2.3.

Congratulations! You have successfully run your first parallel MATLAB program. These results will be examined more closely after the program has been discussed further and a little more is known about what these timing data mean.

**Important Note**: The last argument to the pRUN command determines which parallel computer the program will be run on. You may need to obtain the proper setting from your system administrator; see the book website for details. Setting the last argument to {} runs multiple copies of the program on your local machine and will result in different performance values from those shown in Table 2.3.

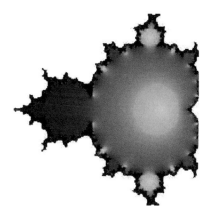

**Figure 2.1. Mandelbrot output.**
Example output from the `pMandelbrot` program.

## 2.1.2 Parallel design

Designing a parallel program begins with a specification of what the program is trying to do, in this case, computing the Mandelbrot set. The Mandelbrot set is computed by the recursive application of the formula

$$f(\mathbf{Z}) = \mathbf{Z} \mathbin{.*} \mathbf{Z} + \mathbf{C}$$

where $\mathbf{Z}$ and $\mathbf{C}$ are complex numbers. The image of the Mandelbrot set is formed by sweeping the parameter $\mathbf{C}$ over its domain in the complex plane:

$$-1.6 < Re(\mathbf{C}) < 0.4, \quad -1 < Im(\mathbf{C}) < 1$$

where $Re()$ and $Im()$ are the real and imaginary parts, respectively. The basic algorithm for computing the Mandelbrot set is shown in Algorithm 2.1 (see caption for details).

**Algorithm 2.1. Mandelbrot serial.**
The algorithm takes as input the size of the matrix to be computed $N$, the maximum number of iterations to be executed $N_{iter}$, and the lower threshold $\epsilon$. The complex matrices $\mathbf{Z}$ and $\mathbf{C}$ are initialized on lines 1 and 2. Lines 5 and 6 compute the next iteration of the Mandelbrot set and rescale the values to the output matrix $\mathbf{W}$. The values that are above threshold are determined in line 7.

$\mathbf{W} : \mathbb{R}_+^{N \times N} = \text{MandelbrotSerial}(N, N_{step}, \epsilon)$

1   $\mathbf{Z}, \mathbf{C} : \mathbb{C}^{N \times N} \quad i_\epsilon = 1 : N^2$
2   $\mathbf{C}(i,j) = (jN/2 - 1.6) + (iN/2 - 1)\sqrt{-1}, \quad i, j = 1 : N$
3   **for** $i_{step} = 1 : N_{step}$
4        **do**
5             $\mathbf{Z}(i_\epsilon) = \mathbf{Z}(i_\epsilon) \ .* \ \mathbf{Z}(i_\epsilon) \ + \ \mathbf{C}(i_\epsilon)$
6             $\mathbf{W}(i_\epsilon) = \exp(-|\mathbf{Z}(i_\epsilon)|)$
7             $i_\epsilon = \arg(\mathbf{W} > \epsilon)$

For our purposes the precise details of the calculation are not important; the most relevant pieces of information are the following two properties:

- Computing the Mandelbrot set involves repeating the same calculation over and over again for a specific parameter $\mathbf{C}(i,j)$.

- The result for one value of $\mathbf{C}(i,j)$ does not depend on the others and can be computed independently (i.e., in parallel).

The first property means the problem has enough concurrency (i.e., there are calculations that can actually be performed at the same time). In general, concurrency in a program is not hard to find. The second property means that this particular concurrency has high data locality (i.e., the data to run each concurrent calculation is local to that $P_{ID}$). Locality is more difficult to find in a program and is the key to obtaining good parallel performance. These two properties are common to many types of calculations and are the main requirements for an embarrassingly parallel program.

The first choice in the parallel design is deciding how to distribute the different parameters among various $P_{ID}$s. This process of deciding how to distribute a problem onto different $P_{ID}$s will be referred to as *mapping* the algorithm onto the parallel computer. The standard way to do this for a fine-grained embarrassingly parallel problem is to give each part of the domain of $\mathbf{C}$ to a different set of $P_{ID}$s. For example, if there were four $P_{ID}$s, the domain could be mapped as shown in Table 2.1. This mapping breaks up the domain in the first dimension and gives different vertical strips to each $P_{ID}$. This mapping results in the parallel algorithm shown using P notation in Algorithm 2.2.

The map-based approach to parallel programming is the basis of distributed array parallel programming and has been implemented many times over (see Chapter 5 and the references therein). More recently a simplified form of the map-based approach has been adapted successfully to handle certain classes of large-scale distributed programming applications [Dean & Ghemawat 2004].

**Table 2.1. Mandelbrot parallel mapping.**

The range of $\mathbf{C}$ is mapped for $N_P = 4$ so that each $P_{ID}$ will compute a different vertical strip.

| $P_{ID}$ | Real Range | Imaginary Range |
|---|---|---|
| 0 | $-1.6 < Re(\mathbf{C}) < -1.1$ | $-1 < Im(\mathbf{C}) < +1$ |
| 1 | $-1.1 < Re(\mathbf{C}) < -0.6$ | $-1 < Im(\mathbf{C}) < +1$ |
| 2 | $-0.6 < Re(\mathbf{C}) < -0.1$ | $-1 < Im(\mathbf{C}) < +1$ |
| 3 | $-0.1 < Re(\mathbf{C}) < +0.4$ | $-1 < Im(\mathbf{C}) < +1$ |

**Algorithm 2.2. Mandelbrot parallel.**

$\mathbf{W} : \mathbb{R}_+^{P(N) \times N} = \text{MANDELBROTPARALLEL}(N, N_{step}, \epsilon, N_P)$

1  $\mathbf{Z}, \mathbf{C} : \mathbb{C}^{P(N) \times N} \quad i_\epsilon = 1, \ldots, N^2/N_P$
2  $\mathbf{C}(i,j) = (jN/2 - 1.6) + (iN/2 - 1)\sqrt{-1}, \quad i,j = 1 : N$
3  **for** $i_{step} = 1 : N_{step}$
4      **do**
5          $\mathbf{Z}.loc(i_\epsilon) = \mathbf{Z}.loc(i_\epsilon) \, .* \, \mathbf{Z}.loc(i_\epsilon) \, + \, \mathbf{C}.loc(i_\epsilon)$
6          $\mathbf{W}.loc(i_\epsilon) = \exp(-|\mathbf{Z}.loc(i_\epsilon)|)$
7          $i_\epsilon = \arg(\mathbf{W}.loc > \epsilon)$

The second choice in the parallel design is to determine how to get each $P_{ID}$ the information it needs to do the computation. In this example, a distributed array $\mathbf{C}$ is used that allows each $P_{ID}$ to determine the part of the domain it should work on. Each $P_{ID}$ then computes on its local part of the matrix $\mathbf{W}$. The leader $P_{ID}$ can then gather the local matrices from the other $P_{ID}$s and assemble and display the final matrix. A visual representation of this parallel design is shown in Figure 2.2.

## 2.1.3  Code

The next step is to write the parallel Mandelbrot program. A standard (and recommended) approach is to begin with a correct serial Mandelbrot program. Debugging parallel programs can be challenging, and it is best to start with something that works and can be checked against as the parallel constructs are added. As discussed in the previous subsection, the parallel code requires three additional pieces of functionality:

- Each $P_{ID}$ creates distributed arrays $\mathbf{W}$, $\mathbf{C}$, and $\mathbf{Z}$ using a map.

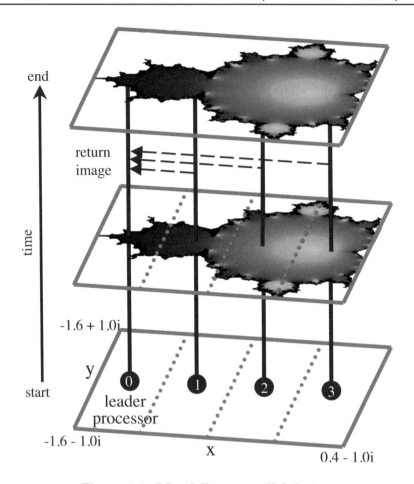

**Figure 2.2. Mandelbrot parallel design.**
Each $P_{ID}$ figures out which part of the domain it needs to compute,
computes the local part of the matrix, and sends it to the leader $P_{ID}$
(dashed lines). The leader $P_{ID}$ then assembles and displays the final
matrix.

- Each $P_{ID}$ determines the part of the domain it will compute by looking at
  the local part of the matrix **C**.

- The leader $P_{ID}$ receives the local pieces of **W** and assembles the final result.

The core of the parallel code is shown in Code Listing 2.1 (see `Examples/`
`Mandelbrot/pMandelbrot.m` for a complete listing). Keep in mind that this same
code is run by every MATLAB instance. The only difference between these instances
is that each has a unique $P_{ID}$ (i.e., `Pid`) that is used to determine which parts of a
distributed array belong to each MATLAB instance.

**Code Listing 2.1.  Mandelbrot parallel MATLAB program.**

```
 1  % Set number of iterations, mesh size and threshold.
 2  N=2400; Niter=20; epsilon = 0.001;
 3  PARALLEL = 1;                          % Set control flag.
 4  Wmap = 1;                              % Create serial map.
 5  if (PARALLEL)
 6     Wmap = map([Np 1],{},0:Np-1);       % Create parallel map.
 7  end
 8  W = zeros(N,N,Wmap);                   % Distributed array
 9  Wloc = local(W);                       % Get local part.
10  myI = global_ind(W,1);                 % Get local i indices.
11  myJ = global_ind(W,2);                 % Get local j indices.
12  [ReC ImC] = meshgrid(myJ./(N/2) -1.6, myI./(N/2) -1 );
13  Cloc = complex(ReC,ImC);               % Initialize C.
14  Zloc = Cloc;                           % Initialize Z.
15  ieps = 1:numel(Wloc);                  % Initialize indices.
16  tic;                                   % Start clock.
17  for i=1:Niter;                         % Compute Mandelbrot set.
18     Zloc(ieps) = Zloc(ieps) .* Zloc(ieps) + Cloc(ieps);
19     Wloc(ieps) = exp(-abs(Zloc(ieps)));
20     ieps = ieps( find(Wloc(ieps) > epsilon) );
21  end
22  W = put_local(W,Wloc);                 % Put back into W;
23  Tcompute = toc;                        % Stop clock.
24  tic;                                   % Start Clock.
25  W1 = agg(W);                           % Gather back to leader.
26  Tcomm = toc;                           % Stop clock.
```

**Lines 3–7** create the parallel map Wmap. The PARALLEL flag is an additional debugging tool that allows the distributed arrays to be turned on and off. Note: this technique can be applied only if all arrays are declared with at least two dimensions (i.e., use zeros(N,N) instead of zeros(N) to create square matrices).

**Lines 8–9** create the distributed array W and have each MATLAB instance retrieve its local part Wloc.

**Lines 10–12** instruct each MATLAB to compute the indices myI and myJ of the distributed array W corresponding to its local part. These indices are then used to construct the starting parameters Cloc each MATLAB uses to perform its part of the calculation.

**Lines 13–21** are the core of the Mandelbrot set algorithm and are the same as in a serial code. In this code, each MATLAB will compute the Mandelbrot set using the local matrices Cloc, Zloc and put the result into Wloc.

In **Lines 22 & 25** each $P_{ID}$ puts its local part of the result Wloc back into the distributed array W. The result is then gathered back to the leader MATLAB (i.e., Pid = 0).

The above code is a good example of the map-based programming approach. After a map `Wmap` is created, it is used to construct a distributed matrix `W` to hold the results of the Mandelbrot set calculation. It is now possible for each MATLAB to use the distributed array to determine the indices it owns using the `global_ind` function. These indices are then used to compute the local part of the domains `Cloc`, which are then used to compute the local Mandelbrot set. The local results `Wloc` are copied back to the distributed array `W` using the `put_local` function. Finally, the `W` matrix is sent to the leader using the `agg` function.

A number of properties of the map-based approach can be observed in this code example:

- Low Code Impact. The program has been converted from a serial program to a parallel program with approximately 10 additional lines of code.

- Serial code is preserved. By setting `PARALLEL=0`, this code can be run in serial without any supporting parallel libraries because `W` will just be a regular MATLAB array.

- Small parallel library footprint. Only five parallel library functions were required: `map`, `local`, `global_ind`, `put_local`, and `agg`.

- Scalable. The code can be run on any problem size or number of processors because the size of the local variables is not required in any part of the calculation and `Wloc`, `Cloc`, and `Zloc` are derived from `W`.

- Bounded communication. Because local variables `Wloc`, `Cloc`, and `Zloc` are used, there is strict control on when communication takes place.

- Map independence. The program will work with a variety of different maps. `Wmap` could be changed to `map([1 Np],{},0:Np-1)` and the code would run correctly.

- Performance guarantee. Because the core algorithm uses only the local variables `Wloc`, `Cloc`, and `Zloc`, which are regular MATLAB numeric arrays, there is a guarantee that there is no hidden performance penalty when running these lines of code in parallel.

### 2.1.4  Debug

As mentioned earlier, parallel debugging brings up many challenges. The primary benefit of the map-based approach is that it lends itself to a well-defined code-debug-test process. A parallel code adds new functionality to a program that has to be debugged independent of its serial functionality. The best way to approach debugging such a program is to do it incrementally. The specific steps are listed in Table 2.2 (more detail on the rationale behind these steps will come later in the book).

Step 1 runs the program in serial on the local machine with the distributed array `W` turned into a regular numeric array. This ensures that the serial code

**Table 2.2. Debugging steps.**

Standard incremental steps for debugging a parallel program. Each step tests specific aspects of the code.

| Step | Mode | Processors | Problem | Debugging Goal |
|------|------|-----------|---------|----------------|
| 1 | PARALLEL=0 | 1 (local) | Small | Serial code correct |
| 2 | PARALLEL=1 | 1 (local) | Small | Parallel code correct |
| 3 | PARALLEL=1 | 2+ (local) | Small | Local communication correct |
| 4 | PARALLEL=1 | 2+ (remote) | Small | Remote communication correct |
| 5 | PARALLEL=1 | 2+ (remote) | Large | Measure performance |

remains correct and the operations `global_ind` and `local` work on the regular numeric arrays. Step 2 runs the program in serial on the local machine with the distributed array W. This step ensures that the operations on W still work when W is distributed. Step 3 runs the program in parallel on the local machine. This step will detect if the domain decomposition is correct, specifically if the computation of Cloc based on `myI` and `myJ` is done properly. It will also detect errors in communication from the `agg` operation. Of all the steps, this is probably the most important and will catch the most errors. Step 4 runs the program in parallel on the remote machine. This step will detect errors introduced by remote communications in the `agg` operation. This will principally detect configuration errors in the installation and setup of the parallel MATLAB software. Step 5 runs the program in parallel on the remote machine but with a problem size of interest. Up to this point, all the testing should have been done on a small problem size. This step allows the performance on a real problem to be measured.

These steps essentially mirror those that were done during the "getting started" section, and each step tests something very specific about the parallel code. In addition, as much as possible, the tests are done locally on small problems that run fastest. Far too often programmers try to debug on large problems (that take a long time to show errors) when these errors could have been found much faster by running on a smaller problem.

## 2.1.5 Test

Testing the Mandelbrot program—assuming that it has been debugged and is giving the right answers—mainly involves looking at how long it took to run and seeing if it is performing as expected. Nearly all the timing data necessary to conduct this analysis was collected in the "getting started" section. Table 2.3 shows the relative compute time (normalized to $N_P = 1$), the launch+communication time, and the compute speedup. These data were collected on a eight processor multicore system and a 16 node multinode system. On the multicore system, all the processors share the same memory. On the multinode system, each node has separate memory and the processors communicate over a network.

The goal of a parallel program is to decrease the computation time of a program. Table 2.3 shows the compute time decreasing as $N_P$ is increased on both

**Table 2.3. Multicore and multinode Mandelbrot performance.**
Relative compute time, absolute launch+communication time, and compute speedup on multicore and multinode computing systems for different values of $N_P$. Performance data are shown for a fixed problem size
($N$ and $N_{iter}$ constant). All values are normalized to column 2 in which
$N_P = 1$ with the distributed arrays turned off (`PARALLEL=0`). Columns
3–7 are the values with distributed arrays turned on (`PARALLEL=1`). The
notation 1*8 means that $N_P = 8$, and all $P_{ID}$s were run on the same processing node with the same shared memory. The notation 16*1 means
that $N_P = 16$, and each $P_{ID}$ was run on a separate processing node
with a separate memory.

| Multicore processors: | 1 | 1*1 | 1*2 | 1*4 | 1*8 | |
|---|---|---|---|---|---|---|
| Relative compute time | 1 | 1.0 | 0.47 | 0.16 | 0.07 | |
| Launch+comm time (sec) | 0.0 | 0.0 | 2.0 | 5.7 | 5.5 | |
| Compute speedup | 1 | 1.0 | 2.1 | 6.2 | 14 | |
| Multinode processors: | 1 | 1*1 | 2*1 | 4*1 | 8*1 | 16*1 |
| Relative compute time | 1 | 1.0 | 0.47 | 0.16 | 0.06 | 0.02 |
| Launch+comm time (sec) | 0.0 | 0.0 | 8.4 | 14.2 | 13.8 | 11.3 |
| Compute speedup | 1 | 1.0 | 2.1 | 6.3 | 18 | 42 |

the multicore and multinode systems. However, a parallel program usually introduces an added time associated with launching and communicating between each
of the MATLAB instances. Table 2.3 shows that launch+communication time increases with $N_P$ and is larger on the multinode system because the launching and
communication take place over a network.

The final analysis is to compute the speedup achieved using the parallel computer. The formula for speedup, $S$, is

$$S(N_P) = \frac{T(N_P = 1)}{T(N_P)}$$

where $T(N_P)$ is the compute time using $N_P$ processors. Applying this formula to the
compute time data produces the speedup values shown in Table 2.3. The speedup
shows the performance of the parts of the code that have been made parallel. This
brings up an obvious, but important, point: parallel computing affects only the
parts of the code that are running in parallel. An important aspect of testing is to
start by measuring the speedup of the part of the program that should be performing
well, because if this is not performing well, the parallel program will never be able
to further make up for the launch+communication overhead.

The compute performance of this program is good and the speedup on the
compute portion of the code is good. [Note: the astute reader may recognize that
the compute speedup is too good (see Section 5.5).] However, since the overhead
increases with $N_P$ the overall performance is limited. This is mostly a byproduct of
running the program for only a few seconds. In most real applications the goal is to
take a program that runs a long time and make it run shorter. As the Mandelbrot

program is run for a much longer period of time (i.e., larger values of $N$ and/or $N_{iter}$), the compute time becomes much larger than the launch+communication time and the compute speedup will be reflective of the overall performance of the parallel application.

## 2.2 Program: ZoomImage (coarse-grained embarrassingly parallel)

The Mandelbrot example illustrated the concept of an embarrassingly parallel program that carries out many independent computations at a fine-grained level by dividing up the elements of a matrix among different processors. In this section, the ZoomImage example is used to demonstrate a coarse-grained embarrassingly parallel program.

The ZoomImage example takes a reference image (in this case a red rectangle on a blue background) and computes a set of new images, each with a slightly different zoom factor. The output is a sequence of images that gives the appearance of rapidly approaching the reference image.

### 2.2.1 Getting started

To run the program start MATLAB and go to the Examples/ZoomImage directory (i.e., type `cd Examples/ZoomImage`). At the prompt, type

```
pZoomImage
```

This runs the program on your local processor and will produce a sequence of images (see Figure 2.3) and timing data similar to

```
Compute Time (sec)              = 22.7613
Launch+Comm Time (sec)          = 0.003693
Performance (Gigaflops)         = 0.84701
```

Record these times for later analysis. Repeat this for each of the following commands:

```
eval(pRUN('pZoomImage',1,{}))
eval(pRUN('pZoomImage',2,{}))
eval(pRUN('pZoomImage',4,{}))
```

These commands run the ZoomImage program on one, two, and four processors. Running on a parallel computer will produce timing values that look similar to Table 2.5.

This completes the "getting started" subsection. These results will be looked at more closely after the program has been discussed a little more and more is known about what the data mean.

**Important Note**: The last argument to the pRUN command determines which parallel computer the program will be run on. You may need to obtain the proper setting from your system administrator; see the book website (http://www.siam.org/

KepnerBook) for details. Setting the last argument to {} runs multiple copies of the program on your local machine and will result in different performance values from those shown in Table 2.5.

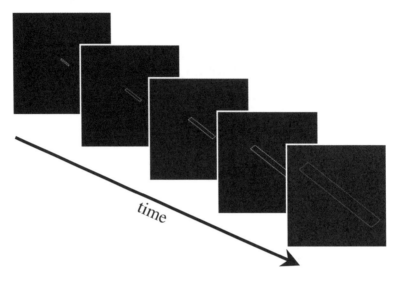

**Figure 2.3. ZoomImage output.**
Example output from the `pZoomImage` program.

### 2.2.2   Parallel design

The basic specification of this program is to compute an $N \times N$ zoomed image $\mathbf{Z}_s$ given a reference image $\mathbf{Z}_0$ and a scale factor $s > 1$. There are many ways to perform this operation. A simple approach is to first blur the reference image and then interpolate the blurred image. The blurring is accomplished by convolving the reference image with an $N_K \times N_K$ kernel matrix $\mathbf{K}_s$ (i.e., $\mathbf{Z}_s^{blur} = \mathbf{K}_s \circ \mathbf{Z}_0$), where the convolution is defined as

$$\mathbf{Z}_s^{blur}(i,j) = \sum_{i'=1}^{N_K} \sum_{j'=1}^{N_K} \mathbf{K}_s(i',j')\mathbf{Z}_0(i-i',j-j')$$

where $N_K = \lceil 5s\sigma \rceil$ and

$$\mathbf{K}_s(i,j) = \frac{1}{\sqrt{2\pi}\sigma} \exp\left[\frac{(i - N_K/2)^2 + (j - N_K/2)^2}{\sigma^2}\right]$$

is a standard Gaussian kernel matrix. The interpolation step is performed using standard bilinear interpolation

$$\mathbf{Z}_s(i,j) = a_{00}\mathbf{Z}_s^{blur}(i_s,j_s) + a_{10}\mathbf{Z}_s^{blur}(i_s+1,j_s)$$
$$+ a_{01}\mathbf{Z}_s^{blur}(i_s,j_s+1) + a_{11}\mathbf{Z}_s^{blur}(i_s+1,j_s+1)$$

where $i_s = \lfloor i/s \rfloor$, $j_s = \lfloor j/s \rfloor$, and

$$a_{00} = (i - i_s)(1 - j + j_s), \quad a_{10} = (i - i_s)(1 - j + j_s)$$
$$a_{01} = (1 - i + i_s)(j - j_s), \quad a_{11} = (i - i_s)(j - j_s)$$

Now consider applying the above mathematics to produce a sequence of zoomed images using as input an $N_s$ element vector of scale factors $\mathbf{s}$. The basic algorithm for computing a set of zoomed images is shown in Algorithm 2.3 (see caption for details).

**Algorithm 2.3. ZoomImage serial.**
The algorithm takes as input an $N \times N$ reference image $\mathbf{Z}_0$, an $N_s$ element vector, $\mathbf{s}$, of scale factors, and $\sigma$ the width of the blurring kernel. The output is an $N \times N \times N_s$ array of zoomed images $\mathbf{Z}$. Line 1 loops over each scale factor in $\mathbf{s}$. Line 3 selects the scale factor. Line 4 performs the convolution of the reference image and line 5 performs the interpolation.

$\mathbf{Z} : \mathbb{R}_+^{N \times N \times N_s} = \text{ZOOMFRAMES}(\mathbf{Z}_0 : \mathbb{R}_+^{N \times N}, \mathbf{s} : \mathbb{R}_+^{N_s}, \sigma)$
1  **for** $i_s = 1 : N_s$
2      **do**
3          $s = \mathbf{s}(i_s)$
4          $\mathbf{Z}_s^{blur} = \mathbf{K}_s \circ \mathbf{Z}_0$
5          $\mathbf{Z}(:, :, i_s) = \text{INTERPOLATE}(\mathbf{Z}_s^{blur}, s)$

For our purposes, the precise details of the calculation are not important; the most relevant pieces of information are the following two properties:

- Computing the set of zoomed images involves repeating the same calculation for different scale factors $\mathbf{s}$ on the same input $\mathbf{Z}_0$.

- The result for one value of $\mathbf{Z}(:, :, i_s)$ does not depend on the others and can be computed independently (i.e., in parallel).

The first property means the problem has enough concurrency (i.e., there are $N_s$ calculations that can actually be performed at the same time). The second property means that computing each $\mathbf{Z}(:, :, i_s)$ has high data locality (i.e., the data necessary to compute each matrix $\mathbf{Z}(:, :, i_s)$ is local to that $P_{ID}$). Locality is more difficult to find in a program and is the key to obtaining good parallel performance. The standard approach to a coarse-grained embarrassingly parallel problem is to give each $P_{ID}$ a different set of scale factors $\mathbf{s}$ to compute and corresponding ownership for a part of the 3D array $\mathbf{Z}$. For example, if there were four processors, the scale factors ranging from 1 to $N_s$ could be mapped as shown in Table 2.4. This mapping results in the parallel algorithm shown using P notation in Algorithm 2.4.

**Table 2.4. ZoomImage parallel mapping.**

For a vector with $N_s$ scale factors, $\mathbf{s}$, mapped onto four processors so that each $P_{ID}$ will compute a different set of scale factors.

| $P_{ID}$ | Scale Factors |
|:---:|:---:|
| 0 | $\mathbf{s}(1 : \lfloor \frac{1}{4}N_s \rfloor)$ |
| 1 | $\mathbf{s}(\lfloor \frac{1}{4}N_s \rfloor + 1 : \lfloor \frac{1}{2}N_s \rfloor)$ |
| 2 | $\mathbf{s}(\lfloor \frac{1}{2}N_s \rfloor + 1 : \lfloor \frac{3}{4}N_s \rfloor)$ |
| 3 | $\mathbf{s}(\lfloor \frac{3}{4}N_s \rfloor + 1 : N_s)$ |

**Algorithm 2.4. ZoomImage parallel.**

The third dimension of the output is split among the different $P_{ID}$s at the declaration (i.e., $\mathbf{Z} : \mathbb{R}_+^{N \times N \times P(N_s)}$). The parallel algorithm simply calls the serial algorithm so that each $P_{ID}$ computes a different set of scale factors. This mapping of indices to $P_{ID}$s is obtained via the $\arg(\mathbf{Z}(1, 1, :)).loc$ operation, which returns the indices of the local part $\mathbf{Z}$.

$$\mathbf{Z} : \mathbb{R}_+^{N \times N \times P(N_s)} = \text{ZoomImageParallel}(\mathbf{Z}_0 : \mathbb{R}_+^{N \times N}, \mathbf{s} : \mathbb{R}_+^{N_s}, \sigma)$$

1  $\mathbf{Z}.loc = \text{ZoomFrames}(\mathbf{Z}_0, \mathbf{s}(\text{ find}(\mathbf{Z}(1, 1, :)).loc\, ), \sigma)$

The second choice in the parallel design is to determine how to get each $P_{ID}$ the scale factors it needs to do the computation. In this design, all the scale factors and the reference image are computed by all the $P_{ID}$s. In general, this approach is preferable to having one $P_{ID}$ compute $\mathbf{S}$ and $\mathbf{Z}_0$ and send them to the other $P_{ID}$s. The specific scale factors are selected by keying off the distributed third dimension of the array $\mathbf{Z}$. Each $P_{ID}$ then computes its images $\mathbf{Z}.loc$. The entire array $\mathbf{Z}$ can then be gathered back to the leader $P_{ID}$. A visual representation of this parallel design for ZoomImage is shown in Figure 2.4.

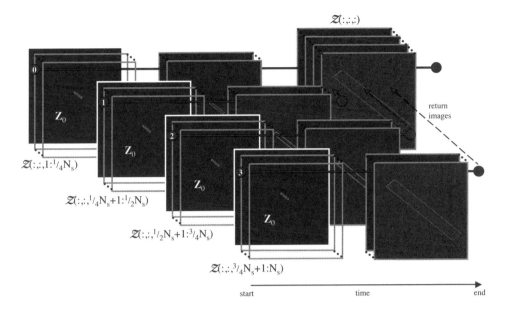

**Figure 2.4. ZoomImage parallel design.**
Each $P_{ID}$ operates on the its local part of the distributed array $\mathcal{Z}$. Once completed, the local parts are sent to the leader $P_{ID}$ (dashed lines). The leader $P_{ID}$ then assembles and displays the final sequence of images.

### 2.2.3 Code

The next step is to write the parallel ZoomImage program. As discussed in the previous subsection, the parallel code requires that three additional pieces of functionality be added to the serial program:

- Each MATLAB instance creates a distributed array $\mathcal{Z}$.

- Each MATLAB determines its scale factors **s** from its local indices of the distributed third dimension of $\mathcal{Z}$.

- The leader MATLAB gathers all the pieces $\mathcal{Z}$.

The core of the parallel code is shown in Code Listing 2.2 below (see `Examples/ZoomImage/pZoomImage.m` for a complete listing). Keep in mind that this same code is run by every MATLAB instance. The only difference between these instances is that each has a unique $P_{ID}$ (i.e., `Pid`) that is used to determine which parts of $\mathcal{Z}$ belong to each MATLAB instance.

**Code Listing 2.2.  ZoomImage parallel MATLAB program.**

```
1   % Set image size, number frames, start and stop scale.
2   N = 128; Ns = 16; Sstart = 32; Send = 1;
3   sigma = 0.5;                        % Width of blur kernel.
4   PARALLEL = 1;                       % Set control flag.
5   Zmap = 1;                           % Create serial map.
6   if (PARALLEL)
7       Zmap = map([1 1 Np],{},0:Np-1); % Create parallel map.
8   end
9   Z = zeros(N,N,Ns,Zmap);             % Distributed array.
10  S = linspace(Sstart,Send,Ns);       % Compute scale factors.
11  disp('Zooming frames...');
12  tic;                                % Start clock.
13  Z0 = referenceFrame(N,0.1,0.8);     % Create reference frame.
14  % Compute local frames.
15  Zloc = zoomFrames(Z0,S( global_ind(Z,3) ),sigma);
16  Tcompute = toc;                     % Stop Clock.
17  Z = put_local(Z,Zloc);              % Insert into Z.
18  tic;                                % Start Clock.
19  Zagg = agg(Z);                      % Aggregate on leader.
20  Tcomm = toc;                        % Start Clock.
```

**Lines 4–8** create the parallel map Zmap. The PARALLEL flag is an additional debugging tool that allows the distributed arrays to be turned on and off, resulting in Z being an ordinary array.

**Line 9** creates the distributed array Z.

**Line 15** uses the global_ind command to instruct each MATLAB to retrieve the indices of the third dimension of distributed array Z corresponding to its local part. These indices are then used to select the scale factors S to use when computing the zoomed images.

**Line 17** has each $P_{ID}$ put its local part Zloc of the result back into the distributed array Z.

**Line 19** gathers the result back to the leader MATLAB (i.e., Pid = 0) using the agg function.

The above ZoomImage code is a good example of the map-based programming approach. After the map Zmap is created, it is used to create a distributed array Z to hold the results. It is now possible for each MATLAB to use the distributed array to determine the indices it owns using the global_ind function. These indices are then used to select the scale factors S to use when computing the zoomed images. The local results are copied back to the distributed array using the put_local function. Finally, the array is sent to the leader using the agg function.

There are a number of properties of the map-based approach that can be observed in the ZoomImage code example.

- Low Code Impact. The program has been converted from a serial program to a parallel program with approximately 10 additional lines of code.

- Serial code is preserved. By setting `PARALLEL=0`, Z becomes a regular array that can be run in serial without any supporting parallel libraries.

- Small parallel library footprint. Only four parallel library functions were required: `map`, `global_ind`, `put_local`, and `agg`.

- Scalable. The code can be run on a variety of problem sizes since all the arrays are parameterized by N. The code can also be run on any number of processors less than Ns since all the local array sizes are derived from the single distributed array Z.

- Bounded communication. Because both the input and output arguments to `zoomFrames` are local variables, no accidental communication can take place inside this function.

- Map independence. The program will work with a variety of different maps as long as the map operates only on the third dimension. For example, a cyclic distribution in this dimension could also be used.

- Performance guarantee. Because the `zoomFrames` function uses local variables, there is a guarantee that there is no hidden performance penalty when running these lines of code.

### 2.2.4   Debug

As mentioned earlier, parallel debugging brings up many challenges. The primary benefit of the map-based approach is that it lends itself to a well-defined code-debug-test process. The specific steps are listed in Table 2.2.

Step 1 runs the program in serial on the local machine with the array Z constructed as an ordinary array. This ensures that the basic serial code is still correct after adding the `global_ind` and `agg` functions. Step 2 runs the program in serial on the local machine with Z as a distributed array and ensures the `zoomFrames` function works properly with its inputs derived from a distributed array. Step 3 runs the program in parallel on the local machine. This step will detect if the parallel decomposition of Z is correct and provides valid indices for selecting scale factors from S. It will also detect errors in communication from the `agg` operation. Of all the steps, this is probably the most important and will catch the most errors. Step 4 runs the program in parallel on the remote machine. This step will detect errors in the `agg` function employing remote communications; these errors are usually due to software installation or configuration issues. Step 5 runs the program in parallel on the remote machine but with a problem size of interest. Up to this point, all the testing should have been done on a small problem size. This step allows the performance on a real problem to be measured.

These steps essentially mirror those that were done during the ZoomImage "getting started" section, and each step tests something very specific about the parallel ZoomImage code. In addition, as much as possible, the tests are done locally on small problems that run fastest.

### 2.2.5  Test

Testing the ZoomImage parallel program—assuming that it has been debugged and is giving the right answers—mainly involves looking at how long it took to run and seeing if it is performing as expected. Nearly all the timing data necessary to conduct this analysis was collected in the "getting started" section (see Table 2.5). The multicore and multinode performances are similar and both show some speedup.

**Table 2.5. Multicore and multinode ZoomImage performance.** Relative compute time, absolute launch+communication time, and compute speedup on multicore and multinode computing systems for different values of $N_P$. Performance data are shown for a fixed problem size ($N$ and $N_s$ constant). All values are normalized to column 2 in which $N_P = 1$ with the distributed arrays turned off (`PARALLEL=0`). Columns 3–7 are the values with distributed arrays turned on (`PARALLEL=1`). The notation 1*8 means that $N_P = 8$, and all $P_{ID}$s were run on the same processing node with the same shared memory. The notation 16*1 means that $N_P = 16$, and each $P_{ID}$ was run on a separate processing node with a separate memory.

| Multicore processors: | 1 | 1*1 | 1*2 | 1*4 | 1*8 | |
|---|---|---|---|---|---|---|
| Relative compute time | 1 | 1.0 | 0.86 | 0.63 | 0.34 | |
| Launch+comm time (sec) | 0.0 | 0.0 | 0.1 | 0.3 | 0.2 | |
| Compute speedup | 1 | 1.0 | 1.2 | 1.6 | 2.9 | |
| Multinode processors: | 1 | 1*1 | 2*1 | 4*1 | 8*1 | 16*1 |
| Relative compute time | 1 | 1.0 | 0.85 | 0.56 | 0.32 | 0.17 |
| Launch+comm time (sec) | 0.0 | 0.0 | 0.16 | 0.17 | 3.4 | 6.5 |
| Compute speedup | 1 | 1.0 | 1.2 | 1.8 | 3.1 | 5.8 |

The goal of a parallel program is to decrease the computation time of a program. Table 2.5 shows the compute time decreasing as $N_P$ is increased on both the multicore and multinode systems. However, a parallel program usually introduces an added time associated with launching and communicating between each of the MATLAB instances. Table 2.5 shows that launch+communication time increases with $N_P$ and is larger on the multinode system because the launching and communication take place over a network.

The speedup on the compute portion of the code is good. [Note: the astute reader may recognize that the compute speedup is not as good as might be hoped (see Section 5.5).] However, since the overhead increases with $N_P$ the overall performance is limited. This is mostly a byproduct of running the program for only a few seconds. In most real applications the goal is to take a program that runs a long time and make it run shorter. As the ZoomImage program is run for a much longer period of time (i.e., larger values of $N$ and/or $N_s$), the compute time becomes much larger than the launch+communication time and the compute speedup will be reflective of the overall performance of the parallel application.

## 2.3 Program: ParallelIO

The previous examples illustrated the concept of an embarrassingly parallel program that carries out many independent computations among different processors. An important element missing from these programs is file IO. Most applications involve some form of file IO. In this section, the ParallelIO example is used to demonstrate how to implement file IO in such a way that it is independent of $N_P$.

The ParallelIO example creates a matrix, writes it to disk, and then reads it back in. The output is the time it takes to complete this operation. One challenge in ParallelIO is to create a program that writes out files in such a way that they can be read in even if $N_P$ changes.

### 2.3.1 Getting started

To run the program, start MATLAB and go to the Examples/IO directory (i.e., type `cd Examples/IO`). At the prompt, type

```
pIO
```

This runs the program on your local processor and will produce timing data similar to

```
Write Time (sec)               = 21.5991
Read Time (sec)                = 2.1681
```

Record these times for later analysis. Repeat this for each of the following commands:

```
eval(pRUN('pIO',1,{}))
eval(pRUN('pIO',2,{}))
eval(pRUN('pIO',4,{}))
```

These commands run the IO program on one, two, and four processors. Running on a parallel computer will produce timing values that look similar to Table 2.6. These results will be reviewed later in the Test subsection.

**Important Note**: The last argument to the `pRUN` command determines which parallel computer the program will be run on. You may need to obtain the proper setting from your system administrator; see the book website (http://www.siam.org/ KepnerBook) for details. Setting the last argument to {} runs multiple copies of the program on your local machine and will result in different performance values from those shown in Table 2.6.

## 2.3.2  Parallel design

The basic specification of the program is to create an $N \times M$ matrix, $\mathbf{X}$, of random numbers, write them to files, and read them in again. The basic algorithm for this operation is shown in Algorithm 2.5 (see caption for details).

**Algorithm 2.5. Serial IO.**
The algorithm writes an $N \times M$ array to $M$ data files and then reads them back into an array. This is done using WRITEMATRIXSERIAL and READMATRIXSERIAL functions, which are also shown.

SERIALIO($\mathbf{X} : \mathbb{R}^{N \times M}, file$)
1   WRITEMATRIXSERIAL($\mathbf{X}, file$)
2   $\mathbf{Y} = $ READMATRIXSERIAL($file$)

WRITEMATRIXSERIAL($\mathbf{X} : \mathbb{R}^{N \times M}, file$)
1   **for** $j = 1 : M$
2       **do**
3           WRITE($\mathbf{X}(:, j), file.j.dat$)

$\mathbf{Y} : \mathbb{R}^{N \times M} = $ READMATRIXSERIAL($file$)
1   **for** $j = 1 : M$
2       **do**
3           $\mathbf{Y}(:, j) = $ READ($file.j.dat$)

The parallel implementation of the IO program is implemented using a distributed array. Each $P_{ID}$ writes just its local part of the array to disk. For example, if $N = 1000$, $M = 32$, and $N_P = 4$, then each $P_{ID}$ would write eight files to disk and each file would contain a 1000-element vector. This mapping results in the parallel algorithm shown using P notation in Algorithm 2.6. One of the advantages of this design is that the files are written so that they can be read in even if the number of processors changes. This is accomplished by creating $M$ unique files instead of creating $N_P$ unique files. A visual representation of the design for the ParallelIO algorithm is shown in Figure 2.5.

**Algorithm 2.6. ParallelIO.**

The algorithm writes an $N \times M$ distributed array to $M$ data files and then reads them back into a distributed array. This is done using WRITEMATRIXPARALLEL and READMATRIXPARALLEL functions. In each of these functions, line 1 gets the global indices of the local part of the distributed array and stores them in the vector $\mathbf{j}_{my}$. Line 2 does a for loop from 1 to the number of elements in $\mathbf{j}_{my}$, which is denoted by $\|\mathbf{j}_{my}\|$. Finally, line 4 does the actual file operation using the global index to determine a unique global filename for the file.

PARALLELIO($\mathbf{X} : \mathbb{R}^{N \times P(M)}, file$)

1   WRITEMATRIXPARALLEL($\mathbf{X}, file$)
2   $\mathbf{Y} = $ READMATRIXPARALLEL($file$)

WRITEMATRIXPARALLEL($\mathbf{X} : \mathbb{R}^{N \times P(M)}, file$)

1   $\mathbf{j}_{my} = $ FIND($\mathbf{X}(1, :)$).$loc$
2   **for** $j = 1 : \|\mathbf{j}_{my}\|$
3       **do**
4           WRITE($\mathbf{X}.loc(:, j), file.\mathbf{j}_{my}(j).dat$)

$\mathbf{Y} : \mathbb{R}^{N \times P(M)} = $ READMATRIXPARALLEL($file$)

1   $\mathbf{j}_{my} = $ FIND($\mathbf{Y}(1, :)$).$loc$
2   **for** $j = 1 : \|\mathbf{j}_{my}\|$
3       **do**
4           $\mathbf{Y}.loc(:, j) = $ READ($file.\mathbf{j}_{my}(j).dat$)

## 2.3.3   Code

The next step is to write the ParallelIO program. As discussed in the previous subsection, the parallel code requires three additional pieces of functionality:

- Each MATLAB instance creates a distributed $\mathbf{X}$ array using a map.

- Each MATLAB determines the vectors it will write out from the distributed array $\mathbf{X}$ and writes out those vectors as unique files.

- Each MATLAB determines the vectors it will read in from the distributed array $\mathbf{Y}$ and reads in the corresponding files.

The core of the parallel code is shown below (see `Examples/IO/pIO.m` for a complete listing). Keep in mind that this same code is run by every MATLAB instance. The only difference between these instances is that each has a unique $P_{ID}$ (i.e., `Pid`) that is used to determine which parts of a distributed array belong to each MATLAB instance (i.e., $\mathbf{X}.loc$ and $\mathbf{Y}.loc$).

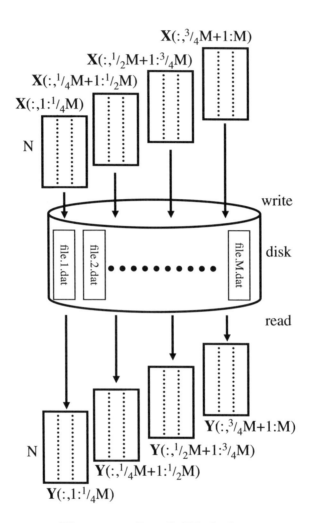

**Figure 2.5. ParallelIO design.**
Each $P_{ID}$ writes the local part of the distributed array **X** to a set of
files (one per vector) and then reads the data into a distributed array
**Y**.

**Code Listing 2.3.   ParallelIO MATLAB program.**

```
 1  % Set the problem dimensions and filename.
 2  N = 1024; M = 32; FILE = './pIOvector';
 3  PARALLEL = 1;                 % Set control flag.
 4  Xmap = 1; Ymap = 1;           % Create serial maps.
 5  if (PARALLEL)                 % Create parallel maps.
 6    Xmap = map([1 Np],{},0:Np-1); Ymap = Xmap;
 7  end
 8  Xrand = rand(N,M,Xmap);       % Create distributed array.
 9  Yrand = zeros(N,M,Ymap);      % Create distributed array.
10  WriteMatrixParallel(Xrand,FILE);        % Write files.
11  Yrand = ReadMatrixParallel(Yrand,FILE); % Read files.
```

```
 1  function WriteParallelMatrix(X,filebase)
 2  myJ = global_ind(X,2);         % Get local indices.
 3  Xlocal = local(X);             % Get local matrix.
 4  for j=1:length(myJ)            % Loop over local indices.
 5    Xj = Xlocal(:,j);            % Get a vector.
 6    filej = [filebase '.'  num2str(myJ(j)) '.mat']; % Filename.
 7    save(filej,'Xj');           % Save vector to a file.
 8  end
```

```
 1  function Y = ReadMatrixParallel(X,file)
 2  Y = X;                             % Create output matrix.
 3  myJ = global_ind(Y,2);             % Get local indices.
 4  Ylocal = local(Y);                 % Create a local matrix.
 5  for j=1:length(myJ)                % Loop over local indices.
 6    filej = [file '.'  num2str(myJ(j)) '.mat']; % Filename.
 7    temp = load(filej,'Xj');         % Read data.
 8    Ylocal(:,j) = temp.Xj;           % Insert column.
 9  end
10  Y = put_local(Y,Ylocal);           % Copy back to Y.
```

In the main program,

**Lines 3–7** create the parallel maps Xmap and Ymap. The PARALLEL flag is an additional debugging tool that allows the distributed arrays X and Y to be turned on and off.

**Lines 8–9** create the distributed matrices X and Y.

**Lines 10–11** write out and read in the distributed matrix.

In the WriteMatrixParallel program,

**Lines 2–3** instruct each MATLAB to retrieve the indices myJ of the distributed matrix corresponding to its local part. These indices are then used to create the filenames of the vectors that are written out.

**Lines 4–8** write out the vectors from `Xloc` to separate files.

In the `ReadMatrixParallel` program,

**Lines 3–4** instruct each MATLAB to retrieve the indices `myJ` of the distributed matrix corresponding to its local part. These indices are then used to select filenames of the vectors that are read.

**Lines 5–9** read in the local vectors of the matrix from separate files into `Yloc`.

**Line 10** creates a distributed array `Y` from the local matrices `Yloc`.

The above code is a good example of the map-based programming approach. After the maps `Xmap` and `Ymap` are created, they are used to create the distributed matrices `X` and `Y`. It is now possible for each MATLAB to use the distributed array to determine the indices it owns using the `global_ind` function. These indices are then used to create the filenames to be associated with the local vectors each $P_{ID}$ will write out and read in.

There are a number of properties of the map-based approach that can be observed in this code example:

- Low Code Impact. The program has been converted from a serial program to a parallel program with approximately 10 additional lines of code.

- Serial code is preserved. By setting `PARALLEL=0`, the distributed arrays `X` and `Y` become ordinary arrays and can be run in serial without any supporting parallel libraries.

- Small parallel library footprint. Only four parallel library functions were required: `map`, `put_local`, `local`, and `global_ind`.

- Scalable. The code can be run on any problem size or number of processors such that $N > N_P$. More importantly, the number of processors used to write the data can be different from the number of processors that need to read in the data.

- Bounded communication. Because local variables are used inside the `Write ParallelMatrix` and `ReadParallelMatrix` functions, there is strict control on when communication takes place.

- Map independence. In this case, the program is less map independent than is ideal. The map and the parallel write and read functions are coupled and will work only for distributed matrices broken along the second dimension. However, the program will work for any distribution in the second dimension (i.e., block, cyclic, or block-cyclic).

- Performance guarantee. Because the `save` and `load` commands are working local variables that are regular MATLAB numeric arrays, there is a guarantee that there is no hidden performance penalty when running these lines of code.

## 2.3.4  Debug

As mentioned earlier, parallel debugging brings up many challenges. The primary benefit of the map-based approach is that it lends itself to a well-defined code-debug-test process. The specific steps are listed in Table 2.2.

Step 1 runs the program in serial on the local machine with the arrays X and Y constructed as ordinary arrays. This ensures that the basic serial code is still correct after applying the `local` and `global_ind` functions. Step 2 runs the program in serial on the local machine with X and Y as distributed arrays and ensures the `WriteParallelMatrix` and `ReadParallelMatrix` functions work properly with distributed arrays as inputs. Step 3 runs the program in parallel on the local machine. This step will detect if the parallel decompositions of X and Y are correct and provide valid indices for creating the filenames to be written and read. Of all the steps, this is probably the most important and will catch the most errors. Step 4 runs the program in parallel on the remote machine. This step will detect errors in the `save` and `load` functions introduced by remote file operations, particularly if the directory to be written to is not visible by all processors. Step 5 runs the program in parallel on the remote machine but with a problem size of interest. Up to this point, all the testing should have been done on a small problem size. This step allows the performance on a real problem to be measured.

These steps essentially mirror those that were done during the ParllelIO "getting started" section, and each step tests something very specific about the parallel code. In addition, as much as possible, the tests are done locally on small problems that run fastest. Far too often programmers try and debug on large problems that take a long time to show errors that could have been found much faster by running on a smaller problem.

### 2.3.5   Test

Testing a parallel program—assuming that it has been debugged and is giving the right answers—mainly involves looking at how long it took to run and seeing if it is performing as expected. Nearly all the timing data necessary to conduct this analysis was collected in the "getting started" section (see Table 2.6).

The first thing to notice is that the timing was broken up into two phases: write and read. While each of these is done in a fully parallel manner, the performance will be limited by the scalability of the file system being written to and read from. In this case, because the problem is not large, the file system is able to absorb the file IO from all the $N_P$. Thus, both the write and read speedups on both the multicore and multinode systems increases with $N_P$.

## 2.4   Why these worked

This chapter has quickly presented several examples and analyzed the design, coding, debugging, and testing required for each of them. Ideally, these examples provide a good feel of how to run a parallel MATLAB program, some knowledge of how to code these programs in parallel, and what to measure to see if the program is producing good performance. The good performance achieved in these programs is due to a number of factors:

- The programs were chosen from applications that were known to perform well (i.e., embarrassingly parallel).

**Table 2.6. Multicore and multinode ParallelIO performance.**
Relative write and read time on multicore and multinode computing
systems for different values of $N_P$. Performance data are shown for
a fixed problem size ($N$ and $M$ constant). All values are normalized
to column 2 in which $N_P = 1$ with the distributed arrays turned off
(PARALLEL=0). Columns 3–7 are the values with distributed arrays
turned on (PARALLEL=1). The notation 1*8 means that $N_P = 8$, and
all $P_{ID}$s were run on the same processing node with the same shared
memory. The notation 16*1 means that $N_P = 16$, and each $P_{ID}$ was
run on a separate processing node with a separate memory.

| Multicore processors: | 1 | 1*1 | 1*2 | 1*4 | 1*8 | |
|---|---|---|---|---|---|---|
| Relative write time | 1 | 1.0 | 0.45 | 0.17 | 0.09 | |
| Relative read time | 1 | 1.0 | 0.67 | 0.20 | 0.15 | |
| Write speedup | 1 | 1.0 | 2.2 | 5.9 | 10.7 | |
| Read speedup | 1 | 1.0 | 1.5 | 4.9 | 6.5 | |
| Multinode processors: | 1 | 1*1 | 2*1 | 4*1 | 8*1 | 16*1 |
| Relative write time | 1 | 1.0 | 0.48 | 0.24 | 0.12 | 0.07 |
| Relative read time | 1 | 1.0 | 0.46 | 0.23 | 0.11 | 0.06 |
| Write speedup | 1 | 1.0 | 2.1 | 4.2 | 8.6 | 13.5 |
| Read speedup | 1 | 1.0 | 2.1 | 4.3 | 8.8 | 17.7 |

- The designs were constructed so as to minimize overhead by maximizing locality.

- The code was also written so as to minimize overhead and the amount of new code required.

- Debugging was done incrementally.

- The performance speedup was measured and compared to what was expected.

The rest of the book will work through these issues in much greater detail. The goal
is to provide the key concepts required to be able to quickly and efficiently produce
well-performing parallel programs like the ones in this chapter.

# References

[Dean & Ghemawat 2004] Jeffrey Dean & Sanjay Ghemawat, MapReduce: Simplified Data Processing on Large Clusters, OSDI'04: Sixth Symposium on Operating System Design and Implementation, San Francisco, CA, December, 2004.

[Mandelbrot 1982] Benoit Mandelbrot, The Fractal Geometry of Nature, 1982, New York: W.H. Freeman.

[Moler 1985] Cleve Moler is believed to have originated this term while at Intel Corporation in 1985.

# Chapter 3

# Interacting with Distributed Arrays

## Summary

A multistage example program with IO is presented to illustrate how such programs can be constructed using distributed arrays. The program creates simulated data from a multichannel sensor and then processes the simulated dataset. This example will also show how to interact with distributed arrays during the debug and test process. In particular, the kinds of information that can be extracted from distributed arrays while running the program are discussed.

This chapter examines a multistage application with IO. It builds on the ideas presented in the previous chapter to create a more complex program using distributed arrays. The main goal is to run the program through the four-step debug process and interactively explore the distributed arrays to see what can be learned at each step. This example will illustrate how to interact with distributed arrays as well as highlight some of the issues multistage parallel programs present. [**Note**: to run this example requires that the example programs and the underlying parallel software be installed. Please see the book website (http://www.siam.org/KepnerBook) for installation instructions.]

The subsequent sections are presented as follows. First is the "getting started" section that runs the example program on a different number of processors and collects timing data. Next, the mathematics of the problem are presented along with a basic parallel design. Third is a look at how the program was written. Fourth, the program will be run again and instructions are provided on ways to probe and explore distributed arrays in an interactive MATLAB session. The chapter concludes with a brief discussion on the advanced topic of parallel pipelines.

The Beamformer program illustrates the concept of a multistage parallel program that is composed of a series of fine-grained embarrassingly parallel operations. First, the Beamformer program simulates the wave pattern received by an array of sensors from a pair of point sources. Next, the program processes the simulated input data by forming beams that focus the energy into specific locations; these data are then written to files. Finally, all the data is gathered together and summed, and the output is displayed.

## 3.1   Getting started

To run the program, start MATLAB and go to the Examples/Beamformer directory (i.e., type cd Examples/Beamformer). At the prompt, type

    pBeamformer

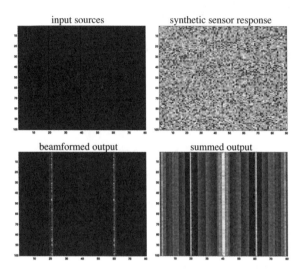

**Figure 3.1. Beamformer output.**
Example output from the pBeamformer program.

This runs the program on your local processor and will produce an image (see Figure 3.1) and timing data similar to

    Compute Time (sec)              = 22.5518
    Launch+Comm Time (sec)          = 0.00576

Record these times for later analysis.  Repeat this for each of the following commands:

    eval(pRUN('pBeamformer',1,{}))
    eval(pRUN('pBeamformer',2,{}))
    eval(pRUN('pBeamformer',4,{}))

These commands run the Beamformer program on one, two, and four processors. Running on a parallel computer will produce timing values that look similar to Table 3.2. We will will return to these results later after we have discussed the program a little and know more about what the data mean.

**Important Note**: The last argument to the pRUN command determines on which parallel computer the program will be run. You may need to obtain the proper setting from your system administrator; see the book website (http://www.siam.org/KepnerBook) for details. Setting the last argument to {} runs multiple copies of the program on your local machine and will result in different performance values from those shown in Table 3.2.

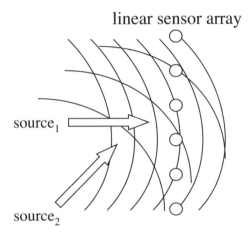

**Figure 3.2. Beamformer physics.**
The Beamformer program simulates the response received at a linear
arrays of sensors produced by two wave sources.

## 3.2 Parallel design

Consider two point sources emitting waves of energy (see Figure 3.2). The energy
could be acoustic (e.g., sound waves in air or water) or electromagnetic (e.g., radio
waves). The first step in the Beamformer program is to compute the combined
energy of these waves received at a linear array of sensors containing $N_s$ sensor
elements over a set of frequencies $N_f$ at a number of different time snapshots $N_t$.
The location of the sources relative to the sensor array elements is stored in the
input tensor

$$\mathcal{X}_0 : \mathbb{R}^{N_t \times N_b \times N_f}$$

where $N_b$ is the number of "beams" or angles that the receivers examine. If source
1 is at a 45° angle, then this can be specified by setting

$$\mathcal{X}_0(:, \lfloor N_b/4 \rfloor, :) = 1$$

Likewise, if source 2 is at a 90° angle, then this can be specified by setting

$$\mathcal{X}_0(:, \lfloor N_b/2 \rfloor, :) = 1$$

Of course, the other values could also be changed if it is desired that the location
of the sources moves between time snapshots or the frequency response varies with
source. For simplicity, uniform sources are used in this example.

The response of the sensors to these sources is stored in the complex valued
tensor $\mathcal{X}_1 : \mathbb{C}^{N_t \times N_s \times N_f}$. Computing this response is achieved by multiplying the
input by a matrix

$$\mathcal{X}_1(i_t, :, i_f) = \mathcal{V}(:, :, i_f) \, * \, \mathcal{X}_0(i_t, :, i_f)^T$$

where $\boldsymbol{\mathcal{V}} : \mathbb{C}^{N_s \times N_b \times N_f}$ is the frequency-dependent tensor of "steering vectors" that transforms waves from the sources into a response at the receiver elements. The simulated response is completed by simply adding random noise to $\boldsymbol{\mathcal{X}}_1$.

The next stage in the processing is to attempt to recover the location of the sources from the noisy data by "beamforming" and summing over the different frequencies. The beamforming is performed by the formula

$$\boldsymbol{\mathcal{X}}_2(i_t, :, i_f) = |\boldsymbol{\mathcal{X}}_1(i_t, :, i_f) \; * \; \boldsymbol{\mathcal{V}}(:, :, i_f)|^2$$

where $\boldsymbol{\mathcal{X}}_2 : \mathbb{R}_+^{N_t \times N_b \times N_f}$. The final summation step is given by

$$\mathbf{X}_3(i_t, i_b) = \sum_{i_f=1}^{N_f} \boldsymbol{\mathcal{X}}_2(i_t, i_b, i_f)$$

where $\mathbf{X}_3 : \mathbb{R}_+^{N_t \times N_b}$ is a matrix showing the angle of each source at each snapshot. In sonar applications, this matrix is called a time-bearing plot.

The basic serial beamforming algorithm is shown in Algorithm 3.1 (see caption for details).

The precise details of the calculation are not important; the most relevant pieces of information are the following properties:

- The computations are performed over three-dimensional arrays with four core dimensions: $N_t$, $N_b$, $N_s$, and $N_f$.

- The algorithm consists of four stages; each stage consists of a for loop over a tensor.

- The first three for loops are over the same loop indices, which implies they can use the same parallel map.

- The final loop involves summing over a different set of loop indices, which implies that data will need to be communicated to complete this operation.

**Algorithm 3.1. Beamformer serial.**

The algorithm takes as input a tensor of sources $\boldsymbol{\mathcal{X}}_0$, a tensor of steering vectors $\boldsymbol{\mathcal{V}}$, a noise variance $\sigma$, and a file header for saving the results. The output is the matrix $\mathbf{X}_3$ that recovers the angular location of the sources as a function of time. The algorithm consists of four distinct for loops. The first creates a simulated response of the sources plus complex random noise ($\mathbf{n}^{\mathbb{C}}_{\mu=0,\sigma}$). The second loop beamforms the data. The third loop writes the beamformed data to a set of files. The final loop sums the beamformed data across frequencies.

$$\mathbf{X}_3 : \mathbb{R}_+^{N_t \times N_b} = \text{BEAMFORMERSERIAL}($$
$$\boldsymbol{\mathcal{X}}_0 : \mathbb{R}^{N_t \times N_b \times N_f}, \boldsymbol{\mathcal{V}} : \mathbb{C}^{N_s \times N_b \times N_f}, \sigma, file)$$

1   $\boldsymbol{\mathcal{X}}_1 : \mathbb{C}^{N_t \times N_s \times N_f} \quad \boldsymbol{\mathcal{X}}_2 : \mathbb{R}_+^{N_t \times N_b \times N_f}$

2   **for** $i_t = 1 : N_t$, $i_f = 1 : N_f$

3         **do** $\triangleright$ Stage 1: create sensor data.

4               $\boldsymbol{\mathcal{X}}_1(i_t, :, i_f) = \boldsymbol{\mathcal{V}}(:, :, i_f) \, * \, \boldsymbol{\mathcal{X}}_0(i_t, :, i_f)^T + \mathbf{n}^{\mathbb{C}}_{\mu=0,\sigma}$

5   **for** $i_t = 1 : N_t$, $i_f = 1 : N_f$

6         **do** $\triangleright$ Stage 2: beamform sensor data.

7               $\boldsymbol{\mathcal{X}}_2(i_t, :, i_f) = |\boldsymbol{\mathcal{X}}_1(i_t, :, i_f) \, * \, \boldsymbol{\mathcal{V}}(:, :, i_f)|^2$

8   **for** $i_f = 1 : N_f$

9         **do** $\triangleright$ Stage 3: write data to files.

10              $\text{WRITE}(\boldsymbol{\mathcal{X}}_2(:, :, i_f), file.i_f.dat)$

11  **for** $i_t = 1 : N_t$, $i_b = 1 : N_b$

12        **do** $\triangleright$ Stage 4: sum along frequency dimension.

13              $\mathbf{X}_3(i_t, i_b) = \sum_{i_f=1}^{N_f} \boldsymbol{\mathcal{X}}_2(i_t, i_b, i_f)$

The first property means the problem has enough concurrency (i.e., there are calculations that can actually be performed at the same time). In general, concurrency in a program is not hard to find. The second property means that this particular concurrency has high data locality (i.e., the data to run each concurrent process is local to that processor). Locality is more difficult to find in a program and is the key to obtaining good parallel performance. The third and fourth properties mean that the locality is the same for the first three stages but different for the fourth stage. These properties are common to many types of calculations and are typical of multistage programs. Typically, each stage of the program is made parallel independently, and communication is then performed between or within the stages as needed. In this particular example, a fine-grained parameter-sweep approach is used within each loop so that each $P_{ID}$ is responsible for a different portion of each array.

The first choice in the parallel design is deciding how to map the arrays to the various $P_{ID}$s. The standard way to do this for a fine-grained embarrassingly parallel problem is to give each part of the domain of the arrays to a different set of $P_{ID}$s. For example, if $N_P = 4$, the domain could be mapped as shown in Table 3.1. This mapping breaks up the domain in the third dimension and gives different pieces of the array to each $P_{ID}$. This mapping results in the parallel algorithm shown using P notation in Algorithm 3.2.

The second choice in the parallel design is to determine how to get each $P_{ID}$ the information it needs to do the computation. This example uses distributed arrays that allow each $P_{ID}$ involved in the computation to determine which part of the domain it should work on. Each $P_{ID}$ then computes its part of the final matrix and sends the data back to the leader $P_{ID}$ (typically the $P_{ID} = 0$). The leader $P_{ID}$ receives all the matrices from the other $P_{ID}$s and then sums and displays the final matrix. A visual representation of this parallel design is shown in Figure 3.3.

### Algorithm 3.2. Beamformer parallel.

The parallel algorithm is similar to the serial algorithm with a few modifications. The most important change is that $\mathcal{X}_{0,1,2}$ are now distributed arrays decomposed in their third dimensions (line 1). The corresponding for loops are also changed so that the index ranges from $i_f = 1$ to $i_f = \|i_f^{my}\|$, which is the size of the local part of the array in the third dimension (lines 3, 6, and 9). Finally, the last stage of the computation is broken up into two for loops. The first for loop sums the beamformed data across frequencies on the local $P_{ID}$ (lines 12–14). This data is then aggregated (line 15) using the distributed array $\tilde{\mathcal{X}}_3$ and the sum is completed (lines 16–18).

$$\mathbf{X}_3 : \mathbb{R}_+^{N_t \times N_b} = \textsc{BeamformerParallel}($$
$$\mathcal{X}_0 : \mathbb{R}^{N_t \times N_b \times P(N_f)}, \mathcal{V} : \mathbb{C}^{N_s \times N_b \times P(N_f)}, \sigma, file)$$

1    $\mathcal{X}_1 : \mathbb{C}^{N_t \times N_s \times P(N_f)}$     $\mathcal{X}_2 : \mathbb{R}_+^{N_t \times N_b \times P(N_f)}$     $\tilde{\mathcal{X}}_3 : \mathbb{R}_+^{N_t \times N_b \times P(N_P)}$

2    $i_f^{my} = \arg(\mathcal{X}_1(1,1,:)).loc$

3    **for** $i_t = 1 : N_t,\, i_f = 1 : \|i_f^{my}\|$

4        **do** $\triangleright$ Stage 1: create sensor data.

5          $\mathcal{X}_1.loc(i_t, :, i_f) = \mathcal{V}(:, :, i_f^{my}(i_f)) \,*\, \mathcal{X}_0.loc(i_t, :, i_f)^T + \mathbf{n}_{\mu=0,\sigma}^{\mathbb{C}}$

6    **for** $i_t = 1 : N_t,\, i_f = 1 : \|i_f^{my}\|$

7        **do** $\triangleright$ Stage 2: beamform sensor data.

8          $\mathcal{X}_2.loc(i_t, :, i_f) = |\mathcal{X}_1.loc(i_t, :, i_f) \,*\, \mathcal{V}(:, :, i_f^{my}(i_f))|^2$

9    **for** $i_f = 1 : \|i_f^{my}\|$

10       **do** $\triangleright$ Stage 3: write data to files.

11         $\textsc{Write}(\mathcal{X}_2(:, :, i_f), file.i_f^{my}(i_f).dat)$

12    **for** $i_t = 1 : N_t,\, i_b = 1 : N_b$

13       **do** $\triangleright$ Stage 4a: sum along local frequency dimension.

14         $\tilde{\mathcal{X}}_3.loc(i_t, i_b, 1) = \sum_{i_f=1}^{\|i_f^{my}\|} \mathcal{X}_2(i_t, i_b, i_f)$

15    $\textsc{Agg}(\tilde{\mathcal{X}}_3)$

16    **for** $i_t = 1 : N_t,\, i_b = 1 : N_b$

17       **do** $\triangleright$ Stage 4b: sum aggregated data.

18         $\mathbf{X}_3(i_t, i_b) = \sum_{i_p=1}^{N_P} \tilde{\mathcal{X}}_3(i_t, i_b, i_P)$

**Table 3.1. Beamformer parallel mapping.**
The range of the arrays is mapped onto four $P_{ID}$s so that each $P_{ID}$ will compute a different piece of the array.

| $P_{ID}$ | Array | Snapshots | Beams/Sensor | Frequencies |
|---|---|---|---|---|
| 0 | $\mathcal{X}_{0,1,2}($ | $1 : N_t,$ | $1 : N_{b/s},$ | $1 : \lfloor \frac{1}{4} N_f \rfloor)$ |
| 1 | $\mathcal{X}_{0,1,2}($ | $1 : N_t,$ | $1 : N_{b/s},$ | $\lfloor \frac{1}{4} N_f \rfloor + 1 : \lfloor \frac{1}{2} N_f \rfloor)$ |
| 2 | $\mathcal{X}_{0,1,2}($ | $1 : N_t,$ | $1 : N_{b/s},$ | $\lfloor \frac{1}{2} N_f \rfloor + 1 : \lfloor \frac{3}{4} N_f \rfloor)$ |
| 3 | $\mathcal{X}_{0,1,2}($ | $1 : N_t,$ | $1 : N_{b/s},$ | $\lfloor \frac{3}{4} N_f \rfloor + 1 : N_f \quad )$ |

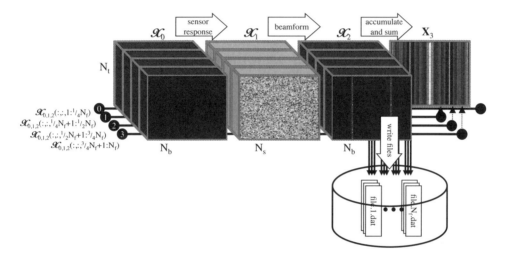

**Figure 3.3. Beamformer parallel design.**
Each stage of the algorithm interacts primarily with two arrays: one for input and one for output. The distributed arrays $\mathcal{X}_{0,1,2}$ are all decomposed in the $N_f$ dimension so that no communication is required in the sensor response, beamform, and write data stages. The final state (accumulate and sum) requires that results all be sent back to $P_{ID} = 0$.

## 3.3   Code

The next step is to write the parallel program. A standard (and recommended) approach is to begin with a correct serial program. Debugging parallel programs can be challenging, and it is best to start with something that works and can be checked against as the parallel constructs are added. As discussed in the previous section, the parallel code requires three additional pieces of functionality:

- Each MATLAB instance creates a set of distributed arrays using a map.

- Each MATLAB determines its part of the domain from the distributed array.

- The leader MATLAB receives the pieces and assembles the final result.

### Code Listing 3.1.  Beamformer parallel MATLAB program.

```
 1  % Number of times, sensors, beams and frequencies.
 2  Nt = 50; Ns = 90; Nb = 40; Nf = 100;
 3  PARALLEL = 1;                          % Set control flag.
 4  Xmap = 1;                              % Create serial map.
 5  if (PARALLEL)
 6    Xmap = map([1 1 Np],{},0:Np-1);  % Create parallel map.
 7  end
 8  X0 = zeros(Nt,Nb,Nf,Xmap);             % Source array.
 9  X1 = complex(zeros(Nt,Ns,Nf,Xmap));% Sensor input.
10  X2 = zeros(Nt,Nb,Nf,Xmap);             % Beamformed output.
11  X3 = zeros(Nt,Nb,Np,Xmap);             % Intermediate sum.
12  myI_f = global_ind(X1,3);              % Get local indices.
13  % Get local parts of arrays and insert two targets in X0.
14  X0loc = local(X0); X1loc = local(X1); X2loc = local(X2);
15  X0loc(:,round(0.25*Nb),:)=1; X0loc(:,round(0.5*Nb),:)=1;

16  for i_t=1:Nt                           % Time snapshots loop.
17    for i_f=1:numel(myI_f)               % Local frequencies loop.
18      X1loc(i_t,:,i_f) = ...    % Shift beams to sensors.
19      (squeeze(myV(:,:,i_f))*squeeze(X0loc(i_t,:,i_f)).')...
20      + sqrt(Ns)*complex(rand(Ns,1),rand(Ns,1));
21    end
22  end

23  for i_t=1:Nt                           % Time snapshots loop.
24    for i_f=1:numel(myI_f)               % Local frequencies loop.
25      X2loc(i_t,:,i_f) = ...    % Sensors back to beams.
26      abs(squeeze(X1loc(i_t,:,i_f))*squeeze(myV(:,:,i_f))).^2;
27    end
28  end

29  for i_f=1:numel(myI_f)                 % Loop over frequencies.
30    X_i_f = squeeze(X2loc(:,:,i_f)); % Get a matrix of data.
31    filename=['dat/Beam_freq.' num2str(myI_f(i_f)) '.mat'];
32    save(filename,'X_i_f');              % Save to a file.
33  end

34  X3 = put_local(X3,sum(X2loc,3));       % Sum local into X3.
35  x3 = squeeze(sum(agg(X3),3));          % Agg and complete sum.
```

The key fragments of the parallel code are shown above (see Examples/ Beamformer/pBeamformer.m for a complete listing). Keep in mind that this same code is run by every MATLAB instance. The only difference between these instances is that each has a unique $P_{ID}$ (i.e., `Pid`) that is used to determine which parts of a distributed array belong to each MATLAB instance.

**Lines 3–7** create the parallel map `Xmap` used to construct the distributed arrays. The `PARALLEL` flag is an additional debugging tool that allows the distributed arrays to be turned on and off.

**Lines 8–11** create the distributed arrays `X1`, `X2`, `X3`, and `X4`. These code lines can reuse `Xmap` because all the distributed arrays are 3D and are to be distributed along the third dimension.

**Line 12** instructs each MATLAB to retrieve the indices of the distributed array corresponding to its local part. These indices are then used to select the frequencies and steering vectors to use when doing the computation.

**Line 14** causes each MATLAB to retrieve its local part of the distributed arrays.

**Lines 16–22** create the simulated sensor response dataset. The loop over the frequency is done over the local indices of each MATLAB.

**Lines 23–28** beamform the simulated sensor data. The loop over the frequency is done over the local indices of each MATLAB.

**Lines 29–33** write the data to a file, with each MATLAB writing one file per frequency that is local to that MATLAB.

**Lines 34–35** aggregate and sum the data.

The above code is a good example of the map-based programming approach. After the map is created, it is used to create the distributed arrays to hold the results. By using the `global_ind` function, it is now possible for each MATLAB to use the distributed array to determine the indices it owns. These indices are then used to select the frequencies and steering vectors used when computing the results. In the first several steps, no communication is required so only the local parts of the distributed arrays are used. The local results are copied back to the distributed array using the `put_local` function. Finally, the array is aggregated and summed on the leader using the `agg` function.

There are a number of properties of the map-based approach that can be observed in this code example:

- Low Code Impact. The program has been converted from a serial program to a parallel program with approximately 10 additional lines of code.

- Serial code is preserved. By setting `PARALLEL=0`, this code can be run in serial without any supporting parallel libraries.

- Small parallel library footprint. Only four parallel library functions were required: `map`, `global_ind`, `local`, `put_local`, and `agg`, as well as the overloaded constructor functions `zeros()`, `complex()`, and `rand()`. [Note: `rand` may produce values in a different order depending on the parallel map.]

- Scalable. The code can be run on any problem size or $N_P$.

- Bounded communication. Because local variables are used, there is strict control on when communication takes place.

- Map independence. The program will work with a variety of different maps.

- Performance guarantee. Because the core algorithm uses local variables that are regular MATLAB numeric arrays, there is a guarantee that there is no hidden performance penalty when running these lines of code.

## 3.4   Interactive debug and test

In this section, the Beamformer program is run in five distinct steps. Step 1 runs the program in serial on the local machine with the distributed arrays turned off. This ensures that the basic serial code is still correct. Step 2 runs the program in serial on the local machine with the distributed arrays turned on. This step ensures that the parallel code is correct. Step 3 runs the program in parallel on the local machine. This step will detect errors introduced by communications. Of all the steps, this is probably the most important and will catch the most errors. Step 4 runs the program in parallel on the remote machine. This step will detect errors introduced by remote communications. Step 5 runs the program in parallel on the remote machine but with a problem size of interest. Up to this point, all the testing should have been done on a small problem size. This step allows the performance on a real problem to be measured.

   In addition to just running the program, descriptions of how to interact with some of the variables will also be provided. To run the program, start MATLAB and go to the Examples/Beamformer directory (i.e., type `cd Examples/Beamformer`).

### 3.4.1   Serial code correct

To put the Beamformer program into a serial mode, edit the `pBeamfomer.m` file and set `PARALLEL=0` and uncomment the last line of the file:

    whos X0 X1 X2 X3 X0loc X1loc X2loc x3 myI_f myV

Next, at the MATLAB prompt, type

    pBeamformer

This will produce the following output:

| Name  | Size        | Bytes   | Class  | Attributes |
|-------|-------------|---------|--------|------------|
| X0    | 50x40x100   | 1600000 | double |            |
| X0loc | 50x40x100   | 1600000 | double |            |
| X1    | 50x90x100   | 7200000 | double | complex    |
| X1loc | 50x90x100   | 7200000 | double | complex    |
| X2    | 50x40x100   | 1600000 | double |            |
| X2loc | 50x40x100   | 1600000 | double |            |
| X3    | 50x40       | 16000   | double |            |
| x3    | 50x40       | 16000   | double |            |
| myI_f | 1x100       | 800     | double |            |
| myV   | 90x40x100   | 5760000 | double | complex    |

Setting `PARALLEL=0` turns off the parallel library by turning the maps into serial maps. Using a serial map as an argument to a MATLAB constructor causes the constructor to return a regular MATLAB array. This effectively is the same as running the program without any distributed arrays. This can be verified by checking that the sizes and classes of the distributed/local variable pairs X0/X0loc, X1/X1loc, X2/X2loc, and X3/x3 are the same. If they are not the same, this is a clue that the arrays are not being declared properly. Running the program in this mode ensures that the serial program is correct.

### 3.4.2 Parallel code correct

To put the Beamformer program back into a parallel mode, edit the `pBeamfomer.m` file and set `PARALLEL=1`. Next, at the MATLAB prompt, type

```
pBeamformer
```

This is also equivalent to typing

```
eval(pRUN('pBeamformer',1,{}))
```

This will produce the following output:

| Name  | Size      | Bytes   | Class  | Attributes |
|-------|-----------|---------|--------|------------|
| X0    | 50x40x100 | 1600928 | dmat   |            |
| X0loc | 50x40x100 | 1600000 | double |            |
| X1    | 50x90x100 | 7200928 | dmat   |            |
| X1loc | 50x90x100 | 7200000 | double | complex    |
| X2    | 50x40x100 | 1600928 | dmat   |            |
| X2loc | 50x40x100 | 1600000 | double |            |
| X3    | 50x40      | 16920   | dmat   |            |
| x3    | 50x40      | 16000   | double |            |
| myI_f | 1x100     | 800     | double |            |
| myV   | 90x40x100 | 5760000 | double | complex    |

Setting `PARALLEL=1` turns on the parallel library by creating distributed maps. Using a distributed map as an argument to a MATLAB constructor causes the constructor to return a distributed MATLAB array. This can be verified by checking the sizes and classes of the distributed/local variable pairs X0/X0loc, X1/X1loc, X2/X2loc, and X3/x3. In this step, the sizes of the arrays should be the same, but the classes of the distributed arrays should be `dmat`. If they are not the same, this is a clue that the arrays are not being declared properly. During this step, running the program ensures that the declaration of the distributed arrays is correct and that any overloaded functions (in this case `zeros`, `rand()`, and `complex`) are working properly.

### 3.4.3 Local communication correct

To run the program using four MATLABs on the local computer system, type the following at the MATLAB prompt:

```
eval(pRUN('pBeamformer',4,{}))
```

This will produce the following output:

```
Name         Size                    Bytes   Class       Attributes
X0           50x40x100              400952   dmat
X0loc        50x40x25               400000   double
X1           50x90x100             1800952   dmat
X1loc        50x90x25              1800000   double      complex
X2           50x40x100              400952   dmat
X2loc        50x40x25               400000   double
X3           50x40x4                 16952   dmat
x3           50x40                   16000   double
myI_f          1x25                    200   double
myV          90x40x25              1440000   double      complex
```

Setting the second argument in the dRUN() command to four launches the program on four MATLABs on the local processor. This can be verified by checking the sizes and classes of the distributed/local variable pairs X0/X0loc, X1/X1loc, X2/X2loc, and X3/x3. In this step, the sizes of the arrays should be different, and the classes of the distributed arrays should be dmat. More specifically, the third dimension of the local array should be 1/4 the size of the third dimension of the corresponding distributed array. If they are not different in this way, this is a clue that the arrays are not being declared properly. In addition, the output from the other MATLABs can viewed by typing the following at the MATLAB prompt:

```
!type MatMPI\*.out
```

This is also equivalent to typing

```
!more MatMPI/*.out
```

The sizes and class types of the distributed and local arrays should follow the same pattern.

During this step, the program is run in parallel on the local machine. This step will detect errors introduced by communications. Of all the steps, this is probably the most important and will catch the most errors.

### 3.4.4 Remote communication correct

To run the program using four MATLABs on a remote computer system, type the following at the MATLAB prompt:

```
eval(pRUN('pBeamformer',4,ParallelMachine))
```

The last argument to the pRUN() command determines on which parallel computer the program will be run. (You may need to obtain the proper setting from your system administrator. See the book website (http://www.siam.org/KepnerBook) for details. The output from this step should be identical to that of the previous step. If the outputs are the same, this is a clue that the way the software is being run on the remote machine is different from how it is being run locally.

### 3.4.5  Measuring performance

Step 5 runs the program in parallel on the remote machine but with a problem size of interest. Up to this point, all the testing should have been done on a small problem size. This step allows the performance on a real problem to be measured. To complete the timing data involves running for the program for a range of $N_P$ (powers of two are typical).

Testing the Beamformer program—assuming that it has been debugged and is giving the right answers—mainly involves looking at how long it took to run and seeing if it is performing as expected. Nearly all the timing data necessary to conduct this analysis was collected in the "getting started" section.

The first test is to compare the performance of running the program using $N_P = 1$ with distributed arrays turned off (`PARALLEL=0`) and distributed arrays turned on (`PARALLEL=1`). Columns 2 and 3 in Table 3.2 provide this data. In this case, the performance differences are negligible and indicate that distributed arrays do not incur a performance penalty. If using distributed arrays with $N_P = 1$ slows things down significantly, then this must be addressed. It is very difficult to get any benefit with $N_P > 1$ if the $N_P = 1$ case is slower than the base serial code. Working only on the local parts of distributed arrays almost guarantees the performance will be the same as when distributed arrays are not being used.

Table 3.2 shows the relative compute time (normalized to $N_P = 1$), the launch+communication time, and the compute speedup. These data were collected on an eight processor multicore system and a 16 node multinode system. On the multicore system, all the processors share the same memory. On the multinode system, each node has separate memory and the processors communicate over a network.

Table 3.2 shows the compute time decreasing as $N_P$ is increased on both the multicore and multinode systems. However, a parallel program usually introduces an added time associated with launching and communicating between each of the MATLAB instances. Table 3.2 shows that launch+communication time increases with $N_P$ and is larger on the multinode system because the launching and communication take place over a network.

The speedup on the compute portion of the code is good. However, since the overhead increases with $N_P$ the overall performance is limited. This is mostly a byproduct of running the program for only a few seconds. In most real applications the goal is to take a program that runs a long time and make it run shorter. As the Beamformer program is run for a much longer period of time (i.e., larger values of $N_t$, $N_s$, $N_b$, and $N_f$), the compute time becomes much larger than the launch+communication time and the compute speedup will be reflective of the overall performance of the parallel application.

## 3.5  Advanced topic: Introduction to parallel pipelines

In the previous sections distributed arrays were used to allow each $P_{ID}$ to operate on a small piece of the overall array. This type of parallelism is often referred to as "data parallelism" since each $P_{ID}$ executes the same line of code but on different pieces

**Table 3.2. Multicore and multinode Beamformer performance.**
Relative compute time, absolute launch+communication time, and compute speedup on multicore and multinode computing systems for different values of $N_P$. Performance data are shown for a fixed problem size ($N_t$, $N_s$, $N_b$, and $N_f$ are constant). All values are normalized to column 2 in which $N_P = 1$ with the distributed arrays turned off (`PARALLEL=0`). Columns 3–7 are the values with distributed arrays turned on (`PARALLEL=1`). The notation 1*8 means that $N_P = 8$, and all $P_{IDS}$ were run on the same processing node with the same shared memory. The notation 16*1 means that $N_P = 16$, and each $P_{ID}$ was run on a separate processing node with a separate memory.

| Multicore processors: | 1 | 1*1 | 1*2 | 1*4 | 1*8 | |
|---|---|---|---|---|---|---|
| Relative compute time | 1 | 1.0 | 0.48 | 0.22 | 0.12 | |
| Launch+comm time (sec) | 0.0 | 0.0 | 0.5 | 0.5 | 1.2 | |
| Compute speedup | 1 | 1.0 | 2.1 | 4.4 | 8.0 | |
| Multinode processors: | 1 | 1*1 | 2*1 | 4*1 | 8*1 | 16*1 |
| Relative compute time | 1 | 1.0 | 0.51 | 0.26 | 0.12 | 0.06 |
| Launch+comm time (sec) | 0.0 | 0.0 | 8.4 | 10.9 | 10.7 | 14.3 |
| Compute speedup | 1 | 1.0 | 2.0 | 3.9 | 8.1 | 15.7 |

of data. In order for data parallelism to work, each $P_{ID}$ must execute the same program. This parallel programming model is referred to as the Single-Program Multiple-Data (SPMD) model.

The Beamformer application also exhibits another type of parallelism because it has multiple stages and it is possible to map different stages to different sets of $P_{ID}$s. This type of parallelism is referred to as task parallelism. To effectively exploit this parallelism requires some modification to the application. Specifically, instead of just processing a single array of input data, it would need to process a long sequence of independent data arrays, which is not an uncommon scenario. In this context, it is possible to set up a parallel pipeline with each stage processing an array of data and then sending it on to a different set of $P_{ID}$s (see Algorithm 3.3). The notation for mapping to the $i$th set of $P_{ID}$s is denoted by $P_{\{i\}}()$. A specific example is shown in Figure 3.4, where the $P_{ID}$ set mapping is given in Table 3.3.

**Table 3.3. Beamformer parallel pipeline mapping.**

| Notation | $P_{IDS}$ | Map |
|---|---|---|
| $P_{\{1\}}()$ | 1, 2, 3 ,4 | map([1 1 4],,1:4) |
| $P_{\{2\}}()$ | 5, 6, 7, 8 | map([1 1 4],,5:8) |
| $P_{\{3\}}()$ | 9, 10, 11, 12 | map([1 1 4],,9:12) |
| $P_{\{4\}}()$ | 0 | map([1 1 1],,0) |

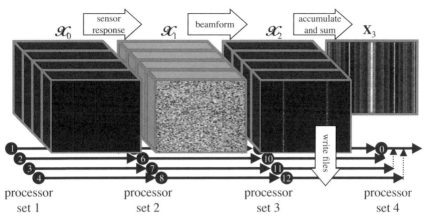

**Figure 3.4. Beamformer parallel pipeline design.**

Each stage of the algorithm is mapped onto a different set of $P_{ID}$s.

**Algorithm 3.3. Beamformer pipeline.**

This algorithm outline illustrates the changes between the parallel Beamformer algorithm and the pipeline parallel Beamformer algorithm. Each distributed array is declared twice (lines 1–3) with a $P_{ID}$ set $\{1\}$, $\{2\}$, $\{3\}$, or $\{4\}$. Assignment between two distributed arrays causes communication to occur between those arrays (lines 8 and 11).

$$\mathbf{X}_3 : \mathbb{R}_+^{P_{\{4\}}(N_t \times N_b)} = \text{BEAMFORMERPIPELINE}($$
$$\boldsymbol{\mathcal{X}}_0 : \mathbb{R}^{N_t \times N_b \times P_{\{1\}}(N_f)}, \boldsymbol{\mathcal{V}} : \mathbb{C}^{N_s \times N_b \times P_{\{1\}}(N_f)}, \sigma, file)$$

$\quad 1 \quad \tilde{\boldsymbol{\mathcal{X}}}_1 : \mathbb{C}^{N_t \times N_s \times P_{\{1\}}(N_f)} \qquad \boldsymbol{\mathcal{X}}_1 : \mathbb{C}^{N_t \times N_s \times P_{\{2\}}(N_f)}$

$\quad 2 \quad \tilde{\boldsymbol{\mathcal{X}}}_2 : \mathbb{R}_+^{N_t \times N_b \times P_{\{2\}}(N_f)} \qquad \boldsymbol{\mathcal{X}}_2 : \mathbb{R}_+^{N_t \times N_b \times P_{\{3\}}(N_f)}$

$\quad 3 \quad \tilde{\boldsymbol{\mathcal{X}}}_3 : \mathbb{R}_+^{N_t \times N_b \times P_{\{3\}}(N_P)}$

$\quad 4 \quad$ **for** $i = 1 : \infty$

$\quad 5 \qquad$ **do** $\triangleright$ Loop over sequences of input data.

$\quad 6 \qquad\quad$ **for** $i_t, i_f$

$\quad 7 \qquad\qquad$ **do** $\triangleright$ Stage 1: create sensor data.

$\quad 8 \qquad\quad \boldsymbol{\mathcal{X}}_1 = \tilde{\boldsymbol{\mathcal{X}}}_1$

$\quad 9 \qquad\quad$ **for** $i_t, i_f$

$\quad 10 \qquad\qquad$ **do** $\triangleright$ Stage 2: beamform sensor data.

$\quad 11 \qquad\quad \boldsymbol{\mathcal{X}}_2 = \tilde{\boldsymbol{\mathcal{X}}}_2$

$\quad 12 \qquad\quad$ **for** $i_f$

$\quad 13 \qquad\qquad$ **do** $\triangleright$ Stage 3: write data to files.

$\quad 14 \qquad\quad$ **for** $i_t, i_b$

$\quad 15 \qquad\qquad$ **do** $\triangleright$ Stage 4a: sum along local frequency dimension.

$\quad 16 \qquad\quad \text{AGG}(\tilde{\boldsymbol{\mathcal{X}}}_3)$

$\quad 17 \qquad\quad$ **for** $i_t, i_b$

$\quad 18 \qquad\qquad$ **do** $\triangleright$ Stage 4b: sum aggregated data.

# Part II

# Advanced Techniques

# Chapter 4

# Parallel Programming Models

**Summary**

A nonembarrassingly parallel example (Blurimage) is used to illustrate the key design, code, debug, and test trade-offs associated with parallel programming. The Blurimage example reveals the breadth of issues associated with applying these steps. In addition, this chapter will also provide a short introduction to the primary parallel programming models: distributed arrays, message passing, and manager/worker.

This chapter focuses on providing more breadth regarding the key design, code, debug, and test trade-offs associated with parallel programming. The goal is to reveal the breadth of issues associated with applying these principles. In addition, this chapter will also provide a short introduction to the primary parallel programming models: distributed array semantics, message passing, and manager/worker. Some of the principles covered in this section include the following:

Design: when to go parallel, classes of parallel programs, parallel programming models, machine model

Coding: different parallel programming styles, impact of code on performance and scalability

Debug: details of the parallel debug process, what errors are found at each step

Testing: performance metrics and predicting performance (relative to machine parameters)

The primary example program used in this chapter is more sophisticated than those shown in Chapter 2 and is designed to expose some of the boundaries of the different parallel programming models.

## 4.1 Design: Knowing when to "go parallel"

The single most important decision in parallel programing is knowing when a parallel computer is required. There are two—and only two—reasons to use a parallel computer:

- Time: a computation is taking a long time on one processor.

- Memory: a computation requires more memory than one processor can provide.

Often both reasons apply. Programs that require a lot of memory often take a long time to run. So, how does a MATLAB programmer determine if either of these conditions apply? A long time is a subjective term. Typically, this means a computation that is taking hours or days, but sometimes ten minutes is too long. Memory is a little less subjective. A computer has a certain amount of memory, and when a program tries to use more than this amount of memory, it will either produce an "out of memory" error or the program will start slowing down dramatically because the operating system will try to use the local storage as memory (this is referred to as "swapping"). Fortunately, MATLAB has several built-in tools that can help determine not only how much time and memory a program is taking but also which specific parts are taking the most time and memory. These tools will be demonstrated by first applying them to a simple image processing program (Blurimage).

### 4.1.1  Memory and performance profiling

Consider a serial application that is taking a long time to run or does not fit on one processor. How does the programmer determine where and how to apply parallel processing to best overcome these issues? The first step is to profile the application and determine what data structures are taking up the most storage and which operations are taking the most time to execute. In this chapter, the Blurimage example program will be used to illustrate this process.

First, start MATLAB and type `cd Examples/Blurimage`. To put the Beamformer program into a serial mode, edit the file `dBeamformer.m` and set `PARALLEL=0`. At the MATLAB prompt, type `profview`, which brings up the profiler. In the "Run this command" field type `Blurimage`. This runs the MATLAB profiler on this program. After a little while, it will produce an image (see Figure 4.1). In the profiler window click on the `dBeamformer` line, which will show profile data similar to Figure 4.2. The profiler provides detailed information on how long each line of the

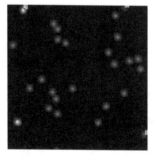

**Figure 4.1. Blurimage output.**

program took to run. To obtain information on the memory storage, type `whos`, which should produce output similar to

```
...
N_x                 1x1                     8   double
N_y                 1x1                     8   double
Nk_x                1x1                     8   double
Nk_y                1x1                     8   double
Z                   1024x1024         8388608   double
Zloc                1024x1024         8388608   double
Zmap                1x1                     8   double
kernel              32x32                8192   double
myI                 1x1024               8192   double
myJ                 1x1024               8192   double
n_blur              1x1                     8   double
...
```

As we can see from Figure 4.2, one function (`conv2`) is taking most of the time, and a very specific variable (`Z`) is taking most of the memory. This is as expected. The Blurimage application is a simple image-filtering program that repeatedly convolves an image with a filter (or kernel). This is one of the most common operations in the field of image processing and is mathematically represented by the double summation formula

$$\mathbf{Z}^{blur}(i,j) = \sum_{i'=1}^{N_K} \sum_{j'=1}^{N_K} \mathbf{K}(i',j')\mathbf{Z}(i-i', j-j')$$

where $i$ and $j$ are pixel indices, $\mathbf{Z}$ and $\mathbf{Z}^{blur}$ are the input and output images, and $K$ is an $N_K$ x $N_K$ filter kernel. The above direct summation involves $2N_K^2$ operations per pixel (the 2 is because there is a multiply and an add). The serial algorithm for this program is shown in Algorithm 4.1.

**Algorithm 4.1. Blurimage serial.**
The algorithm takes as input an $N_x \times N_y$ reference image $\mathbf{Z}$ and an $N_K \times N_K$ kernel $\mathbf{K}$, and $N_{blur}$ is the number of times to blur the image. The output is $N_x \times N_y$ blurred image $\mathbf{Z}$.

$\mathbf{Z} : \mathbb{R}_+^{N_x \times N_y} = \text{BLURIMAGE}(\mathbf{Z} : \mathbb{R}_+^{N_x \times N_y}, \mathbf{K} : \mathbb{R}_+^{N_K \times N_K}, N_{blur})$
1   **for** $i_{blur} = 1 : N_{blur}$
2       **do**
3          $\mathbf{Z} = \mathbf{K} \circ \mathbf{Z}$

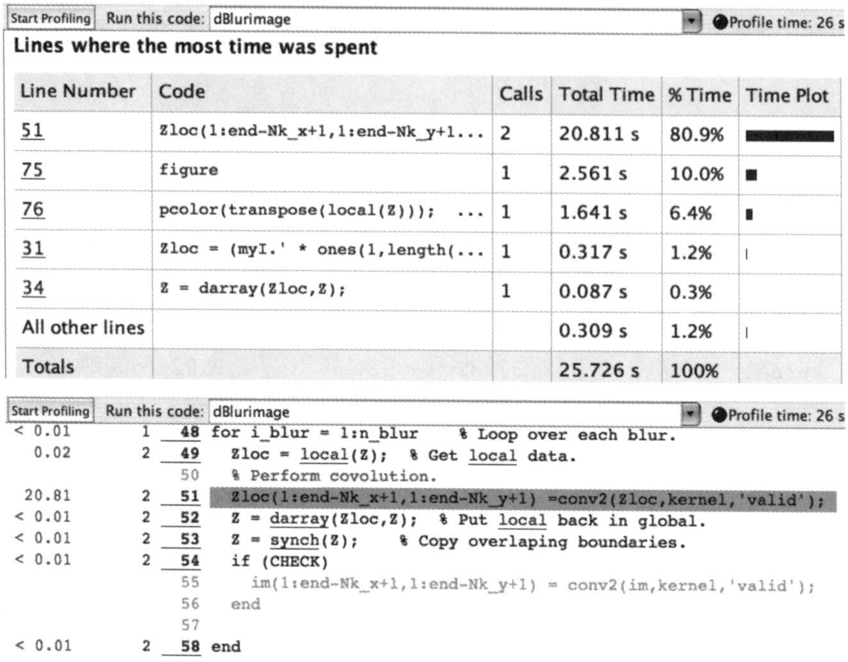

| Start Profiling | Run this code: dBlurimage | | | ▼ ●Profile time: 26 s | | |

**Lines where the most time was spent**

| Line Number | Code | Calls | Total Time | % Time | Time Plot |
|---|---|---|---|---|---|
| 51 | Zloc(1:end-Nk_x+1,1:end-Nk_y+1... | 2 | 20.811 s | 80.9% | ▬▬▬▬▬ |
| 75 | figure | 1 | 2.561 s | 10.0% | ▪ |
| 76 | pcolor(transpose(local(Z)));  ... | 1 | 1.641 s | 6.4% | ▪ |
| 31 | Zloc = (myI.' * ones(1,length(... | 1 | 0.317 s | 1.2% | ǀ |
| 34 | Z = darray(Zloc,Z); | 1 | 0.087 s | 0.3% | |
| All other lines | | | 0.309 s | 1.2% | ǀ |
| Totals | | | 25.726 s | 100% | |

| Start Profiling | Run this code: dBlurimage | | | ▼ ●Profile time: 26 s |

```
< 0.01      1   48  for i_blur = 1:n_blur     % Loop over each blur.
  0.02      2   49      Zloc = local(Z);  % Get local data.
                50      % Perform covolution.
 20.81      2   51      Zloc(1:end-Nk_x+1,1:end-Nk_y+1) =conv2(Zloc,kernel,'valid');
< 0.01      2   52      Z = darray(Zloc,Z);   % Put local back in global.
< 0.01      2   53      Z = synch(Z);     % Copy overlaping boundaries.
< 0.01      2   54      if (CHECK)
                55          im(1:end-Nk_x+1,1:end-Nk_y+1) = conv2(im,kernel,'valid');
                56      end
                57
< 0.01      2   58  end
```

**Figure 4.2. Blurimage profiler results.**
Profiler records the total time and the number of times each function or
line of code is called. This profile indicates that the conv2 function is
consuming the majority of the time.

The convolution traverses each point (or pixel) of the image, multiplies all
the other points around the pixel by the values in the filter, and then sums these
together to produce a new pixel value. This type of program is a good target for
parallelization because a single function is consuming all the time and a single data
structure is occupying all the storage. The Blurimage program is in many respects
similar to the Mandelbrot program shown in Chapter 2, with one small but very
important difference. In the Mandelbrot program, each point in the image could be
computed independently of the others. In Blurimage, each point depends upon the
values surrounding that point. This subtle difference will have a significant impact
on how the program can be parallelized. In fact, this type of nonlocal dependency
is characteristic of many programs.

So how can a parallel computer be best used in this situation? This question
brings up another very important principle: the best parallel program is a good
serial program. Parallel computing adds unavoidable complexities to any program.
It is better to first try and solve the performance issues using other means, if
possible. So the first step is to optimize the serial code for time and memory.

• Time

    – Can the data structures be allocated up front instead of dynamically?

- Can vectorized statements be used instead of for loops?

- Are there very long for loops that can be replaced by shorter for loops?

- Can a C, C++, or Fortran routine that would do a key function much faster be written and linked in?

- Memory

  - Are there unnecessary duplicates of variables?

  - Can variables be cleared after they are used?

  - Can arrays be used instead of cell arrays or structures?

  - Can smaller data types be used (e.g., int8 instead of double)?

  - Can the problem be worked on one piece at a time and intermediate results stored to disk?

These are just a few optimization hints. For more information on MATLAB optimization please see [McGarrity 2007]. Since this book is about parallel computing, it will be assumed that the starting point is a well-optimized serial program that can overcome time and memory limitations only through the use of parallel computing. In the Blurimage example, most of the computations are consumed by a single MATLAB function (`conv2`) and most of the memory is consumed by a single data array (`image`), leaving little room for additional optimization of the serial program.

## 4.1.2   Parallel programming patterns

After deciding that a parallel computer is indeed the appropriate solution to the time and/or memory constraints, the next question is how to parallelize the program. When one is choosing a parallel design, it is good to follow the classic engineering principle: the best way to solve a problem is to know the answer ahead of time. More specifically, there are many classical parallel computing problems with known solutions (several of these were presented in Chapter 2). The best approach is to determine which of these classical problems is most similar to the specific problem at hand and to then follow that approach. This approach is sometime referred to as pattern-based programming (see [Mattson et al. 2004]). This book will provide many such examples, and a brief taxonomy is given in Table 4.1. However, selecting the appropriate pattern to follow is just the first step in the design process. Our goal is to provide insight on the entire process necessary to produce a well-performing application.

Most likely this table is not very useful to you at this point because you are not very familiar with these programs. Don't worry—these programs will be covered in greater detail throughout the book. However, several of them have already been covered (see the examples in Chapter 2) and are among the most important. If your particular application is well represented by one of the examples in Chapter 2, then you may already know what you need to make it a parallel program. If, after looking over the examples in this book, you find that your problem doesn't fit into

**Table 4.1. Taxonomy of parallel applications.**
List of parallel programs covered in this book (see Chapter 7 for more detailed descriptions). Name is the common name for the application or benchmark. Description provides a short description of what the program is trying to do. Communication is the type of communication required to implement the program in parallel. Programming model is the "best" programming model for this problem.

| Name (Chapter) | Description | Communication | Programming Model |
|---|---|---|---|
| AddOne (1) | Parameter Sweep | Scatter/Gather | Array or manager/worker |
| Mandelbrot (2) | Parameter Sweep | Scatter/Gather | Array or manager/worker |
| ParallelIO (2) | Parallel File IO | None | Any |
| ZoomImage (2) | Zoom in on an image | Scatter/Gather | Array or manager/worker |
| Beamformer (3) | Sensor Processing | Pipeline | Array |
| Blurimage (4) | Filter a large image | Nearest neighbor | Array |
| Benchmark Suite: HPC Challenge | | | |
| STREAM (8) | Add large vectors | None | Any |
| RandomAccess (9) | Update large vector | All-to-all | Array & Messages |
| 1D FFT (10) | FFT a large vector | All-to-all | Array |
| HPL (11) | LU factorization | All-to-all | Array & Messages |

any of these, the next best thing to do is to discuss your problem with someone who is familiar with parallel programming in your domain. Finally, you may be required to design your own solution, in which case you are reading the right book. Table 4.1 also introduces two new terms that haven't been covered yet. The first is the communication pattern required by the program. The second term is the parallel programming model.

**Parallel communication patterns**

The communication pattern is the standard way parallel programming experts classify programs. Four of the most common patterns are shown in Figure 4.3. The first is the scatter/gather model, which was used in many of the examples in Chapter 2. In this pattern, a single $P_{ID}$ scatters data to all the other $P_{ID}$s and then waits for answers to come back. This pattern can be implemented by any of the parallel programming models. For the most part, the manager/worker model is limited to only this communication pattern. The next pattern is pipelining, whereby each $P_{ID}$ receives data, processes it, and then sends it to another $P_{ID}$. This pipeline pattern is typical of many sensor data processing applications. The nearest-neighbor pattern usually involves organizing the $P_{ID}$s into a virtual grid; each $P_{ID}$ then communicates only with its nearest neighbors. Blurimage falls into this pattern. Finally, the all-to-all pattern means any $P_{ID}$ may try and communicate with any other $P_{ID}$.

Most of the examples in Chapter 2 fall into the scatter/gather pattern. This is probably the most common pattern and also has the benefit of being relatively easy to implement using any of the programming models. In general, the distributed array programming model will be used to implement these types of applications because it is the simplest (i.e., requires the fewest changes to a serial program).

Blurimage has a nearest-neighbor communication pattern, which is easiest to implement with a distributed array programming model. The three programming models covered in this book are distributed arrays, message passing, and manager/worker. In certain all-to-all programs, a message passing approach or a hybrid distributed array and message passing approach is best. These will be covered in greater detail in Chapters 9 and 11.

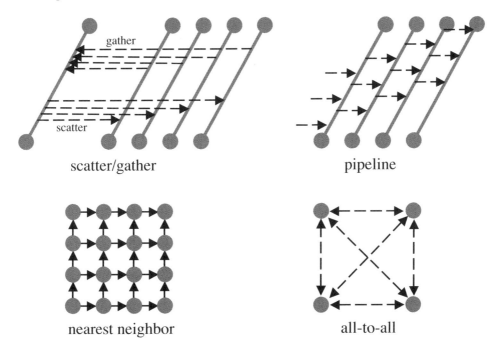

**Figure 4.3. Standard parallel communication patterns.**
In scatter/gather, a single $P_{ID}$ scatters data to all the other $P_{ID}$s and then waits for answers to come back. Pipelining involves each $P_{ID}$ receiving data, processing it, and then sending it on to another $P_{ID}$. The nearest-neighbor pattern usually involves organizing the $P_{ID}$s into a virtual grid; each $P_{ID}$ then communicates only with its nearest neighbors. In the all-to-all pattern, any $P_{ID}$ may try and communicate with any other $P_{ID}$.

**Parallel programming models**

The manager/worker model is the simplest parallel programming model. It is used when a problem can be broken up into a set of completely independent tasks that the workers (clients) can process without communicating with each other. The central constraint of the manager/worker model is that each worker communicates only with the leader (server) and requires no knowledge about what the other workers are doing. This constraint is very powerful and is enormously simplifying. Furthermore, it has proved very robust and the vast majority of networked programs follow this model.

The message passing model is in many respects the opposite of the manager/worker model. The message passing model requires that any $P_{ID}$ be able to send and receive messages from any other $P_{ID}$. The infrastructure of the message passing model is fairly simple. This infrastructure is most typically instantiated in the parallel computing community via the Message Passing Interface (MPI) standard [Gropp et al. 1999]. The message passing model requires that each processor have a unique identifier ($P_{ID}$) and know how many other processors ($N_P$) are working together on a problem (in MPI terminology ($P_{ID}$) and ($N_P$) are referred to as the processor "rank" and the "size" of the MPI world). Any parallel program can be implemented using the message passing model. The primary drawback of this model is that the programmer must manage every individual message in the system; therefore, the model often requires a great deal of additional code and may be extremely difficult to debug. Nevertheless, there are certain parallel programs that can be implemented only with a message passing model.

The distributed array model is a compromise between the two models. Distributed arrays impose additional constraints on the program, which allow complex programs to be written relatively simply. In many respects, it is the most natural parallel programming model for MATLAB because it is implemented using arrays, which are the core data type in MATLAB. Briefly, the distributed array model creates distributed arrays in which each $P_{ID}$ stores or owns a piece of the whole array. Additional information is stored in the array so that every $P_{ID}$ knows which parts of the array the other $P_{ID}$s have. How the arrays are broken up among the $P_{ID}$s is specified by a map [Lebak et al. 2005]. For example, Figure 4.4 shows a matrix broken up by rows, columns, rows and columns, and columns with some overlap. The different mappings are useful concepts to have even if the distributed array model is not being used. The concept of breaking up arrays in different ways is one of the key ideas in parallel computing.

Computations on distributed matrices are usually performed using the "owner computes" rule, which means that each $P_{ID}$ is responsible for doing a computation on the data it is storing locally. Maps can become quite complex and express virtually arbitrary distributions. One example of this complexity is the case in which a boundary of an array is required by more than one $P_{ID}$. The Blurimage example has this requirement because a convolution needs data around each point.

### 4.1.3  Blurimage parallel design

It is easiest to understand these models through specific examples. In this section, we will discuss implementing the Blurimage example using all three programming models; this approach should give some understanding as to the trade-offs involved in employing each model. The different parallel designs for Blurimage are shown in Figure 4.5.

In the manager/worker design, the manager sends a part of the image along with the boundary to each $P_{ID}$. The workers perform the convolution and send

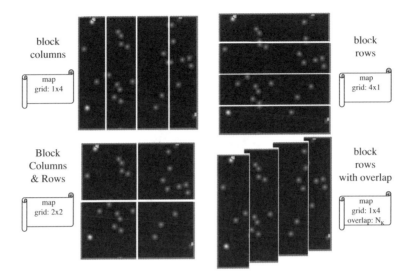

**Figure 4.4. Distributed array mappings.**
Different parallel mappings of a two-dimensional array. Arrays can be broken up in any dimension. A block mapping means that each $P_{ID}$ holds a contiguous piece of the array. Overlap allows the boundaries of an array to be stored on two neighboring $P_{ID}$s.

the convolved answer back. This process of scattering and gathering the image is repeated for each iteration of the convolution. This model has two primary challenges. First, if the reason the program is being run in parallel is because the image is prohibitively large (which is often the case), then the manager/worker model won't work because the leader will have difficulty holding the entire image. Second, the multiple scatters and gathers may be time-consuming, and they are unnecessary. At each iteration, $N_x N_y + N_K N_y N_P$ pixels need to be communicated or $8 + 8N_K N_P/N_x$ bytes per pixel (assuming 8-byte pixels). The term computation-to-communication ratio is used for an important measure of how compute-intensive a parallel program is. The higher this ratio, the faster this program will run well on a parallel computer. In this case, this ratio in operations per byte sent is

$$\text{Computation/Communication} = 2N_K^2/(8 + 8N_K N_P/N_x) \approx \frac{1}{4}N_K^2$$

For $N_K = 32$, this implies a ratio of 256.

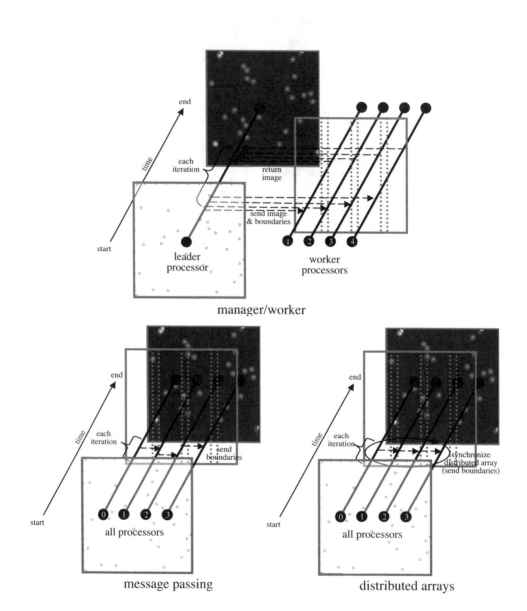

**Figure 4.5. Blurimage parallel designs.**
Manager/worker, message passing, and distributed array parallel designs for the Blurimage program. Dashed lines indicate communication between $P_{ID}$s.

**Algorithm 4.2. Blurimage manager/worker.**

The algorithm consists of two programs: a manager program and a worker program. The manager program runs on one computer and sends the input to each of the workers (line 5) and receives the output when the worker is done performing the convolution (line 7). The worker program runs on $N_P$ processors, receives the input from the manager (line 3), performs the convolution (line 4), and sends the output (minus the boundary) back (line 5).

$$\mathbf{Z} : \mathbb{R}_+^{N_x \times N_y} = \text{BLURIMAGEMANAGER}($$
$$\mathbf{Z} : \mathbb{R}_+^{N_x \times N_y}, \mathbf{K} : \mathbb{R}_+^{N_K \times N_K}, N_{blur})$$

1   $i_{start} = \lfloor N_x(0 : N_P - 1)/N_P \rfloor + 1$
2   $i_{end} = \lfloor N_x(1 : N_P)/N_P \rfloor + 1$
3   **for** $i_{blur} = 1 : N_{blur}$
4       **do for** $P_{ID} = 1 : N_P$
5           **do** $\text{SEND}(P_{ID}, \mathbf{Z}(i_{start}(P_{ID}) : \min(i_{end}(P_{ID}) + N_K, N_X), :))$
6       **for** $P_{ID} = 1 : N_P$
7           **do** $\mathbf{Z}(i_{start}(P_{ID}) : i_{end}(P_{ID}), :) = \text{RECEIVE}(P_{ID})$

$\text{BLURIMAGEWORKER}(\mathbf{K} : \mathbb{R}_+^{N_K \times N_K}, N_{blur})$

1   **for** $i_{blur} = 1 : N_{blur}$
2       **do**
3           $\mathbf{Z} = \text{RECEIVE}(manager)$
4           $\mathbf{Z} = \mathbf{K} \circ \mathbf{Z}$
5           $\text{SEND}(manager, \mathbf{Z}(1 : end - N_K, :))$

The message passing design overcomes both of these issues by having each $P_{ID}$ initialize and store just the part of the image it works on, plus the additional boundary points it needs to do its computation. Between each iteration, the only required communication is updating the boundary points with the new values computed by the adjacent $P_{ID}$. This results in only $N_K N_y N_P$ pixels being sent per iteration (or $8 N_K N_P / N_x$ byte per pixel). The resulting computation-to-communication ratio in operations per byte is

$$\text{Computation/Communication} = 2 N_K^2 / (8 N_K N_P / N_x) = \frac{1}{4} N_K N_x / N_P$$

For $N_K = 32$ and $N_x / N_P = 1024$, this implies a ratio of 8192, which is 32 times higher than the ratio for the manager/worker algorithm. This means that the message passing algorithm does approximately 32 times less communication than the manager/worker algorithm.

This communication step involves determining who the adjacent $P_{ID}$s are, packaging up the data, sending it, and receiving it. At one level, this operation is relatively straightforward because every $P_{ID}$ is actually doing nearly the same thing. Unfortunately, exactly what each $P_{ID}$ does is slightly different. No two $P_{ID}$s will be sending or receiving the same data to or from the same $P_{ID}$s. Coding and debugging these types of communications require a great deal of bookkeeping and are highly error prone.

**Algorithm 4.3. Blurimage message passing.**
The algorithm consists of one program run on all $P_{ID}$s. Each $P_{ID}$ works only $\tilde{\mathbf{Z}}$, which is its $N_x/N_P + N_K \times N_y$ of the whole image. At each iteration, each $P_{ID}$ explicitly sends (line 4) and receives (line 6) boundary to/from its neighboring $P_{ID}$s and then performs the convolution (line 7).

$$\tilde{\mathbf{Z}} : \mathbb{R}_+^{N_x/N_P + N_K \times N_y} = \text{BLURIMAGEMESSAGEPASSING}($$
$$\tilde{\mathbf{Z}} : \mathbb{R}_+^{N_x/N_P + N_k \times N_y}, \mathbf{K} : \mathbb{R}_+^{N_K \times N_K}, N_{blur})$$

1  **for** $i_{blur} = 1 : N_{blur}$
2      **do**
3          **if** $(P_{ID} > 1)$
4              **do** SEND$(P_{ID} - 1, \tilde{\mathbf{Z}}(1 : N_K, :))$
5          **if** $(P_{ID} < N_P)$
6              **do** $\tilde{\mathbf{Z}}(N_x/N_P : N_x/N_P + N_K, :) = \text{RECEIVE}(P_{ID} + 1)$
7          $\tilde{\mathbf{Z}} = \mathbf{K} \circ \tilde{\mathbf{Z}}$

**Algorithm 4.4. Blurimage distributed array.**
The algorithm is similar to the serial algorithm with the following differences. First, a distributed $\mathbf{Z}$ is declared with $N_K$ of overlapping boundary information using the notation $P_{ovN_K}()$. Second, each $P_{ID}$ performs the convolution on its local part of the image (line 3). Finally, the boundary conditions are synchronized using (line 4), which causes the neighboring $P_{ID}$s to communicate their overlapping boundaries.

$$\mathbf{Z} : \mathbb{R}_+^{P_{ov(N_K)}(N_x) \times N_y} = \text{BLURIMAGEDISTRIBUTEDARRAY}($$
$$\mathbf{Z} : \mathbb{R}_+^{P_{ov(N_K)}(N_x) \times N_y}, \mathbf{K} : \mathbb{R}_+^{N_K \times N_K}, N_{blur})$$

1  **for** $i_{blur} = 1 : N_{blur}$
2      **do**
3          $\mathbf{Z}.loc = \mathbf{K} \circ \mathbf{Z}.loc$
4          SYNCH$(\mathbf{Z})$

The distributed array design allows the same communication pattern as in the message passing design (and has the same computation-to-communication ratio) but in a way that is much easier to code. A single distributed image is created across $P_{ID}$s, with a specified overlap between $P_{ID}$s. Each $P_{ID}$ performs the convolution operation on its local data, and the updating of the boundary conditions is done with a single distributed synchronization command that determines that only the boundaries need to be sent to the nearest neighbors and manages all the required messages and array indexing.

## 4.2  Coding

In the previous section, the concept of the communication pattern was introduced. This pattern has strong implications on which programming model to use. In the testing section, it will be apparent that the programming model can have a large impact on performance (usually because different programming models support different communication patterns to a greater or lesser degree). In addition, the parallel programming model can also have a large impact on the complexity of writing the program. In fact, it is often better to use a simpler programming model (e.g., manager/worker) that gives worse performance than a more difficult programming model (e.g., message passing) that gives higher performance.

This section discusses parallelizing the example using each of these programming models and the trade-offs involved. Because of the length of the manager/worker and message passing codes, only the distributed array version will be shown and run.

There are several important goals that should be kept in mind in converting the serial program to a parallel program. The first goal is to achieve reasonable performance by expressing the parallelism in the problem so that every processor is fully utilized while minimizing the overhead of communication. The second goal, which is often at odds with the first, is to minimize the complexity of the program. This complexity can be measured by looking at several factors:

- Code expansion. How much bigger is the parallel code than the serial code?

- Distribution of code changes. Are the changes localized or are they made throughout the code?

- Scaling. Are the functions parameterized by $N_P$ and the problem size? Is the explicit use of parameters, such as $N_P$ or $P_{ID}$, minimized?

- Testing. How many more tests need to be run in order to know that the program is running correctly?

- Debugging. Is the parallel code still a valid serial code? Does the code support a straightforward process to go from serial to parallel?

### 4.2.1  Manager/worker

This approach to implementing parallel MATLAB programs has been around the longest. Manager/worker approaches [Choy & Edelman 1999, Morrow et al. 1998, Dean et al. 2005] use MATLAB as the users' front-end as a manager of a set of workers. The workers may or may not run MATLAB. For example, StarP keeps the distributed arrays on a parallel server, which calls the necessary routines from parallel libraries such as ScaLAPACK and FFTW. These approaches often provide the best performance once the data are transferred to the server. However, these approaches are limited to those functions that have been specifically linked to a parallel library. pMatlab can be run in this mode, although in the case of pMatlab the back-end server is MATLAB running on each $P_{ID}$ and the user is responsible for breaking up the calculation into embarrassingly parallel tasks that can be independently scheduled onto the workers.

In this section, a brief outline of the manager/worker implementation of the **Blurimage** program is described. The key conceptual difference between the manager/worker model and the other programming models is that there are two (and possibly three) different roles performed by different computers. There is a user MATLAB that initiates the program, breaks up the work into tasks, and sends them out to a job manager. The job manager then dispatches the tasks to multiple worker $P_{ID}$s, who then send their results back to the job manager for the user MATLAB to pick up.

The manager/worker code requires that four additional pieces of functionality be added to the basic serial algorithm:

- Manager computes the part of images each worker should get.

- Manager launches each worker with its piece of the image.

- Workers send their pieces of the image back to leader and then exit.

- Manager receives image pieces and assembles the final image.

In the manager code, the manager $P_{ID}$ computes the range of the image that each worker is responsible for and places these into the **i_start** and **i_stop** index arrays. These indices are then used to copy the pieces of the image (including the overlapping edges) into the **image_overlap_cell** array, which has one entry per $P_{ID}$. Next, **dfeval** is called, which scatters the image to the workers; the workers perform the convolution, and the results are gathered back to the leader. Finally, the returned cell array is converted back into an image using the **cell2mat** command. Adding this functionality to the code has a number of implications.

**Code expansion**. Going from a serial program to a manager/worker program usually results in a modest increase in the size of the code.

**Distribution of code changes**. This is the most significant impact of the manager/worker program because the program will need to be broken into two pieces and each line of code needs to be assigned to one of the two programs.

**Scaling.** Typically, manager/worker programs partition problems based on some preset task size and then vary the task size based on the overall size of the problem. Unfortunately, this often results in many small tasks that cannot employ the manager/worker model efficiently. To fix this problem, a manager/worker code can be parameterized based on the number of workers, thus resulting in a more efficient code. Unfortunately, this parameterization eliminates one of the main benefits of a manager worker code: no explicit dependence on $N_P$.

**Testing.** The number of test cases is reduced because serial testing is no longer meaningful.

**Debugging.** This is probably the biggest disadvantage of this approach. In the manager/worker model, the serial program is lost and it is no longer possible to cleanly run the program serially. Thus, there is no clean process for systematically isolating and testing specific aspects of the parallel functionality. This lack of a process significantly increases code development time as it becomes more difficult to isolate and track down bugs.

From a coding perspective, this manager/worker model does an excellent job of keeping the program small and simple. The elimination of the ability to run the program cleanly in a serial mode creates testing difficulties. From a performance standpoint, the manager/worker program requires that the pieces of the image be sent back to the leader and rebroadcast to the workers at every iteration, thus introducing a large overhead. In addition, and perhaps more importantly, because the leader must store the entire image, this program is limited to processing an image that will fit in the memory of the leader.

## 4.2.2 Message passing

In this section, a brief outline of the message passing implementation of the Blurimage program is described. The message passing approach [Kepner 2004, Zollweg 2006, Hudak 2008] requires the user to explicitly send messages within the code. These approaches often implement a variant of the Message Passing Interface (MPI) standard [Gropp et al. 1999]. Message passing allows any $P_{ID}$ to directly communicate with any other $P_{ID}$ and provides the minimum required functionality to implement any parallel program.

Like the distributed array model, a message passing program runs the same program on every $P_{ID}$ but operates on slightly different data. This is referred to as the same Single-Program Multiple-Data (SPMD, pronounced "spim-dee") execution model [Flynn 1972]. The key conceptual difference between the distributed array model and the message passing model is that the message passing between computers must be managed explicitly. In a message passing program, there are two key pieces of data that the program uses to guide its actions: the number of processors, $N_P$, and the processor ID, $P_{ID}$. Using this information, each $P_{ID}$ determines the part of the problem it is working on and which other $P_{ID}$s it needs to communicate with.

The message passing code requires that four additional pieces of functionality be added to the basic serial algorithm:

- Each $P_{ID}$ determines the size of its local image.

- Each $P_{ID}$ determines the identity of its neighbor $P_{ID}$s.

- Each $P_{ID}$ sends boundary data to its neighbor.

- Each $P_{ID}$ receives boundary from its neighbor.

The code consists of one program run on all $P_{ID}$s. Each $P_{ID}$ works only on its local portion of the image. The exact size of this local image must be explicitly calculated. At each iteration, each $P_{ID}$ explicitly sends and receives boundary data to/from its neighboring $P_{ID}$s and then performs the convolution. Adding this functionality to the code has a number of implications.

**Code expansion**. Going from a serial program to a message passing program usually results in a large increase in the size of the code. Serial programs converted to parallel programs with message passing typically increase in size by 25% to 50%; in contrast, manager/worker and distributed array approaches typically increase the code size by only approximately 5% [Funk & Kepner 2005].

**Distribution of code changes**. Message passing programs typically require changes to a program at its lowest levels and often result in highly unlocalized code changes.

**Scaling.** Message passing codes usually require the least amount of communication of any programming model and often exhibit the best performance scaling. Unfortunately, message passing programs inherently depend upon $N_P$ and $P_{ID}$. These concepts are used throughout the program. If properly done, this can be done in a parameterized way. However, this requires a lot of effort to check for edge conditions as the $N_P$ or the input data size scale.

**Testing.** The number of test cases is reduced because serial testing is no longer meaningful.

**Debugging.** Users who are already familiar with messaging find these approaches powerful, but the learning curve is steep for the typical user because explicit message passing is a lower level of abstraction and requires users to deal directly with deadlocks, synchronization, and other low-level parallel programming concepts. As in the manager/worker model, the serial program is lost and it is no longer possible to cleanly run the program serially. Thus, there is no clean process for systematically isolating and testing specific aspects of the parallel functionality. This lack of a process significantly increases code development time as it becomes more difficult to isolate and track down bugs.

In spite of these difficulties, a message passing capability is a requirement for both the manager/worker and distributed array approaches. Furthermore, message passing is often the most efficient way to implement a program, and certain programs with complex communication patterns can be implemented only with direct message passing. Thus, any complete parallel solution must provide a mechanism for accessing the underlying messaging layer.

In this instance, the message passing program and the distributed array program perform the same communication, and there is no performance advantage to using message passing. The main disadvantage of the message passing program is that it is significantly more complicated. The code is bigger, the changes to the serial program are not localized, and it is difficult to test.

## 4.2.3  Distributed arrays

The design of the distributed array program has already been discussed and was illustrated in Figure 4.5. The distributed array implementation follows a similar approach to Mandelbrot and the other programs described in Chapter 2. The distributed array code requires four additional pieces of functionality:

- Create a map and a distributed image with overlapping edges.

- Perform the convolution on the local part of the image.

- Synchronize the boundaries.

- The leader aggregates the image pieces and assembles the final image.

The core of the distributed array code is shown below (see `Examples/Blurimage/pBlurimage.m` for a complete listing).

In this instance, the distributed array model provides the best of both the manager/worker and message passing worlds. The code is small, simple, and easy to test, as is the manager/worker program. In addition, the memory and communication are scalable as in the message passing program.

**Code Listing 4.1.  Blurimage parallel MATLAB program.**

```
 1  % Set image size (scaled by Np), filter size and blur.
 2  Nx = 1024*Np; Ny = 1024; Nk = 32; Nblur = 2;
 3  PARALLEL = 1;              % Set control flag.
 4  Zmap = 1;                  % Create serial map.
 5  if (PARALLEL)              % Parallel map with overlap.
 6     Zmap = map([Np 1],{},0:Np-1,[Nk 0]);
 7  end
 8  Z = zeros(Nx,Ny,Zmap) + 1.e-4;      % 2D distributed array.
 9  [ii jj] = find(sprand(Nx,Ny,1e-4)); % Create non-zeros.
10  for i=1:numel(ii)
11     Z(ii(i),jj(i))=1;       % Insert non-zeros.
12  end
13  myI = global_ind(Z,1);     % Get local i indices.
14  myJ = global_ind(Z,2);     % Get local j indices.
15  kernel = ones(Nk,Nk);      % Create kernel.
16  Z = synch(Z);              % Synchronize boundary conditions.
17  for iblur = 1:Nblur        % Loop over each blur.
18     Zloc = local(Z);        % Get local data.
19     Zloc(1:end-Nk+1,1:end-Nk+1) = conv2(Zloc,kernel,'valid');
20     Z = put_local(Z,Zloc);  % Put local back in global.
21     Z = synch(Z);           % Copy overlapping boundaries.
22  end
```

## 4.3 Debug

The goal of debugging a parallel program is to achieve high performance on running the problem of interest. In theory, this can be done as soon as the program has been written. In practice, there are many additional functions that have been added to the program, and each of these should be debugged independently. In addition, a parallel program is usually targeting a problem that takes a long time to run, but debugging is much faster if the program runs to completion quickly. The process for negotiating these competing goals was used in Chapter 2. This process is depicted in Figure 4.6 and consists of four primary steps. It is extremely important that these steps are performed iteratively. If an error is found at one step, it is best to go back to the beginning and try to debug the error at the lowest numbered step.

The first step is to take a serial code and add the basic distributed array functionality using a `map`. This code is then run on one processor locally:

```
eval(pRUN('pBlurimage',1,{}))
```

The goal is to determine if the distributed array code is syntactically correct. Typically, the errors that are caught in this step have to do with the conversion of the arrays to distributed arrays.

The second step is to test the parameterization of the code in terms of $N_P$. This code is then run using multiple MATLAB instances on the local machine:

```
eval(pRUN('pBlurimage',2,ParallelMachine))
```

The goal is to determine if the decomposition is syntactically correct. Typically, the errors that are caught in this step have to do with the arithmetic of the decomposition.

The third step usually does not require additional coding but simply involves running on remote machines:

```
eval(pRUN('pBlurimage',2,ParallelMachine))
```

This step principally tests the underlying mechanisms for distributing the data and remotely running the program. Typically, the errors that are caught in this step have to do with the configuration of parallel software installation or the file system. For example, a function required to run the program exists on the local machine but is not available on the remote machine.

The fourth step also usually does not require additional coding but simply involves running on remote machines while setting $N_P$ to ever-increasing larger values and increasing the problem to the target size.

```
eval(pRUN('pBlurimage',4,ParallelMachine))
```

The goal is to start looking at the performance of the program and determine if it is achieving the desired performance.

## 4.4   Testing

In the previous section, the distributed array version of the Blurimage program was run for a variety of problem sizes. In addition to the visual output, each run also displayed the performance of the program measured in gigaflops (one billion floating

get it right                                                            make it fast

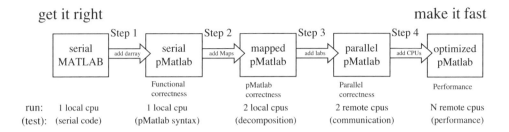

Figure 4.6. Four-step debug process.

At each step, the minimum amount of functionality is added and a test is run that specifically tests that functionality.

point operations per second). The next question is, Are these values good or bad? In other words, is `pBlurimage` a well-written parallel program?

Answering this question requires gathering the performance data and conducting a little further analysis. Dividing the performance by the performance achieved on one processor yields the parallel speedup achieved. Table 4.2 shows the relative compute time (normalized to $N_P = 1$), the launch time, and the relative performance. These data were collected on an eight processor multicore system and a 16 node multinode system. On the multicore system, all the processors share the same memory. On the multinode system, each node has separate memory and the processors communicate over a network.

**Table 4.2. Multicore and multinode Blurimage performance.**
Relative compute time, absolute launch+communication time, and compute speedup on multicore and multinode computing systems for different values of $N_P$. Performance data are shown for a scaled problem size ($N_x \propto N_P$). All values are normalized to column 2 in which $N_P = 1$ with the distributed arrays turned off (`PARALLEL=0`). Columns 3–7 are the values with distributed arrays turned on (`PARALLEL=1`). The notation 1*8 means that $N_P = 8$, and all $P_{ID}$s were run on the same processing node with the same shared memory. The notation 16*1 means that $N_P = 16$, and each $P_{ID}$ was run on a separate processing node with a separate memory.

| Multicore processors: | 1 | 1*1 | 1*2 | 1*4 | 1*8 | |
|---|---|---|---|---|---|---|
| Relative compute time | 1 | 1.0 | 0.85 | 0.87 | 0.86 | |
| Launch time (sec) | 0.0 | 0.0 | 0.7 | 1.2 | 1.8 | |
| Relative performance | 1 | 1.0 | 2.3 | 4.6 | 9.3 | |
| Multinode processors: | 1 | 1*1 | 2*1 | 4*1 | 8*1 | 16*1 |
| Relative compute time | 1 | 1.0 | 1.0 | 1.0 | 1.0 | 1.0 |
| Launch time (sec) | 0.0 | 0.0 | 8.0 | 8.0 | 7.8 | 7.8 |
| Relative performance | 1 | 1.0 | 2.0 | 4.0 | 7.9 | 15.9 |

Comparing the performance of running the program using $N_P = 1$ with distributed arrays turned off (`PARALLEL=0`) and distributed arrays turned on (`PARALLEL=1`) indicates that distributed arrays do not incur a performance penalty. If using distributed arrays with $N_P = 1$ slows things down significantly, then this must be addressed. It is very difficult to get any benefit with $N_P > 1$ if the $N_P = 1$ case is slower than the base serial code. Working only on the local parts of distributed arrays almost guarantees the performance will be the same as when distributed arrays are not being used.

Table 3.2 shows the compute time decreasing as $N_P$ is increased on both the multicore and multinode systems. However, a parallel program usually introduces an added time associated with launching and communicating between each of the MATLAB instances. Table 4.2 shows that launch+communication time increases with $N_P$ and is larger on the multinode system because the launching and communication take place over a network.

Blurimage was run on a scaled problem size (i.e., $N_x \propto N_P$). The execution time will remain approximately the same as $N_P$ increases. The performance increases because the total work done also increases with $N_P$.

## 4.5   Performance summary

Recall that in the Blurimage algorithm $O(N_K^2)$ operations are required to compute each pixel. The manager/worker implementation does a good job of distributing the computations so that an equal number of image pixels are on each $P_{ID}$. Therefore, the performance of the computations should scale with $N_P$. However, in the manager/worker implementation, the entire image needs to be sent back and forth from the leader to the workers at each step. In other words, every pixel that is computed is sent twice. Ignoring constants, this produces a computation-to-communication ratio of $O(N_K^2)$ operations per pixel sent, which for $N_K = 16$ implies a ratio of 256. This ratio is comparable to what is found on typical parallel machines. Therefore, an efficiency of 0.5 may actually be about all that can be achieved using the manager/worker design.

Given that the manager/worker design limits the performance of this application, how well would the message passing and distributed array models do? The computation in both models remains the same as in the manager/worker case: $O(N_K^2)$ per pixel. Both the message passing and distributed array designs use the nearest-neighbor communication pattern. In this pattern, only a small fraction of the image pixels needs to be communicated: $O(N_K/N_I)$, for a $N_I \times N_I$ image. This nearest-neighbor pattern results in a computation-to-communication ratio of $O(N_K N_I)$ operations per pixel sent, which for $N_I = 1024$ implies a ratio of around 16,000. This number is much higher than in the manager/worker designs. Therefore, both the message passing and distributed array designs should perform well with increasing $N_P$ as shown in Table 4.2.

## 4.6   Summary

The goal of this chapter has been to rapidly introduce nearly all the concepts that are covered in the book:

Design: when to go parallel, classes of parallel programs, parallel programming models, machine model.

Coding: different parallel programming styles, impact of code on performance and scalability.

Debug: details of the parallel debug process, what errors are found at each step.

Testing: performance metrics and predicting performance (relative to machine parameters).

Fortunately, this is pretty much all there is. There will be very few new concepts introduced in the rest of this book. The remainder of the book will be spent looking at these concepts in greater detail and providing you with sufficient proficiency in them to apply them to your own programs.

# References

[Choy & Edelman 1999] Ron Choy and Alan Edelman, Parallel MATLAB: Doing it right. Proceedings of the IEEE (Feb. 2005), Vol. 93, No. 2, pp. 331–341.

[Dean et al. 2005] Loren Dean, Silvina Grad-Freilich, J. Kepner, and A. Reuther, Distributed and Parallel Computing with MATLAB. Tutorial presented at Supercomputing 2005, Nov. 12, 2005, Seattle, WA.

[Flynn 1972] Michael Flynn, Some computer organizations and their effectiveness, IEEE Trans. Comput., Vol. C-21, p. 948, 1972.

[Funk & Kepner 2005] Andrew Funk, Jeremy Kepner, Loren Hochstein, and Victor Basili, A Relative Development Time Productivity Metric for HPC Systems, HPEC Workshop, Sep. 20–22, 2005, Lexington, MA.

[Gropp et al. 1999] William Gropp, Ewing Lusk, and Anthony Skjellum, Using MPI: Portable Parallel Programing with the Message Passing Interface, Cambridge, MA: MIT Press, 1999.

[Hudak 2008] Dave Hudak, Blue Collar MPI, http://www.bluecollarcomputing.org

[Kepner 2004] Jeremy Kepner and Stan Ahalt, MatlabMPI, Journal of Parallel and Distributed Computing, Vol. 64, No. 8, pp. 997–1005, 2004.

[Lebak et al. 2005] James Lebak, Jeremy Kepner, Henry Hoffmann, and Edward Rutledge, Parallel VSIPL++: An open standard software library for high-performance parallel signal processing, 2005, Proceedings of the IEEE: Special Issue on Program Generalization, Optimization, and Platform Adaptation, Jose Moura (editor).

[Mattson et al. 2004] Timothy G. Mattson, Beverly A. Sanders, and Berna L. Massingill, Patterns for Parallel Programming 2004, Pearson Education, Boston, MA.

[McGarrity 2007] Stuart McGarrity, Programming Patterns: Maximizing Code Performance by Optimizing Memory Access, The MathWorks News & Notes - June 2007.

[Morrow et al. 1998] G. Morrow and R. A. van de Geijn, Parallel Linear Algebra Server for Matlab-like Environments. In Proceedings of Supercomputing 1998, Orlando, FL, November 1998.

[Zollweg 2006] John Zollweg, Cornell Multitask Toolbox for MATLAB, 2006, http://www.tc.cornell.edu/services/support/forms/cmtm.p2.htm

# Chapter 5

# Advanced Distributed Array Programming

**Summary**

Effectively using distributed arrays requires understanding the underlying technology that is used to implement them. MATLAB distributed arrays are generally implemented in a library using object-oriented operator overloading techniques. The core data structure in the library is a distributed numerical array whose distribution onto multiple processors is specified with a map construct. Communication operations between distributed arrays are abstracted away from the user. The types of data distributions supported by the maps are typically drawn from the class of $N$-dimensional block-cyclic distributions with overlap. Block distributions are the most commonly used. Cyclic distributions are often useful for addressing load-balancing issues. The distributed array library is built on a point-to-point messaging library such as the Message Passing Interface (MPI). The messaging library sets the fundamental limit on communication performance in the distributed array library.

## 5.1 Introduction

The essence of a distributed array library is its ability to support parallel redistribution between distributed arrays

$$\mathbf{B} = \mathbf{A}$$

In the simple case where $\mathbf{A}$ and $\mathbf{B}$ are identically mapped (e.g., $\mathbf{A}, \mathbf{B} : \mathbb{R}^{P(N) \times N}$), the operation is fairly straightforward. Each $P_{ID}$ would simply copy its local part of $\mathbf{A}$ to its local part of $\mathbf{B}$; in other words

$$\mathbf{B}.loc = \mathbf{A}.loc$$

[Recall that the $P()$ notation causes the specified dimension to be split into uniform blocks among $N_P$ processors.] In a more complex case such as $\mathbf{A} : \mathbb{R}^{P(N) \times N}$ and

$\mathbf{B} : \mathbb{R}^{P(N) \times N}$, the underlying distributed array library needs to determine which
$P_{IDS}$ "own" which data elements and send the corresponding data elements to
the appropriate $P_{IDS}$. Chapters 2 and 3 illustrated more complex examples that
included overlapping edges and pipelining of data between sets of $P_{IDS}$. The types
of data distributions supported by the maps are typically drawn from the class of $N$-
dimensional block-cyclic overlapped distributions. Ultimately, it is the distributed
array library that must figure this out and do so in a way that is easy to use and is
efficient.

## 5.2   Pure versus fragmented distributed arrays

Distributed array programming in MATLAB has a number of antecedents, most notably pMatlab [Bliss & Kepner 2007], StarP [Choy & Edelman 1999], Falcon [Falcon],
and hierarchical array extensions [Kim & Kepner 2006, Bikshandi et al. 2006].
These approaches provide a mechanism for creating arrays that are distributed
across multiple processors. Distributed arrays have a long history in other languages, for example, Fortran [Koelbel 1994, Numrich & Reid 1998] and C
[El-Ghazawi et al. 2005], as well as in many C++ libraries such as
POOMA [Cummings et al. 1998], GA Toolkit [Nieplocha et al. 2002], PVL
[Rutledge & Kepner 1999], and Parallel VSIPL++ [Lebak et al. 2005]. The distributed array approach allows the user to view a distributed object as a single
entity as opposed to multiple pieces. This approach allows operations on the array
as a whole or on local parts of the array. Additionally, these libraries are com-
patible with communication libraries (such as MPI) and are amenable to hybrid
shared/distributed memory implementations.

   Distributed arrays can be used in both pure distributed array and fragmented
distributed array programming models (see Figure 5.1). The pure distributed array
model presents an entirely global view of a distributed array. Specifically, once
created with an appropriate map object, distributed arrays are treated the same as
nondistributed ones. When using this programming model, the user never accesses
the local part of the array and all operations (such as matrix multiplies, FFTs,
convolutions, etc.) are performed on the global structure. The benefits of pure
distributed arrays are ease of programming and the highest level of abstraction.
The drawbacks include the need to implement parallel versions of serial operations
and the library performance overhead this incurs.

   The fragmented distributed array model maintains a high level of abstraction
but allows access to local parts of the arrays. Specifically, distributed arrays are
created in the same manner as pure distributed arrays; however, the operations can
be performed on just the local part of the arrays. Later, the global structure can
be updated with locally computed results. This approach allows greater flexibility.
Additionally, this approach does not require function coverage or implementation of
parallel versions of all existing serial functions. Furthermore, fragmented distributed
array programs often achieve better performance by eliminating the library overhead
on local computations.

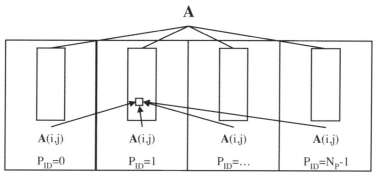

pure distributed array

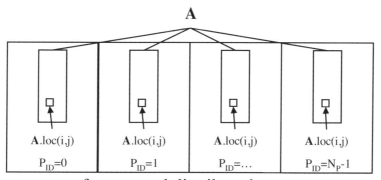

fragmented distributed array

**Figure 5.1. Pure versus fragmented distributed arrays.**
The top half of the figure illustrates pure distributed arrays. Matrix **A** is distributed among $N_P$ processors. Element $i, j$ is referenced on all the processors. In pure distributed arrays, the index $i, j$ is a global index that references the same element on all processors (on $P_{ID} = 0$ that element is local; on all other $P_{ID}$s it is remote). The lower half of the figure illustrates fragmented distributed arrays. Here, each $P_{ID}$ references element $i, j$ local to the $P_{ID}$; thus, each $P_{ID}$ references a different element in the global matrix.

The distributed array libraries used in this book support both pure and fragmented distributed array programming models and allows combining distributed arrays with direct message passing for optimized performance. Both fragmented and pure distributed array programming models use the same distributed array data structure, allowing conversion between the two. While the library does use message passing in the library routines, a typical user does not have to explicitly incorporate messages into the code.

## 5.3   MATLAB distributed array interface and architecture design

The primary challenge in implementing a parallel computation library is how to balance the conflicting goals of ease of use, high performance, and ease of implementation. With respect to distributed arrays in MATLAB, each of these goals can be defined in a measurable way (see Table 5.1); in Chapter 6, these metrics are explored in greater detail. The performance metrics are typical of those used throughout the high performance computing community and primarily look at the computation and memory overhead of programs written using parallel MATLAB relative to serial programs written using MATLAB and parallel programs written using C with MPI. The metrics for ease of use and ease of implementation are derived from the software engineering community (see [Johnson 2004, Johnson 2005] and [Kepner 2004] and papers therein) and look at code size, programmer effort, and required programmer expertise. These metrics have a subjective element; nevertheless, they are useful tools for measuring progress toward programmer goals. The rest of this section discusses the particular choices made in implementing a distributed array library to satisfy these goals.

## 5.4   Maps and distributions

The first step in writing a parallel program is to start with a functionally correct serial program. The conversion from serial to parallel requires the user to add new constructs to the code. Distributed array programming adopts a separation-of-concerns approach to this process that makes the functionality of the program orthogonal to mapping it onto a parallel architecture. A serial program is made parallel by adding maps to arrays to create distributed arrays. Maps contain only information about how an array is broken up onto multiple $P_{ID}$s, and the addition of a map should not change the functional correctness of a program. A map is composed of a grid specifying how each dimension is partitioned; a distribution that selects either a block, cyclic, or block-cyclic partitioning; and a list of $P_{ID}$s that defines which $P_{ID}$s actually hold the data.

The concept of using maps to describe array distributions has a long history. The ideas for parallel MATLAB maps are principally drawn from the High Performance Fortran (HPF) community [Loveman 1993, Zosel 1993], the MIT Lincoln Laboratory Space-Time Adaptive Processing Library (STAPL) [DeLuca et al. 1997], and the Parallel Vector Library (PVL) [Lebak et al. 2005]. MATLAB distributed arrays explicitly support data parallelism; however, implicit task parallelism can be implemented through careful mapping of data arrays.

The distributed array map construct is defined by three components: (1) grid description, (2) distribution description, and (3) a $P_{ID}$ list. The grid description together with the $P_{ID}$ list describes where the data object is distributed, while the distribution describes how the object is distributed. Depending on the underlying implementation, MATLAB distributed arrays can support any combination of block-cyclic distributions. The API defining these distributions is shown in Figure 5.2.

**Table 5.1. Distributed array design goals.**
Metrics are defined for each of the high-level distributed array library design goals: ease of use, performance, and ease of implementation. These metrics lead to specific approaches for addressing the goals in a measurable way.

| Goal | Ease of use |
|---|---|
| Metrics | -Time for a user to produce a well-performing parallel code from a serial code.<br>-Fraction of serial code that has to be modified.<br>-Expertise required to achieve good performance. |
| Approach | -Separate functional coding from mapping onto a parallel architecture.<br>-Abstract message passing away from the user.<br>-Ensure that simple (embarrassingly) parallel programs are simple to express.<br>-Provide a simple mechanism for globally turning pMatlab constructs on and off.<br>-Ensure backward compatibility with serial MATLAB.<br>-Provide a well-defined and repeatable process for migrating from serial to parallel code. |
| **Goal** | **High performance** |
| Metrics | -Execution time and memory overhead as compared to serial MATLAB, the underlying communication library, and C+MPI benchmarks. |
| Approach | -Use underlying serial MATLAB routines wherever possible (even if it means slightly larger user code).<br>-Minimize the use of overloaded functions whose performance depends upon how distributed arrays are mapped.<br>-Provide a simple mechanism for using lower-level communication when necessary. |
| **Goal** | **Ease of implementation** |
| Metrics | -Time to implement a well-performing parallel library.<br>-Size of library code.<br>-Number of objects.<br>-Number of overloaded functions.<br>-Functional and performance test coverage. |
| Approach | -Utilize a layered design that separates math and communication.<br>-Leverage well-understood PGAS and data redistribution constructs.<br>-Minimize the use of overloaded functions.<br>-Develop a "pure" MATLAB implementation to minimize code size and maximize portability. |

Block distribution is typically the default distribution, which can be specified simply by passing in the dimension to be distributed to the map constructor. Cyclic and block-cyclic distributions require the user to provide more information. Distributions can be defined for each dimension, and each dimension could potentially have a different distribution scheme. Additionally, if only a single distribution is specified and the grid indicates that more than one dimension is distributed, that distribution is applied to each dimension.

Some applications, particularly image processing, require data overlap, or replicating rows or columns of data on neighboring $P_{ID}$s. This capability is also supported through the map interface. If overlap is necessary, it is specified with additional arguments. In Figure 5.2, the fourth argument indicates that there is 0 overlap between rows and 1 column overlap between columns. Overlap can be defined for any dimension and does not have to be the same across dimensions.

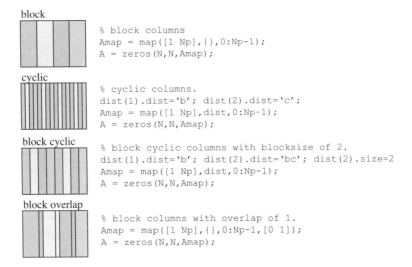

block

```
% block columns
Amap = map([1 Np],{},0:Np-1);
A = zeros(N,N,Amap);
```

cyclic

```
% cyclic columns.
dist(1).dist='b'; dist(2).dist='c';
Amap = map([1 Np],dist,0:Np-1);
A = zeros(N,N,Amap);
```

block cyclic

```
% block cyclic columns with blocksize of 2.
dist(1).dist='b'; dist(2).dist='bc'; dist(2).size=2
Amap = map([1 Np],dist,0:Np-1);
A = zeros(N,N,Amap);
```

block overlap

```
% block columns with overlap of 1.
Amap = map([1 Np],{},0:Np-1,[0 1]);
A = zeros(N,N,Amap);
```

**Figure 5.2. Block-cyclic distributions.**
Block distribution divides the object evenly among available $P_{ID}$s.
Cyclic distribution places a single element on each available $P_{ID}$ and
then repeats. Block-cyclic distribution places the specified number of
elements on each available $P_{ID}$ and then repeats. Overlap allows boundary elements to be present on neighboring $P_{ID}$s.

While maps introduce a new construct and potentially reduce the ease of programming, they have significant advantages over both manager/worker and message
passing approaches. Specifically, maps are scalable, allow optimal distributions for
different algorithms, and support pipelining.

Maps are scalable in both the size of the data and $N_P$. Maps allow the user
to separate the task of mapping the application from the task of writing the application. Different sets of maps do not require changes to be made to the application
code. Specifically, the distribution of the data and $N_P$ can be changed without
making any changes to the algorithm. Separating mapping of the program from
the functional programming is an important design approach in a parallel MATLAB
library.

Maps make it easy to specify different distributions to support different algorithms. Optimal or suggested distributions exist for many specific computations.
For example, matrix multiply operations are most efficient on processor grids that
are transposes of each other. Column- and row-wise FFT operations become embarrassingly parallel if the dimension along which the array is broken up matches
the dimension on which the FFT is performed.

Perhaps the most powerful aspect of the map concept is its applicability to a
wide range of circumstances. Maps allow simple parallel programs to be declared
simply while still supporting very complex applications. For example, as discussed

in Chapter 4, maps also allow the user to set up pipelines in the computation, thus
supporting implicit task parallelism. Pipelining is a common approach to hiding the
latency of communication between stages. The following slight change in the maps
(see Algorithm 4.3) can be used to set up a pipeline in which the first set of $P_{IDS}$
($\tilde{\mathfrak{X}}_1 : \mathbb{C}^{N_t \times N_s \times P_{\{1\}}(N_f)}$) performs the first part of the computation and the second
set of $P_{IDS}$ ($\tilde{\mathfrak{X}}_2 : \mathbb{C}^{N_t \times N_s \times P_{\{2\}}(N_f)}$) performs the second part, etc. When a $P_{ID}$
encounters such a map, it first checks if it has any data to operate on. If the $P_{ID}$ does
not have any data, it proceeds to the next line. In the case of the above mappings,
the first set of $P_{IDS}$ will simply perform the first stage of the computation, send
data to the second set of $P_{IDS}$, skip the other stages, and proceed to process the
next set of data. Likewise, the second set of $P_{IDS}$ will skip the first stage of the
computation, receive data from the first set of $P_{IDS}$, and perform the second stage
of the computation.

## 5.5  Parallel support functions

Every distributed array implementation must provide a set of functions for managing and working with distributed arrays that have no serial equivalents. The set
of distributed array parallel support functions is shown in Table 5.2. These functions allow the user to aggregate data onto one or many $P_{IDS}$, determine which
global indices are local to which $P_{IDS}$, and get/put data from/to the local part of
a distributed array. This set of functions is relatively small and requires minimal
changes to the user's original code. These functions, in addition to map definitions,
represent the core of MATLAB distributed array syntax. To support the development process discussed, all of these functions have been overloaded to also work on
serial MATLAB arrays so that the code will still work if the maps have been turned
off.

There are many different possible map distributions that can be supported
in a distributed array library. Limiting the library to $N$-dimensional block-cyclic
distributions with overlap still leaves a large number of possibilities. A selection of
these, along with their notation and syntax, is shown in Table 5.3.

### 5.5.1  Cyclic distributions and parallel load balancing

Of the many distributions described in the previous section, one-dimensional block
distributions are by far the most commonly used. Interestingly, the next most
commonly used distribution tends to be the one-dimensional cyclic distribution.

Cyclic distributions are one of the most useful distributions for increasing the
performance of embarrassingly parallel computations. Specifically, cyclic distributions are useful for dealing with the widespread issue of parallel load balancing,
which refers to how uniformly the work is distributed among the different $P_{IDS}$.
For example, if a particular computation is spread over $N_P$ processors, let $T(P_{ID})$
be the time it takes for each processor to complete its part of the work. Ideally, the
time should be approximately the same on all the processors, and this will be the
time it takes for the whole computation. However, the total time on $N_P$ processors

**Table 5.2. Distributed array parallel support functions.**
Set of functions with no serial equivalents that need to be provided by
a distributed array library.

| Math | Function | Description |
|------|----------|-------------|
| $P_{ID}$ | Pid | The identity of each program instance currently running the program. |
| $N_P$ | Np | Number of MATLAB instances currently running the program. |
| $P()$ | map | Constructs a map. |
| $\mathbf{B} : \mathbb{R}^{P(N) \times N}$ | zeros | Constructs a distributed array. |
| $\mathbf{A}.loc$ | local | Returns the local part of the distributed array. |
| $\arg(\mathbf{A}).loc$ | global_ind | Returns the global indices local to the current $P_{ID}$. |
| $\mathbf{A} = \mathbf{B}$ | = | Redistributes data from one distributed array to another. |
| $\tilde{\mathbf{A}} = \mathbf{A}$ | agg | Gathers the parts of a distributed array onto one or more $P_{ID}$s. |
| $Synch(\mathbf{A})$ | synch | Synchronizes the data in a distributed array with overlap. |

is actually

$$T(N_P) = \max_{P_{ID}} T(P_{ID})$$

Thus, if any one processor takes a lot longer than the others, it will directly impact
the total run of the calculation. When this occurs, there is a load imbalance across
the processors. The load imbalance is generally defined as

$$\text{Load Imbalance} = \max_{P_{ID}} T(P_{ID}) / \min_{P_{ID}} T(P_{ID})$$

Ideally, this value is very nearly 1. The larger the load imbalance, the more
processors are sitting idle.

One of the most common sources of load imbalance is when the execution time
of a program depends upon the value of an input parameter. For example, suppose
a calculation is to be repeated over each of the $N$ values in an input parameter
vector $\mathbf{x}$. Let $T(\mathbf{x}(i))$ be the time it takes to execute the calculation with $i$th input
parameter $\mathbf{x}(i)$. If there are any correlations in these times with the parameter
index $i$, this will result in a load imbalance. For example, suppose there is a small
linear increase in execution time with parameter index

$$T(\mathbf{x}(i + 1)) = T(\mathbf{x}(i)) + \epsilon$$

or

$$T(\mathbf{x}(i)) = T(\mathbf{x}(1)) + i\epsilon$$

If the input parameter is distributed among processors using a standard block distribution (e.g., $\mathbf{x} : \mathbb{R}^{P(N)}$), then clearly the processor $P_{ID} = N_P$ will take longer

**Table 5.3. Distributed array distributions.**

Notation and syntax for describing different distributed array distributions.

| Math | Function | Distribution |
|------|----------|--------------|
| $P(N_1) \times N_2$ | map([Np 1],{},0:Np-1) | 1D block in 1st dimension |
| $N_1 \times P(N_2)$ | map([1 Np],{},0:Np-1) | 1D block in 2nd dimension |
| $P(N_1) \times P(N_2)$ | map([Np/2 2],{},0:Np-1) | 2D block in 1st and 2nd dimensions |
| $P(N_1 \times N_2)$ | map([Np/2 2],,0:Np-1) | 2D block in 1st and 2nd dimensions |
| $P_b(N)$ | map([Np 1],{},0:Np-1) | Explicit block |
| $P_c(N)$ | dist.dist='c' map([Np 1],dist,0:Np-1) | Explicit cyclic |
| $P_{bc(B)}(N)$ | dist.dist='bc'; dist.size=B; map([Np 1],dist,0:Np-1) | Block-cyclic [$B = 1$ is same as $P_c$] |
| $P_{ov(B)}(N)$ | map([Np 1],,0:Np-1,[0 B]) | Overlap with size $B$ |
| $P_S(N)$ | map([Np/2 2],{},S) | Block over set of $P_{IDS}$ $S$ |

to do its work than will processor $P_{ID} = 1$. The resulting load imbalance will be (assuming $T(\mathbf{x}(1)) = 1$)

$$\text{Load Imbalance} = \frac{\sum_{i=N-N/N_P}^{i=N} 1 + i\epsilon}{\sum_{i=1}^{i=N/N_P} 1 + i\epsilon}$$
$$\approx \frac{1 + \epsilon(N - N/2N_P)}{1 + \epsilon N/2N_P}$$
$$\approx 1 + \epsilon N$$

For the typical values $N = 1000$, $\epsilon = 0.01$, and $N_P = 50$, the resulting load imbalance is $\sim 10$.

A simple technique for alleviating this load imbalance is to break up the correlations between execution time and parameter index by using a cyclic distribution (e.g., $\mathbf{x} : \mathbb{R}^{P_c(N)}$). In this case, the load imbalance works out to be

$$\text{Load Imbalance} =\approx 1 + \epsilon N_P$$

which for typical values results in a load imbalance of $\sim 1.05$.

### Example: Mandelbrot using cyclic distribution

To get a feel of what load imbalance is like in practice, rerun the Mandelbrot program (see Chapter 2) on four processors. Start MATLAB and go to the Examples/Mandelbrot directory (i.e., type **cd Examples/Mandelbrot**). At the prompt, type

```
eval(pRUN('pMandelbrot',4,{}))
```

This runs the program on your local processor and will produce timing data similar to

```
Compute Time (sec)                  = 6.0421
Launch+Comm Time (sec)              = 14.2262
```

In addition, the output from the other MATLABs can viewed by typing the following at the MATLAB prompt:

```
!type MatMPI\*.out
```

On UNIX systems, this is also equivalent to typing

```
!more MatMPI/*.out
```

Running on a parallel computer will produce timing values that look similar to the first line of Table 5.4. These results show that $P_{ID}$s 1 and 2 take nearly twice as long as $P_{ID}$s 0 and 3. The overall compute speedup will be minimum speedup achieved across all $P_{ID}$, which is approximately 3.1.

To complete timing data, edit the file Examples/Mandelbrot/pMandelbrot.m and uncomment the lines

```
dist(1).dist = 'c';  dist(2).dist = 'b';
Wmap = map([Np 1],dist,0:Np-1);
```

This will switch the distribution from block to cyclic. Now rerun the calculation by typing

```
eval(pRUN('pMandelbrot',4,{}))
```

Running on a parallel computer will produce timing values that look similar to the second line of Table 5.4. These results show that all the processors take approximately the same time and that this time is between the maximum and the minimum time taken in the block case. Thus, the overall execution time will be faster using the cyclic distribution because it has better load balancing.

**Important Note**: The last argument to the pRUN command determines which parallel computer the program will be run on. You may need to obtain the proper setting from your system administrator. See the book website (http://www.siam.org/KepnerBook) for details. Setting the last argument to {} runs multiple copies of the program on your local machine and will result in different performance values from those shown in Table 5.4.

The improvement in compute performance of the Mandelbrot program using a cyclic distribution is typical of many applications that experience load imbalance. In the specific case of the Mandelbrot program, the algorithm does repeated calculations over a range of input parameters $\mathbf{Z}$ that cover a region of the complex plane. For each parameter, the calculation is repeated until it reaches a certain value. Values near the center of the region take more steps to reach this criterion than do values near the edge. A block distribution results in more work being done by the middle $P_{ID}$s (1 and 2) and less work done by the edge $P_{ID}$s (0 and 3). A cyclic distribution evenly distributes the work across the different processors.

**Table 5.4. Mandelbrot load imbalance.**
Relative compute time and compute speedup for each $P_{ID}$ in a $N_P = 4$ run of the Mandelbrot program on a multinode system. Results are shown using a block distribution and a cyclic distribution and are normalized to the $N_P = 1$ execution time.

| $P_{ID}$ | 0 | 1 | 2 | 3 |
|---|---|---|---|---|
| **Block** | | | | |
| Relative compute time | 0.15 | 0.31 | 0.31 | 0.15 |
| Compute speedup | 6.33 | 3.16 | 3.19 | 6.33 |
| **Cyclic** | | | | |
| Relative compute time | 0.24 | 0.24 | 0.24 | 0.24 |
| Compute speedup | 4.21 | 4.20 | 4.23 | 4.20 |

## 5.6  Concurrency versus locality

A key initial step in developing a parallel algorithm is identifying sets of operations that can be done in parallel or concurrently. More specifically, concurrent operations are sets of operations that do not depend upon the order in which they are performed. Fortunately, identifying concurrency in a MATLAB program is straightforward because most programs are based on arrays, which are naturally concurrent. Any operation on one or more arrays that results in a new array can be performed concurrently over all the elements in the output array. In fact, concurrency in most MATLAB programs is ubiquitous; thus, writing programs that run in parallel is not difficult. The real challenge is writing parallel programs that run fast. The key step to writing these programs is identifying concurrency in the program that will also result in a high degree of locality. Such a program is able to execute its concurrent operations with a minimal amount of data coming from other $P_{ID}$s (see Figure 5.3).

The distributed array programming model is unique among all the parallel programming models in that locality is usually addressed first by the simple act of creating a distributed array. The concurrency in the problem can then be derived from the locality, thus leading to a well-performing parallel program. In contrast, other parallel programming models usually have the programmer address the concurrency and then deal with the more difficult locality problem as an afterthought. The primary use of the parallel support functions `local` and `global_ind` is to allow programmers to extract locality and concurrency from their distributed arrays.

To illustrate these concepts, consider the AddOne program discussed in Chapter 1. The essence of this program is the operation

$$\mathbf{Y} = \mathbf{X} + 1$$

where $\mathbf{X}, \mathbf{Y} : \mathbb{R}^{N \times N}$. This program has $N^2$ operations which can be performed concurrently. The size of the concurrency is often referred to as the degrees of parallelism. Most any parallel mapping of $\mathbf{X}$ and $\mathbf{Y}$ will expose this concurrency. If $\mathbf{X}, \mathbf{Y} : \mathbb{R}^{P(N) \times N}$, the resulting algorithm will expose $N$ degrees of parallelism (as long as $N > N_P$). More degrees of parallelism can be exposed if both dimensions

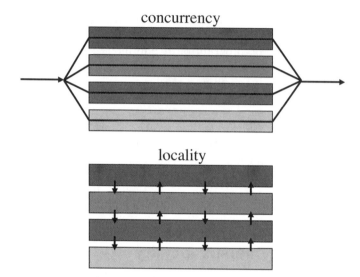

**Figure 5.3. Concurrency and locality.**
Concurrency describes how many operations can be done in parallel at
any one time. Locality refers to how much data needs to be moved to
complete the parallel operations.

of the array are distributed. For example, if $\mathbf{X}, \mathbf{Y} : \mathbb{R}^{P(N) \times P(N)}$ or equivalently
$\mathbf{X}, \mathbf{Y} : \mathbb{R}^{P(N \times N)}$, then $N^2$ degrees of parallelism are exposed.

A program's locality can be measured using the computation-to-communication
ratio $W/D$, where $W$ is the number of operations performed and $D$ is the total
amount of data moved between $P_{ID}$s. The AddOne program will have a high degree of locality if $\mathbf{X}$ and $\mathbf{Y}$ are mapped the same because no data needs to be
communicated. The resulting computation-to-communication ratio will be

$$W/D = N^2/0 \to \infty$$

On the other hand, if $\mathbf{X} : \mathbb{R}^{P(N) \times N}$ and $\mathbf{Y} : \mathbb{R}^{N \times P(N)}$, then data will have to be communicated for almost every operation to be completed. The resulting computation-
to-communication ratio will be

$$W/D = N^2/(N^2(N_P - 1)/N_P) = N_P/(N_P - 1) \approx 1$$

The MATLAB version of the AddOne program can be explicitly written to
show the concurrency as follows:

```
X = zeros(N,N);
Y = zeros(N,N);
for i=1:N
  for j=1:N
```

```
        Y(i,j) = X(i,j) + 1;
    end
end
```

Making the above code parallel can be done by simply applying a map to the constructors of X and Y:

```
XYmap = map([Np 1],{},0:Np-1);
X = zeros(N,N,XYmap);
Y = zeros(N,N,XYmap);
for i=1:N
  for j=1:N
    Y(i,j) = X(i,j) + 1;
  end
end
```

The resulting program clearly has good locality since both X and Y use the same map. However, the relationship between concurrency and locality is implicit. A slightly longer way to write this program, which will guarantee that the locality is enforced, is

```
XYmap = map([Np 1],{},0:Np-1);
Xloc = local(zeros(N,N,XYmap));
Yloc = local(zeros(N,N,XYmap));
for i=1:size(Xloc,1)
  for j=1:size(Xloc,2)
    Yloc(i,j) = Xloc(i,j) + 1;
  end
end
```

In this case, the connection between concurrency and locality is explicit. Typically, writing in this way results in the best performance.

## 5.7   Ease of implementation

The ease of use and high performance goals are well understood by the parallel computing community. Unfortunately, implementing these goals in a middleware library often proves to be quite costly. A typical distributed array C++ library can be 50,000 lines of code and require several programmer-years to implement. The distributed array libraries implemented for MATLAB have adopted several strategies to reduce implementation costs. The common theme among these strategies is finding the minimum set of features that will still allow users to write well-performing programs.

One of the key choices in implementing a distributed array library is which data distributions to support. At one extreme, it can be argued that most users are satisfied by one-dimensional block distributions. At the other extreme, one can find applications that require truly arbitrary distributions of array indices to $P_{ID}$s. Current MATLAB distributed array implementations have chosen to support a set of distributions that lies somewhere between these two extremes. In general, these distributions support $N$-dimensional block-cyclic distributions with overlap because the problem of redistribution between any two such distributions (see Section 3.3) has been solved a number of times by different parallel computing technologies.

Overloading the MATLAB `subsasgn` (subscripted assignment) operator supports data redistribution between arrays using the = operation. The next question is what other functions to support and for which distributions. Table 5.5 shows an enumeration of different levels of distributed array support. The ability to work with the local part of a distributed array and its indices has also been demonstrated repeatedly. The big challenge is overloading all mathematical functions in a library to work well with every combination of input distributions. As discussed in Section 2.2, this capability is extremely difficult to implement and is not entirely necessary if users are willing to tolerate the slightly less elegant coding style associated with fragmented distributed arrays. Thus, most MATLAB distributed array libraries provide a rich set of data distributions, but a relatively modest set of overloaded functions, which are mainly focused on array construction functions, array index support functions, and the various element-wise operations $(+, -, .^*, ./)$.

The final implementation choice is the language for writing the distributed array library. In this respect, MATLAB is unique in that it is a high-level array-based language that has sufficient language abstraction to allow implementing a distributed array library in MATLAB with minimal reliance on other languages. This approach minimizes the code size and maximizes portability. For example, it is possible to implement the majority of the distributed array functionality with only about 3,000 lines of code and the introduction of only two new objects (maps and distributed arrays). Such an approach guarantees that the code will run wherever MATLAB runs.

## 5.8   Implementation specifics

This section discusses the implementation details of distributed arrays in MATLAB. The basic design of a distributed array library builds on concepts from the Parallel Vector Library (PVL) [Lebak et al. 2005] and StarP [Choy & Edelman 1999] and uses MPI concepts [Kepner & Ahalt 2004] for the communication layer. Figure 5.4 illustrates the layered architecture of the parallel library. In the layered architecture, the distributed array library implements distributed constructs, such as distributed matrices and higher-dimensional arrays. In addition, the distributed library provides parallel implementations of a select number of functions such as redistribution, Fast Fourier Transform (FFT), and matrix multiplication. However, it is usually simpler for a user to create a parallel implementation of a function focused on his/her particular data sizes and data distributions of interests than to provide generic parallel implementations of functions that will give good performance for all data distributions and data sizes. The distributed array library uses the parallelism-through-polymorphism approach as discussed in [Choy & Edelman 1999]. Monomorphic languages require that each variable is of only one type; on the other hand, in polymorphic languages, variables can be of different types and polymorphic functions

**Table 5.5. Implementation levels.**
Levels of parallel support for data and functions. Note: support for data distribution is assumed to include support for overlap in any distributed dimension. Data4/Op1 has been successfully implemented many times. Data1/Op2 may be possible but has not yet been demonstrated.

| Data Level | Description of Support |
|---|---|
| Data0 | Distribution of data is not supported [not a parallel implementation]. |
| Data1 | One dimension of data may be block distributed. |
| Data2 | Two dimensions of data may be block distributed. |
| Data3 | Any and all dimensions of data may be block distributed. |
| Data4 | Any and all dimensions of data may be block or cyclically distributed. |
| **Operations Level** | **Description of Support** |
| Op0 | No distributed operations supported [not a parallel implementation]. |
| Op1 | Distributed assignment, get, and put operations, and support for obtaining data and indices of local data from a distributed object. |
| Op2 | Distributed operation support (the implementation must state which operations those are). |

can operate on different types of variables [Abadi et al. 1991]. The concept of polymorphism is inherent in the MATLAB language: variable types do not have to be defined, variable types can change during the execution of the program, and many functions operate on a variety of data types such as double, single, complex, etc.

In the distributed array library, this concept is taken one step further. The polymorphism is exploited by introducing the map object. Map objects belong to a MATLAB class and are created by specifying the grid description, distribution description, and the processor list, as discussed in the previous sections. The map object can then be passed to a MATLAB constructor, such as `rand`, `zeros`, or `ones`. The constructors are overloaded, and when a map object is passed into a constructor, the library creates a variable of type distributed, i.e., a distributed array.

As discussed previously, a subset of functions, such as plus, minus, fft, mtimes, and all element-wise operations, are overloaded to operate on distributed array objects. When one uses a pure distributed array programming model and an overloaded function, the distributed array object can be treated as a regular array. Functions that operate only on the local part of the distributed array (element-wise operations) simply perform the operations requested on the local array, which is a standard MATLAB numerical type specified at array creation. Functions that require communication, such as redistribution (or `subsasgn` in MATLAB syntax), use messaging as the communication layer.

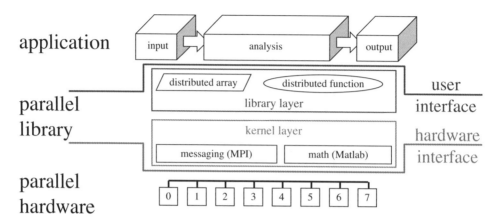

**Figure 5.4. Layered library architecture.**
The distributed array library implements distributed constructs, such as
vectors, matrices, and multidimensional arrays and parallel algorithms
that operate on those constructs, such as redistribution, FFT, and matrix multiplication. Point-to-point communication and serial functions
are implemented in the kernel layer and called by the library layer.

The primary goal of using a parallel computer is to improve run time performance. The first step in achieving high performance is to minimize the overhead of
using distributed array constructs as compared to their serial equivalents. Unfortunately, the ideal "pure" distributed array case in which all the required functions
have been overloaded tends to run slowly. Furthermore, it is impractical (and unnecessary) to provide optimized implementations of the approximately 8,000 built-
in MATLAB functions for every combination of array distributions. Instead, it is
much simpler to have the programmer employ a coding style that uses some fragmented distributed array constructs. This style is less elegant but provides strict
guarantees on performance. Fundamentally, the best-performing distributed array
programs are those that use only distributed arrays for executing interprocessor
communication.

## 5.8.1   Program execution

All distributed array code resides within a generic code framework (see Figure 5.5)
for initializing the distributed array library (pRUN), determining the number of
MATLAB instances being run (Np), determining the ID of the local processor (Pid),
and finalizing the library when the computation is complete (pRUN). The distributed
array program uses the Single-Program Multiple-Data (SPMD) execution model
[Flynn 1972]. The user runs a distributed array program by calling the pRUN command to launch and initialize the multiple instances of MATLAB required to run in
parallel. Figure 5.5 shows an example RUN.m script using pRUN to launch four copies
of the dIO.m script (see Chapter 2).

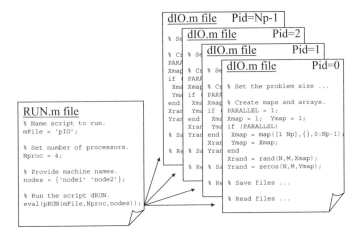

**Figure 5.5. Execution framework.**
A distributed array program (`dIO.m`) is launched using the `pRUN` command shown in the `RUN.m` file, which sets the number of processors and the precise machines to run on. `pRUN.m` starts $N_P$ instances of MATLAB, each with a different `Pid`. Within the distributed array program the distributed array environment is initialized and the number of processors (`Np`) and local `Pid` can be obtained. The program is completed when the `dIO.m` script finishes and the MATLAB instance is automatically exited by the `pRUN` command.

## 5.9   Array redistribution

Arguably, the fundamental operation of a distributed array library is the redistribution of data between two distributed arrays. Algorithmically, this can be concisely written as $\mathbf{B} = \mathbf{A}$, with arrays such as $\mathbf{A} : \mathbb{R}^{P(N) \times N}$ and $\mathbf{B} : \mathbb{R}^{P(N) \times N}$. In code, this is simply

```
Amap = map([Np 1],{},0:Np-1);
Bmap = map([1 Np],{},0:Np-1);
A = rand(N,N,Amap);
B = zeros(N,N,Bmap);
B(:,:) = A;
```

An efficient and general technique for data redistribution is PITFALLS (Processor Indexed Tagged FAmiLy of Line Segments) [Ramaswamy & Banerjee 1995], which is a mathematical representation of the data distribution based on treating each dimension in the array as a separate family of line segments. Additionally, [Ramaswamy & Banerjee 1995] provides an algorithm for determining which pairs of $P_{ID}$s need to communicate when redistribution is required and exactly what data needs to be sent.

The redistribution technique begins with defining a Line Segment (LS), which represents a contiguous set of indices in one dimension of an array. For a distributed array an LS describes the set of indices that are local to a particular $P_{ID}$. An LS can be represented by a pair of numbers $(l, r)$, where $l$ is the starting index and $r$ is the ending index. Computing a redistribution from one distributed array to another involves repeatedly determining the intersection of two LS's $L_1 = (l_1, r_1)$ and $L_2 = (l_2, r_2)$ using the formula

$$L_1 \cap L_2 = (\max(l_1, l_2), \min(r_1, r_2)$$

If $\max(l_1, l_2) > \min(r_1, r_2)$, the intersection is empty.

A FAmiLy of Line Segments (FALLS) represents a sequence of evenly spaced LS's and is denoted by the tuple $(l, r, s, n)$, where $n$ is the number of line segments and $s$ is the stride between any to $l$. Thus the $i$th line segment is given by

$$L^i = (l, r) + i \times s$$

Building on this concept, a PITFALLS structure is defined by the following tuple:
$$\text{PITFALLS} = (l, r, s, n, d, N_P)$$

where

$l$ : starting index

$r$ : ending index

$s$ : stride between successive $l$'s

$n$ : number of equally spaced, equally sized blocks of elements per processor

$d$ : spacing between $l$'s of successive processor FALLS

$N_P$ : number of processors

A PITFALLS structure describes a set of evenly spaced FALLS on $N_P$ processors. The FALLS on $P_{ID}$ is given by

$$\text{FALLS}(P_{ID}) = (l + (P_{ID} - 1) \times d, r + (P_{ID} - 1) \times d, s, n)$$

Thus, the $i$th line segment on $P_{ID}$ is given by

$$L^i(P_{ID}) = (l, r) + (P_{ID} - 1) \times d + i \times s$$

The PITFALLS structure can be readily computed from the map found in a distributed array and can be used to quickly determine which array elements belong to a given processor (and vice versa).

The PITFALLS intersection algorithm is used to determine the necessary messages for redistribution between two distributed arrays and is used by the `subsasgn` operation. The algorithm can be applied to each dimension of the array, thus allowing efficient redistribution of arbitrary dimensional arrays. The algorithm intersects the PITFALLS structures for each dimension. If intersections in all of the dimensions are nonempty, the size and the content of the messages that need to be sent between each processor are computed. The intersection algorithm reduces the number of necessary computation by exploiting the periodicity of block-cyclic distributions. Additionally, the PITFALLS structure is also used within the referencing operation, `subsref`, to determine which processor owns which piece of the distributed array. For a detailed discussion of the algorithm and its efficiency see [Ramaswamy & Banerjee 1995].

## 5.10   Message passing layer

One of the core advantages of distributed arrays is the relative ease of specifying very complex data redistributions between arrays. The result is that only a very small number of underlying communication functions are necessary for building a distributed array library. At the user level, only two functions are required: `SendMsg` and `RecvMsg`. These are then built on top of a handful of MPI functions. The MPI functions typically used by distributed array library are listed in Table 5.6.

**Table 5.6. MPI functions.**
The core set of MPI functions required by a distributed array library.

| Function | Description |
| --- | --- |
| MPI_Init | Initializes MPI. |
| MPI_Comm_size | Gets the number of processors in a communication. |
| MPI_Comm_rank | Gets the rank of current processor within a communicator. |
| MPI_Send | Sends a message to a processor. |
| MPI_Recv | Receives a message from a processor. |
| MPI_Finalize | Finalizes MPI. |

The small number of required communication functions also allows very different communication protocols to be used underneath the library. An extreme example is MatlabMPI [Kepner & Ahalt 2004], where the actual communication is done via file I/O (see Figure 5.6) through a common file system. The advantage of this approach is that the MatlabMPI library is very small (~300 lines) and is highly portable. The price for this portability is that while MatlabMPI performance is comparable to traditional MPI for large messages, its latency for small messages is much higher (see Figure 5.8). A distributed array library that used MatlabMPI will tag each message it sends with a unique tag to achieve synchronization. Specifically, each communication increments a global message tag on all $P_{IDs}$ in the scope. MatlabMPI also provides effectively an infinite buffer due to its file I/O communication scheme. Both the tag management by the distributed array library and the infinite buffer prevent deadlocks from occurring.

The performance of a messaging library is fundamentally set by its message size versus latency curve. This curve shows the time it takes for messages of a given size to be sent between two processors. A simple algorithm for measuring this is shown in Algorithm 5.1.

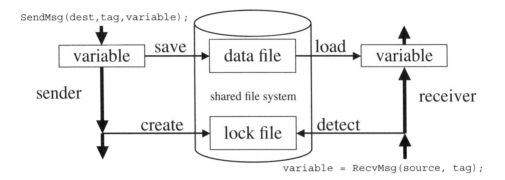

**Figure 5.6. MatlabMPI file I/O based communication.**
MatlabMPI uses file I/O to implement point-to-point communication.
The sender writes variables to a buffer file and then writes a lock file.
The receiver waits until it sees the lock file; it then reads in the buffer
file.

**Algorithm 5.1. Network speedtest.**
Send messages of different sizes between two processors and times the
result.

$\mathbf{t}_m : \mathbb{R}^{N_m} = \text{SPEEDTEST}(N_m)$

1   $P_{ID}^{send} = (P_{ID} - 1 \mod N_P) + 1$
2   $P_{ID}^{recv} = (P_{ID} + 1 \mod N_P) + 1$
3   **for** $i = 1 : N_m,$
4       **do**
5           $\mathbf{d}_{send}, \mathbf{d}_{recv} : \mathbb{R}^{2^i}$
6           $\text{CLOCKSTART}()$
7               $\text{SEND}(\mathbf{d}_{send}, P_{ID}^{send}, i)$
8               $\mathbf{d}_{recv} = \text{RECEIVE}(P_{ID}^{recv}, i)$
9           $\mathbf{t}_m(i) = \text{CLOCKSTOP}()$

The corresponding program can be run by starting MATLAB and going to the
Examples/Speedtest directory (i.e., type `cd Examples/Speedtest`). At the prompt
type

```
eval(pRUN('pSpeedtest',2,{}))
```

This command runs the program on two processors. Because `pSpeedtest` does
only communication, it won't run on just one processor. After the program has
completed type

```
load speedtest.1.mat
loglog(ByteSize,TotalTime)
loglog(ByteSize,Bandwidth)
```

The results will be plots that look something like Figure 5.7. The pSpeedtest program runs over multiple trials, resulting in one curve for each trial of the program. The plot of message latency versus message size shows how long it takes to send a message of a given size between two processors. Note that the first data point is much higher. This is the delay due to the first processor waiting for the others to start. This delay is sometimes referred to as the launch skew. The time corresponding to the flat part of the message latency curve (at small messages) measures the latency of the communication network. The plot of bandwidth versus message size shows the rate at which data is sent over the network. The bandwidth corresponding to the flat part of the bandwidth curve (at large messages) measures the bandwidth of the communication network.

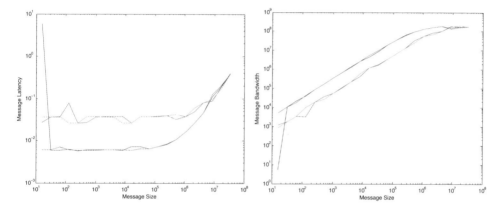

**Figure 5.7. Network speedtest results.**

The Speedtest program can be run with different underlying communication libraries to compare their relative performance. Figure 5.8 shows the latency and bandwidth curves for two different message passing libraries. Both libraries have approximately the same bandwidth and will perform approximately the same in applications that send lots of large messages. However, clearly one has lower latency and is better suited for sending lots of small messages.

When designing a distributed array library it is important to ensure that the overhead incurred by the library does not significantly impact performance. From a library perspective, this means that the performance of the communication operations using the overloaded subsasgn operator should be as close as possible to the equivalent message passing code without distributed arrays. Figure 5.9 shows the performance of an all-to-all redistribution operation using just message passing, distributed array assignment, and the special transpose_grid function. These results are typical for a distributed array library. Redistribution using B(:,:) = A is typically 2x slower than doing the same operation by explicitly writing out all the SendMsg and RecvMsg operations. This overhead is usually due to several factors. First, a generalized redistribution needs to support all possible distributions and does a lot of checking to determine which data needs to be sent where. Second, distributed arrays usually require that some additional copies of the variables be

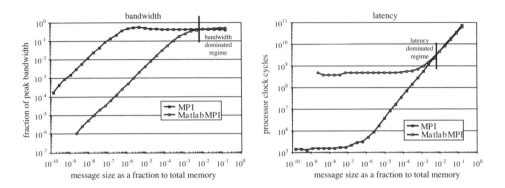

**Figure 5.8. MatlabMPI versus MPI.**
Bandwidth and latency versus message size. Bandwidth is given as fraction of the peak underlying link bandwidth. Latency is given in terms of processor cycles. For large messages the performance is comparable. For small messages the latency of MatlabMPI is much higher.

stored. Third, distribution specific optimizations (such as ordering the messages to minimize bottlenecks) are difficult to exploit. Functions that are customized for particular distributions can achieve the same performance as message passing.

From an application perspective minimizing overhead means using algorithms that use fewer larger messages instead of many smaller messages. The relative performance of a well-implemented program can essentially be derived from the performance of the underlying message passing library. Obviously, embarrassingly parallel computations that have little communication will deliver good performance. Applications that do bulk communication of distributed arrays (e.g., all-to-all or broadcast) tend to fall into the large message regime and deliver reasonable performance. Applications that require many random small messages will perform less well.

## 5.11   Performance concepts

The previous subsection provided some details on how a distributed array library in MATLAB is actually built. Several performance concepts can be extracted from these details, which can be helpful when using distributed arrays to build parallel MATLAB programs.

### 5.11.1   Performance, performance, performance

The *only* reason to create a parallel program is make a program run faster. Unfortunately, it is easy to get caught up in the complexities of just getting a parallel application up and running and lose sight of the ultimate goal. At every point in the development, the performance of each piece should be checked. If the individual

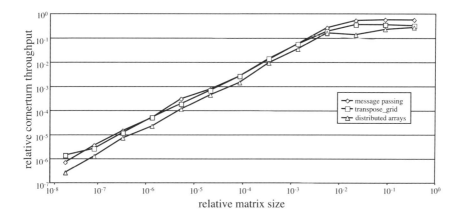

**Figure 5.9. Array communication overhead.**
Relative all-to-all performance for a pure message passing implementation, an `A(:,:) = B` implementation, and a `transpose_grid` implementation. The X-axis represents size of each matrix relative to node
memory. The Y-axis represents throughput relative to peak bandwidth.

pieces of a parallel application are built without attention paid to performance, it is
very difficult to "retrofit" performance into the application later. In a large project,
usually there needs to be a a "performance hawk," who has the authority to reject
changes to the program that degrade performance. The reason for this is that most
programmers are naturally far more interested in functionality than spending the
time to regression test performance.

## 5.11.2   Benchmarks

It is important to have reasonable performance expectations. The simplest way
to obtain these is by having one or two benchmark codes that are simpler than
the "real" application but capture the essence of what the application is trying to
do. Using this benchmark code, it is usually much easier to explore the effects of
adding processors and changing the maps of distributed arrays. By understanding
a benchmark it then becomes much clearer how a real application should perform,
and it can highlight where effort needs to be placed to improve performance.

## 5.11.3   Minimize overhead

Using distributed arrays simplifies the development of parallel programs but adds
some overhead for serial applications. It is important to compare the single processor
performance of a distributed array program to a nondistributed array program. If
the distributed array program is slower by even 10%, this can have a large impact
on the performance when the program is run on many processors. This effect is
called Amdahl's Law (see next chapter).

## 5.11.4   Embarrassingly parallel implies linear speedup

If an application is embarrassingly parallel (i.e., has no communication), then it should speed up linearly with the number of processors. For example, on 10 processors that application should run in 1/10th the time it takes to run on 1 processor. If this isn't the case, then it means something is wrong with the application (e.g., load imbalance) or the underlying distributed array library (e.g., launch skew).

## 5.11.5   Algorithm and mapping are orthogonal

Specifying the algorithm and specifying the parallelism should be orthogonal. The map should be the sole repository of all information that describes the parallelism and should be independent of the algorithm. A distributed array is thus a regular array plus a map. Changing the map should change only the performance and not change the correctness of the result.

## 5.11.6   Do no harm

All serial codes are not good parallel codes, but all good parallel codes must also run well in serial. The last thing a user wants is to add a bunch of constructs that pollute their code so that it is no longer a workable serial MATLAB code that can run without parallel support (and share with their colleagues, who may not have parallel libraries installed).

## 5.11.7   Watch the SLOC

A distributed array library can be implemented in a relatively small number of Software Lines of Code (SLOC). 5000 SLOC is a reasonable amount. Unfortunately, as the library grows, it becomes increasingly difficult to maintain performance. Thus there is a delicate balance between increased functionality and increased performance.

## 5.11.8   No free lunch

Parallel library programming is mostly "fool's gold." If a hard problem looks like it has an easy solution, then it is probably wrong; otherwise, we would have already had it by now. It is a sobering fact that much smarter folks (than us) with a lot more money have failed miserably in this field before us. Just read the work produced in the late 1980s and early 1990s and it is apparent that the typical person in the field had a much deeper understanding of parallelism than most of us do.

## 5.11.9   Four easy steps

Distributed array libraries are generally implemented with a specific incremental code development process. All of these steps, making the code parallel, managing the communication, and debugging, need to be directly supported by the library. Our experience with many parallel MATLAB users has resulted in a standardized and repeatable process (see previous chapters) for quickly going from a serial code to a well-performing parallel code. This process is very important, as the natural tendency of new parallel MATLAB users is to add parallel functions and immediately attempt to run large problems on a large number of processors.

### Step 1: Add serial maps

The four-step process begins by adding distributed matrices to the serial program but then assigning all the maps to a value of 1 and verifying the program with $N_P = 1$ on the local machine.

Take the serial code and add maps to the key arrays and use these to generate parallel for loops; then turn off all the maps. Running this code should produce the exact same serial code as before with the same answers and serial performance. As you can imagine, this step reveals all kinds of bugs which are relatively easy to take care of in this restricted context.

To support this step the distributed array library provides a number of features. All constructors must key off a map object. Constructors that work without an explicit map object can't be turned off, so these should be avoided. All functions must work and make sense on both serial and distributed arrays. Otherwise, the code will break when they try and run it in serial. Most libraries have serial "stubs" of all its functions for this reason. Functions that don't work in serial should be avoided. This will result in code that is still perfectly good serial code that can be shared with others who may not necessarily care if it runs in parallel.

### Step 2: Turn on parallel maps

The second step is to turn the maps on and to run the program again with $N_P = 1$, which will verify that the overloaded constructs in the distributed array library are working properly. It is also important to look at the relative performance of the first and second steps, as this will indicate if any unforeseen overheads are incurred by using the distributed array constructs.

This checks that the serial answers and serial performance are still correct in the presence of distributed arrays. This step reveals all kinds of bugs which are relatively easy to take care of in this restricted context. In addition, it shows if there are any immediate performance overheads (e.g., from using distributed array functions), which need to be addressed before trying to go parallel.

The distributed array library supports this step with the same technology that is used to support Step 1: maps that can be readily turned on and off. In addition, all the parallel support functions need to work on regular arrays. Finally, the overhead of any overloaded functions needs to be minimized; otherwise, simply using distributed arrays slows the program down, which makes speeding the program up with parallelism even harder.

### Step 3: Scale on workstation

The next step involves running the program with multiple instances of MATLAB on a local workstation. Typically, running with $N_P = 2$, 3, and 4 works best and will exercise the code adequately. Often $N_P = 3$ is particularly helpful because the array sizes (i.e., $N$) are typically not evenly divisible by 3 and will discover that accidentally assumes $N$ mod $N_P = 0$.

Step 3 is the most important step in the debugging process as it is the first step that actually tests parallelism. This step verifies that any dimensions derived from distributed arrays are being used correctly. In addition, if any communication is required, it will first be exercised in this step.

Supporting this step requires that the distributed array library allow multiple instances of MATLAB to be launched on the same computer. This requires that the launch time and memory footprint of each MATLAB instance be minimized. In addition, communications need to be able to proceed without deadlocking. Finally, there must be a clear mechanism for observing the output of all the running instances of MATLAB.

### Step 4: Scale on parallel system

The final step is to actually run the program on a parallel computing system with $N_P > 1$. Most users (to their detriment) jump to this step immediately. When first running on such a system, the main goal is to make sure that the program launches and the parallel communication is still functioning correctly. If the program ran well in Step 3, then Step 4 will mainly test that the software is installed correctly and that the parallel computer is properly configured.

Up to this point, all runs should have been performed on a small problem size (i.e., small $N$) that runs quickly. Too often programmers immediately try and run on large problems that take a very long time to show errors. Only after the program has run successfully on a parallel computer is it OK to start increasing the problem size.

This step is the ultimate goal of using the distributed array library, and usually supporting this case well is the focus of most parallel library development. The primary features a distributed array library needs to support this step are easy installation and configuration. In addition, scaling the problem size means that the library must make it easy to do this independent of $N_P$. This is the primary benefit of the map-based approach that allows $N_P$ and $N$ to change without changing the functioning of the code.

Finally, it is important to always debug problems at the lowest numbered step, which tends to run more quickly and allows software bugs to be isolated more rapidly.

## 5.12  User results

The true measure of success for any technology is its effectiveness for real users. Table 5.7 highlights several projects that are using the above parallel MATLAB techniques [Reuther et al. 2004]. The projects are drawn from the hundreds of users and are representative of the user base. Of particular interest are the columns showing the time to parallelize and what parallelization enables. The time to parallelize shows both how quickly MATLAB code can be converted from serial code to parallel code as well as how quickly the user is able to get the parallel code running on a parallel computer. The applications that parallelization enables include scenarios in which larger data sets, more thorough parameter set exploration, and more complex simulations can be considered. While we usually provide users with some initial guidance regarding algorithm parallelization, the users quickly feel comfortable writing new parallel code.

**Table 5.7. Selected user application results.**
The first and last columns provide a brief description of the code and what the parallel version of the code has enabled. The middle column shows the estimated time to write the original serial code and the additional time to parallelize the code with distributed arrays and get it running well on the parallel computer.

| Code description | Serial effort (hours) / Parallel effort (hours) | Parallel enabled more or faster |
|---|---|---|
| Sensor simulations | 2000 / 8 | Higher fidelity radar |
| First-principles LADAR | 1300 / 1 | Speckle image simulations |
| Sensor simulations | 40 / 0.4 | Parameter space studies |
| Sensor simulations | 900 / 0.75 | Monte Carlos |
| Laser propagation | 40 / 1 | Run time |
| Polynomial approx. | 700 / 8 | Faster training algorithm |
| Ground motion tracker | 600 / 3 | Faster/larger data sets |
| Automatic target ID | 650 / 40 | Target classes/scenarios |
| Hyperspectral analysis | 960 / 6 | Larger datasets of images |

Nearly all of these applications involve embarrassingly parallel problems. Because MATLAB is such an array-oriented language users find distributed arrays a very natural way to express embarrassingly parallel problems. For these types of applications the coding overhead is much smaller than message passing. In addition, distributed arrays naturally decompose problems into their largest natural units, which maximizes the local performance. In contrast a client/server approach tends to decompose problems into their smallest functional units and incur a higher overhead. The users of distributed arrays find that the functions the distributed array library provides are sufficient to parallelize their applications and gain significant performance increases. The users take advantage of both distributed arrays, which they often use as container classes, and distributed indices, in situations where distributed for loops are required. Majority of the users use fragmented distributed arrays and find fragmented distributed easy to use and intuitive for their problems.

# References

[Abadi et al. 1991] M. Abadi, L. Cardelli, B. Pierce, and G. Plotkin, Dynamic Typing in a Statically Typed Language, ACM Transactions on Programming Languages and Systems 13(2), Pages: 237–268, 1991.

[Bikshandi et al. 2006] G. Bikshandi, J. Guo, D. Hoeflinger, G. Almasi, B. Fraguela, M. Garzaran, D. Padua, and C. von Praun, Programming for Parallelism and Locality with Hierarchically Tiled Arrays. In Proceedings of the Eleventh ACM SIGPLAN Symposium on Principles and Practice of Parallel Programming (PPoPP06), New York, March 2006.

[Bliss & Kepner 2007] Nadya Bliss and Jeremy Kepner, pMATLAB Parallel MATLAB Library, International Journal of High Performance Computing Applications Special Issue on High Productivity Languages and Models (editors: J. Kepner and H. Zima), SAGE Publications, Volume 21, Number 3, pages 336–359 (August 2007).

[Choy & Edelman 1999] Ron Choy and Alan Edelman, 2005, Parallel MATLAB: Doing it Right. Proceedings of the IEEE 93(2), Pages 331–341.

[Cummings et al. 1998] J. C. Cummings, J. A. Crotinger, S. W. Haney, W. F. Humphrey, S. R. Karmesin, J. V. Reynders, S. A. Smith, and T. J. Williams, Rapid Application Development and Enhanced Code Interoperability Using the POOMA Framework. In Proceedings of the SIAM Workshop on Object-Oriented Methods and Code Interoperability in Scientific and Engineering Computing (OO98), Oct. 1998.

[DeLuca et al. 1997] Cecelia DeLuca, Curtis Heisey, Robert Bond, and James Daly, A Portable Object-Based Parallel Library and Layered Framework for Real-Time Radar Signal Processing. In Proc. 1st Conf. International Scientific Computing in Object-Oriented Parallel Environments (ISCOPE 97), Pages: 241–248.

[El-Ghazawi et al. 2005] Tariq El-Ghazawi, William Carlson, Thomas Sterling, and Kathy Yelick, UPC: Distributed Shared Memory Programming, John Wiley and Sons, May, 2005.

[Falcon] Falcon Project: Fast Array Language Computation, http://polaris.cs.uiuc.edu/falcon/

[Flynn 1972] Michael Flynn, Some Computer Organizations and Their Effectiveness, IEEE Trans. Comput., Vol. C-21, p. 948, 1972.

[Johnson 2004] Phil Johnson (editor), Proceedings of 26th International Conference on Software Engineering (ICSE 2004), Edinburgh, Scotland, UK, May 23–28.

[Johnson 2005] Phil Johnson (editor), Proceedings of 27th International Conference on Software Engineering (ICSE 2005), St. Louis, MO, May 15–21.

[Kepner & Ahalt 2004] Jeremy Kepner and Stan Ahalt, MatlabMPI, Journal of Parallel and Distributed Computing, 2004, Volume 64, Issue 8, Pages: 997–1005.

[Kepner 2004] Jeremy Kepner (editor), 2004. Special issue on HPC Productivity, International Journal of High Performance Computing Applications, 18(4).

[Kim & Kepner 2006] Hahn Kim and Jeremy Kepner, Parallel Out-of-Core Programming in Matlab Using the PGAS Model, presented at The Second Conference on Partitioned Global Address Space Programming Models, October 3–4, 2006, Washington DC.

[Koelbel 1994] Charles Koelbel, The High Performance Fortran Handbook, MIT Press, 1994.

[Lebak et al. 2005] James Lebak, Jeremy Kepner, Henry Hoffmann, and Edward Rutledge, 2005, Parallel VSIPL++: An Open Standard Software Library for High-Performance Parallel Signal Processing, Proceedings of the IEEE 93(2), Pages 313–330.

[Loveman 1993] D.B. Loveman, High Performance Fortran. Parallel and Distributed Technology: Systems and Applications, IEEE 1(1), 1993.

[Nieplocha et al. 2002] J. Nieplocha, R. Harrison, M. Krishnan, B. Palmer, and V. Tipparaju, Combining Shared and Distributed Memory Models: Evolution and Recent Advancements of the Global Array Toolkit. In Proceedings of POOHL2002 Workshop of ICS-2002, New York, 2002.

[Numrich & Reid 1998] R. Numrich and J. Reid, Co-array Fortran for parallel programming. ACM SIGPLAN Fortran Forum, Volume 17 , Issue 2 (August 1998), Pages: 1–31.

[Ramaswamy & Banerjee 1995] S. Ramaswamy and P. Banerjee, Automatic Generation of Efficient Array Redistribution Routines for Distributed Memory Multicomputers. In Proceedings of the Fifth Symposium on the Frontiers of Massively Parallel Computation (Frontiers '95), McClean, VA, February 6–9.

[Reuther et al. 2004] Albert Reuther, Tim Currie, Jeremy Kepner, Hahn Kim, Andrew McCabe, Micheal Moore, and Nadya Travinin, LLgrid: Enabling On-Demand Grid Computing with gridMatlab and pMatlab. In Proceedings of High Performance Embedded Computing Workshop (HPEC2004), Lexington, MA, September 28–30, 2004.

[Rutledge & Kepner 1999] Eddie Rutledge and Jeremy Kepner, PVL: An Object Oriented Software Library for Parallel Signal Processing, Cluster 2001, October 9, 2001, Newport Beach, CA.

[Zosel 1993] M.E. Zosel, High performance Fortran: An overview. Compcon Spring 93, Digest of Papers, San Francisco, CA, February 22–26, 1993.

# Chapter 6

# Performance Metrics and Software Architecture

**Summary**

Performance metrics are an invaluable tool for implementing parallel programs that perform well while minimizing software cost. This chapter defines a number of performance metrics and shows how they can be applied to make better decisions about implementing an application. In the process of presenting these metrics, a canonical parallel computing system is defined and the performance implications of various parallel programming models are discussed.

## 6.1 Introduction

Well-performing parallel MATLAB programs are difficult to write because of the large number of additional factors that must be considered beyond the basic functional correctness of the program. These factors include

**Performance:** latency and throughput

**Efficiency:** processing, bandwidth, and memory

**Software Cost:** code size and portability

**Hardware cost:** size and power

Performance metrics are an important tool that allows the parallel MATLAB programmer to make informed design and implementation choices.

This chapter will primarily focus on the performance metrics and software architectures for implementing parallel applications that minimize software cost while meeting as many of the other requirements as possible. In particular, we will focus on the various software architectures that can be used to exploit parallel computing to achieve high performance. In this context, the dominating factors in a parallel software architecture are

**Type of parallelism:** data, task, pipeline, and/or round-robin

**Parallel programming model:** message passing, manager/worker, and global arrays

**Programming environment:** languages and/or libraries

The approaches for dealing with these issues are best illustrated in the context of concrete examples. This chapter will draw upon the examples described in the previous chapters: AddOne, Mandelbrot, ZoomImage, ParallelIO, Beamformer, and Blurimage.

Section 6.2 defines several parallel application metrics and applies them to the example programs presented in the previous chapters. Section 6.3 provides a definition of a typical parallel computer and how it can be characterized to understand its impact on a parallel application. Section 6.4 presents the software impacts of different parallel programming models. Finally, Section 6.5 defines the system performance, efficiency, form factor, and software cost metrics that we will use for assessing the implementation.

## 6.2 Characterizing a parallel application

Different programs have different parallel characteristics. A good parallel design for one application may be a bad parallel design for a different application. This naturally raises the following question: what characteristics of a parallel program will most impact its parallel design? For the purposes of mapping the algorithm onto a parallel computer, the most relevant characteristics are

**Core data structures:** the array(s) at each stage of the program that will consume the largest amount of memory and upon which most of the computations will be performed.

**Computational complexity** ($W$)**:** the total operations performed (or work done) and how they depend upon the algorithmic parameters.

**Operations per data element** ($W_{element}$)**:** the number of operations performed (or work done) on each data element.

**Degrees of Parallelism** (DoP)**:** the parallelism inherent in the algorithm and how it relates to the core data structures.

**Communication complexity** ($D$)**:** the total number of data elements moved to execute the parallel algorithm.

**Computation-to-communication ratio** ($W/D$)**:** the amount of computation performed per data element moved.

Some of these characteristics for the programs described in Chapters 1–4 are summarized in Table 6.1.

### 6.2.1 Characteristics of the example programs

The AddOne program (see Chapter 1) simply adds 1 to an $N \times N$ matrix $\mathbf{X}$; thus, the total work done is $W = N^2$ and the work done per matrix element is $W_{element} = 1$.

The parallel AddOne algorithm splits the matrix in the first dimension so there are $N$ degrees of parallelism, implying that, at most, $N_P = N$ processors could be effectively used with this algorithm. Finally, this algorithm doesn't require communication, so the total data sent is $D = 0$ and $W/D \to \infty$.

The Mandelbrot program (see Section 2.1) iteratively performs element-wise multiplies on an $N \times N$ complex matrix **Z** and exponentially scales the result with the `exp()` function. Complex multiplication typically requires $\sim 5$ operations, and the exponentially function typically can be evaluated in $\sim 15$ operations, resulting in $\sim 20$ operations performed per element per step. Thus, the work done per matrix element is $W_{element} \sim 20 N_{step}$ and the total work is $W \sim 20 N_{step} N^2$. The parallel Mandelbrot algorithm splits the matrix in the first dimension so there are $N$ degrees of parallelism, implying that, at most, $N_P = N$ processors could be effectively used with this algorithm. The parallel program sends the matrix back to the leader processor for display so $D = N^2$ data elements are communicated, resulting in a computation-to-communication ratio of $W/D \sim 20 N_{step}$ operations per data element sent.

The ZoomImage program (see Section 2.2) performs a convolution and interpolation on each of the $N \times N$ images in an $N \times N \times N_s$ tensor $\mathcal{Z}$. Each convolution performs $2 N_K^2$ operations per pixel. Each interpolation performs $\sim 10$ operations per pixel. The resulting work per data element is $W_{element} \sim 2 N_K^2 + 10$. The total work is $W \sim (2 N_K^2 + 10) N^2 N_s$. The parallel ZoomImage algorithm processes each image independently so there are $N_s$ degrees of parallelism, implying that, at most, $N_P = N_s$ processors could be effectively used with this algorithm. The parallel program sends the entire tensor back to the leader processor for display so $D = N^2 N_s$ data elements are communicated, resulting in a computation-to-communication ratio of $W/D \sim 2 N_K^2 + 10$ operations per data element sent.

The ParallelIO program (see Section 2.3) performs no computation and simply writes out and reads in an $N \times M$ matrix **X**. Thus $W = 0$ and $W_{element} = 0$. The ParallelIO program splits the matrix in the second dimension, resulting in $M$ degrees of parallelism. Technically, the ParallelIO program does not communicate between processors but writes files to a storage device. If the storage device is accessed via a network, then this is equivalent to sending $D = NM$ data elements. Using this value of $D$, it is apparent that the computation-to-communication ratio will be $W/D = 0$.

The Blurimage program (see Chapter 4) performs a convolution on an $N_x \times N_y$ image **Z**. Each convolution performs $2 N_K^2$ operations per pixel, and the resulting work per data element is $W_{element} = 2 N_K^2 N_{blur}$. The total work is $W = 2 N_K^2 N_x N_y N_{blur}$. The parallel Blurimage distributed array algorithm splits the image in the first dimension, but each processor holds $N_K$ additional columns of overlapping boundary data so that it can perform the convolution. Without this overlap, there would be $N_x$ degrees of parallelism. However, if $N_x/N_P < N_K$, the algorithm won't work because the overlap will be larger than the part of the image held on one processor. Thus, the actual degrees of parallelism are $N_x/N_K$, so the maximum number of processors that can be used is $N_P = N_x/N_K$. The Blurimage distributed array algorithm communicates the overlapping boundary data after each iteration of the algorithm, resulting in $D = N_P N_K N_y N_{blur}$ data elements being sent. The corresponding computation-to-communication ratio is $W/D = 2N_K N_x / N_P$ operations per data element sent.

The Beamformer program (see Chapter 3) consists of four stages that create synthetic sensor data, beamform the data, write it out, and then sum along the third dimension. Stage 1 multiplies an $N_s \times N_b$ complex matrix by each of the $N_t \times N_b$ real matrices in the $N_t \times N_b \times N_f$ array $\mathbf{X}_0$. Each matrix multiply performs $W_{element} = 2N_b$. The total work is $W = 4N_t N_b N_f N_s$. The parallel Beamformer algorithm splits the image in the third dimension, resulting in $N_f$ degrees of parallelism. No communication is required in this stage, so $D = 0$ and $W/D \to \infty$. The characteristics of stage 2 are identical to stage 1 except that the matrix multiply is complex followed by an absolute magnitude and the second dimension of $\mathbf{X}_1$ is $N_s$ instead of $N_b$, resulting in $W_{element} = 13N_s$. Stage 3 writes the data to storage, and its characteristics are similar to those of the ParallelIO example. Stage 4 sums the $N_t \times N_b \times N_f$ real array $\tilde{\mathbf{X}}_3$ along the third dimension performing $W_{element} = 1$. The parallel algorithm first performs these sums locally and then aggregates the results onto the leader processor that sums the $N_P$ matrices together. This results in $D = N_t N_b N_P$ and $W/D = N_f / N_P$.

## Implications

The application characteristics listed in Table 6.1 provide most of the salient features of a parallel implementation.

The core data array shows the size of the problem from which it can be determined if the problem will even fit on one processor. If this problem size doesn't change with the number of processors, it is called a "fixed" problem size and for some $N_P$ there will be enough memory to hold the problem. If the problem size changes with the number of processors, it is called a "scaled" problem size. For example, in the dBlurimage program, $N_x = 1024N_P$, so the problem size scales linearly with $N_P$. [Note: for historical reasons, sometimes the performance of an algorithm on fixed problem sizes is referred to as "strong" scaling, while the performance on scaled problems is referred to as "weak" scaling.]

The compute complexity ($W$) shows how many total operations need to be performed. Dividing this number by the speed of a system (in operations per second) provides an estimate of the total time to execute these operations.

**Table 6.1. Parallel algorithm characteristics.**

Various computational characteristics of the example programs discussed in Chapters 1–4.

| Program | Data Array | $W$ Compute Complexity (operations) | $W_{element}$ Operations/ Element | Degrees of Parallelism | $D$ Communication Complexity (Elements Sent) | $W/D$ Computation/ Communication (Ops/Element) |
|---|---|---|---|---|---|---|
| AddOne | $\mathbf{X} : \mathbb{R}^{P(N) \times N}$ | $N^2$ | $1$ | $N$ | $0$ | $\infty$ |
| Mandelbrot | $\mathbf{Z} : \mathbb{C}^{P(N) \times N}$ | $20 N_{step} N^2$ | $20 N_{step}$ | $N$ | $N^2$ | $20 N_{step}$ |
| ZoomImage | $\mathbf{Z} : \mathbb{R}_+^{N \times N \times P(N_s)}$ | $(2N_K^2 + 10) N^2 N_s$ | $2N_K^2 + 10$ | $N_s$ | $N^2 N_s$ | $2N_K^2 + 10$ |
| ParallelIO | $\mathbf{X} : \mathbb{R}^{N \times P(M)}$ | $0$ | $0$ | $M$ | $2NM$ | $0$ |
| Blurimage | $\mathbf{Z} : \mathbb{R}_+^{P_{ov(N_K)}(N_x) \times N_y}$ | $2N_K^2 N_x N_y N_{blur}$ | $2N_K^2 N_{blur}$ | $N_x/N_K$ | $N_P N_K N_y N_{blur}$ | $2N_K N_x/N_P$ |
| Beamformer | | | | | | |
| Stage 1 | $\mathcal{X}_0 : \mathbb{R}^{N_t \times N_b \times P(N_f)}$ | $4N_t N_b N_f N_s$ | $4N_b$ | $N_f$ | $0$ | $\infty$ |
| Stage 2 | $\mathcal{X}_1 : \mathbb{C}^{N_t \times N_s \times P(N_f)}$ | $13 N_t N_b N_f N_s$ | $4N_s$ | $N_f$ | $0$ | $\infty$ |
| Stage 3 | $\mathcal{X}_2 : \mathbb{R}^{N_t \times N_b \times P(N_f)}$ | $0$ | $0$ | $N_f$ | $N_t N_b N_f$ | $0$ |
| Stage 4 | $\tilde{\mathcal{X}}_3 : \mathbb{R}^{N_t \times N_b \times P(N_P)}$ | $N_t N_b N_f$ | $N_f$ | $N_f$ | $N_t N_b N_P$ | $N_f/N_P$ |

The operations per data element value ($W_{element}$) provides a sense of how compute intensive ($W_{element} > 100$) or data intensive ($W_{element} < 10$) the algorithm is. In general, compute-intensive algorithms are more likely to run well at high efficiency than will data-intensive algorithms.

The degrees of parallelism indicate which dimension the algorithm is distributed along. This indicates how many processors can be effectively utilized. Also, for multistage applications, if the parallel dimension and degrees of parallelism are the same at every stage, then no additional communication needs to be done between stages.

The communication complexity ($D$) shows how many total data elements need to be communicated. Dividing this number by the bandwidth of the communication channel (in data elements per second) provides an estimate of the total time to communicate these data elements.

The computation-to-communication ratio ($W/D$) provides a sense of how compute intensive ($W/D > 100$) or communication intensive ($W/D < 10$) the algorithm is. In general, compute-intensive algorithms are more likely to run well on parallel computers than will data-intensive algorithms. For many algorithms, $W_{element}$ and $W/D$ are very similar.

## 6.2.2  Serial performance metrics

The program characteristics described in Table 6.1 provide a lot of information, but none of them are performance metrics. Obtaining performance metrics from these characteristics requires incorporating a timeframe over which the operations are performed or the data elements are sent.

Bandwidth is a key parameter in describing the overall performance requirements of the system. Consider a generic application that repeatedly reads in $D$ data elements at a time and performs $W_{element}$ operations on each data element. Furthermore, let $T_{input}$ be the time that we wish this processing to take. For example, $T_{input}$ might be the time interval between the arrival of successive sets of $D$ data elements. In this case, it is necessary to complete the operations on one dataset before the next one arrives to prevent them from "piling up." More generally, $T_{input}$ can simply be the desired time to process $D$ data elements.

The required bandwidth $BW_{input}$ (in elements per second) is given by

$$BW_{input} = D/T_{input}$$

More generally, if the application has multiple stages, the bandwidth of $i$th stage is

$$BW^i_{input} = D^i/T_{input}$$

A simple approach for estimating the overall required processing rate is to multiply the bandwidth by the number of operations per data element required. Thus the rate of performance goal $R^i_{goal}$ is

$$R^i_{goal} = W^i_{element}BW^i_{input} = W^i/T_{input}$$

When the desired performance rate is less than what can be achieved using one processor, a parallel solution needs to be employed.

---

**Processor Sizing.** Estimating how many processors will be necessary to meet a particular performance goal is an important part of developing a good parallel implementation. An algorithm that is good for 20 processors may not work for 200 processors if there are insufficient degrees of parallelism. A basic processor sizing estimate consists of

> **Computational complexity analysis:** estimates the total amount of work that needs to be done by the application.

> **Throughput analysis:** converts the total work done into a rate at which this work must be performed.

> **Processor performance:** estimates what the performance of the algorithm will be on a single processor.

After the above analysis has been completed, the nominal processor size (in terms of number of processors) is estimated by dividing the required throughput by the processing rate

$$N_P^{est} \approx \sum_i \frac{R_{goal}^i}{\epsilon_{comp}^i R_{peak}}$$

where $\epsilon_{comp}^i$ is the efficiency at which a processor with peak performance $R_{peak}$ (in operations/second) can perform the work in stage $i$.

---

## 6.2.3   Degrees of parallelism

The term "degrees of parallelism" mentioned in the previous section refers to the amount of parallelism available for a given parallel algorithm. Consider a generic algorithm with multiple stages in which there may be different parallel opportunities at each stage. These different types of parallelism can be roughly grouped into three categories (see Figure 6.1).

> **Coarse-grained (round-robin):** this is the highest level of parallelism and exploits the fact that each input can be processed independently of the others. This form of parallelism usually requires the least amount of communication between processors but requires the most memory and has the highest latency.

> **Task/pipeline:** this decomposes different stages of the processing into a pipeline. The output of one stage is fed into the input of another so that at any given time each stage is working on a different dataset.

> **Data parallelism:** this is the finest grained parallelism and decomposes each input into smaller pieces.

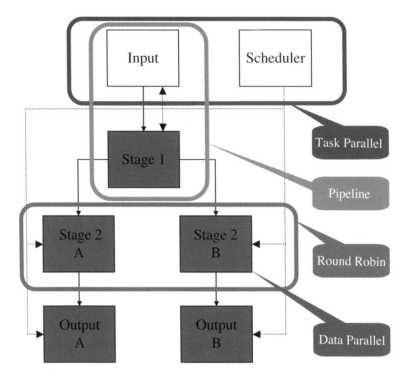

**Figure 6.1. Types of parallelism.**
Within a generic application, there may be many different types of parallelism that can be exploited: task (coarse-grained), pipeline, round-robin (coarse-grained), and data (fine-grained).

A parallel mapping describes how many processors are used in each stage. The goal of parallel mapping is to best allocate these processors to achieve the desired performance goal. The mapping of an application can be parameterized as follows:

$N_{coarse} \equiv$ number of different problems or pipelines

$N_{stage} \equiv$ number of stages in the pipeline

$N_{stage}^i \equiv$ the number of processors used at stage $i$ in the pipeline

These parameters must satisfy the constraint that the sum of all the processors used at every stage in every pipeline is equal to the total number of processors $N_P$:

$$N_P = N_{coarse} \sum_{i=1}^{N_{stage}} N_{stage}^i$$

There are several important special cases of the above description. First is the pure coarse-grained parallel case, in which each processor is given an entire dataset to process and neither fine-grained parallelism nor pipeline parallelism is exploited:

$$N_{coarse} = N_P, \quad N_{stage} = 1, \quad N_{stage}^1 = 1$$

Next is the pure pipeline parallel case. This case is limited in that the total number of processors cannot be more than the number of stages in the pipeline:

$$N_{coarse} = 1, \quad N_{stage} = N_P, \quad N_{stage}^i = 1$$

Finally, there is the pure data-parallel case in which only fine-grained parallelism is exploited:

$$N_{coarse} = 1, \quad N_{stage} = 1, \quad N_{stage}^1 = N_P$$

## 6.2.4   Parallel performance metrics (no communication)

In the absence of any communication and IO cost, all of these parallel approaches will take the same time to process an input frame of data (where there are assumed to be $N_{frame}$ instances)

$$T_{comp}(N_P) = \frac{W^{tot}}{\epsilon_{comp} R_{peak} N_P} \propto \frac{W^{tot}}{N_P}$$

where $W^{tot}$ is the total computational operations or work required to process a set of data elements at each stage (see Table 6.1) and is given by

$$W^{tot} \equiv \sum_{i=1}^{N_{stage}} W^i = W^{1a} + W^{1b} + W^{1cd} + W^{1e} + W^2$$

The computational speedup will be linear in the number of processors:

$$S_{comp}(N_P) \equiv \frac{T_{comp}(1)}{T_{comp}(N_P)} = N_P$$

Likewise, in the zero communication case, the latency (i.e., the time to get the first answer) is the number of stages times the longest time it takes to process any one stage:

$$T_{latency}(N_P) = N_{stage} \max_i (T_{latency}^i(N_{stage}^i))$$

where

$$T_{latency}(N_{stage}^i) = \frac{W_{stage}^i}{\epsilon_{comp} R_{peak} N_{stage}^i}$$

This is because no one stage can progress until the previous stage has also finished. The latency speedup in this case is

$$S_{latency}(N_P) \equiv \frac{T_{latency}(1)}{T_{latency}(N_P)}$$

The total memory required for the different approaches is

$$M(N_P) = N_{coarse} \sum_{i=1}^{N_{stage}} \frac{M_{stage}^i}{N_{stage}^i}$$

Perhaps more importantly is the max amount of memory required by any particular processor:

$$M_{cpu-max}(N_P) = \max_i (M_{stage}^i / N_{stage}^i)$$

## 6.2.5  Parallel performance metrics (with communication)

Of course, assuming no communication and storage costs is a bad assumption, and essentially the entire goal of designing a parallel implementation is to minimize these costs. Nevertheless, the above models are useful in that they provide upper bounds on performance. In addition, the speedup and memory footprint definitions are unaltered when communication is included.

In the case of fine-grained parallelism, communication is required between steps in which the directionality of the parallelism changes. In turn, the directionality change requires that a corner turn be performed to reorganize the data to exploit the parallelism. The time to communicate data between steps $i$ and $i+1$ is given by

$$T_{comm}^{i \rightarrow i+1}(N_{stage}^i \rightarrow N_{stage}^{i+1}) = \frac{D^{i \rightarrow i+1}}{BW_{eff}(N_{stage}^i \rightarrow N_{stage}^{i+1})}$$

where $D^{i \rightarrow i+1}$ is the amount of data (in bytes) moved between steps $i$ and $i+1$ and $BW_{eff}(N_{stage}^i \rightarrow N_{stage}^{i+1})$ is the effective bandwidth (in bytes/second) between the processors, which is given by

$$BW_{eff}(N_{stage}^i \rightarrow N_{stage}^{i+1}) = \epsilon_{comm}^{i \rightarrow i+1} BW_{peak}(N_{stage}^i \rightarrow N_{stage}^{i+1})$$

$BW_{peak}(N_{stage}^i \rightarrow N_{stage}^{i+1})$ is the peak bandwidth from the processors in stage $i$ to the processors in stage $i+1$. A more detailed model of this performance requires a model of the processor interconnect, which is given the next section.

The implication of the communication on various cases is as follows. For the pure pipeline case (assuming that computation and communication can be overlapped), compute time and latency are

$$T_{tot}(N_P) = \max_i (\max(T_{latency}^i(1), T_{comm}^{i \rightarrow i+1}(1 \rightarrow 1)))/N_{coarse}$$

$$T_{latency}(N_P) = 2N_{stage} \max_i (\max(T_{latency}^i(1), T_{comm}^{i \rightarrow i+1}(1 \rightarrow 1)))$$

If communication and computation cannot be overlapped, then the inner max(,) function is replaced by addition. In this case, the principal benefit of pipeline parallelism is that it is determined by the max (instead of the sum) of the stage times. The price for improved performance is increased latency, which is proportional to the number of computation and communication stages. There is a nominal impact on the memory footprint.

For the pure data-parallel case, compute time and latency are

$$T_{tot}(N_P) = \frac{T_{comp}(N_P) + T_{comm}(N_P)}{N_{coarse}}$$

$$T_{latency}(N_P) = T_{comp}(N_P) + T_{comm}(N_P)$$

where

$$T_{comm}(N_P) = \sum_i T_{comm}^{i \to i+1}(N_P \to N_P)$$

In general, in a pure data-parallel approach, it is hard to overlap computation and communication. The principal benefit of data parallelism is that the compute time is reduced as long as it is not offset by the required communication. This approach also reduces the latency in a similar fashion. This approach also provides a linear reduction in the memory footprint.

For the combined pipeline parallel case, we have

$$T_{tot}(N_P) = \max_i(\max(T_{comp}(N_{stage}^i), T_{comm}^{i \to i+1}(N_{stage}^i \to N_{stage}^{i+1})))/N_{coarse}$$

$$T_{latency}(N_P) = 2N_{stage} \max_i(\max(T_{comp}(N_{stage}^i), T_{comm}^{i \to i+1}(N_{stage}^i \to N_{stage}^{i+1})))$$

This approach provides an overall reduction in computation time and allows for overlapping computation and communication and a reduction in the memory footprint. As we shall see later, this is often the approach of choice for parallel signal processing systems.

## 6.2.6  Amdahl's Law

Perhaps the most important concept in designing parallel implementations is managing overhead. Assume that the total amount of work that needs to be done can be broken up into a part that can be done in parallel and a part that can be done only in serial (i.e., on one processor):

$$W_{tot} = W_{||} + W_{|}$$

The execution time then scales as follows:

$$T_{comp}(N_P) \propto W_{||}/N_P + W_{|}$$

which translates into a speedup of

$$S_{comp}(N_P) = \frac{W_{tot}}{W_{||}/N_P + W_{|}}$$

If we normalize with respect to $W_{tot}$, this translates to

$$S_{comp}(N_P) = \frac{1}{w_{||}/N_P + w_{|}}$$

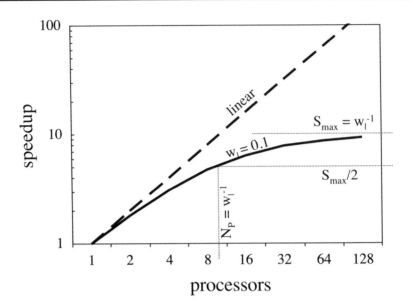

**Figure 6.2. Amdahl's Law.**
Plot showing speedup of a program with an Amdahl fraction of $w_| = 0.1$.
Dotted lines show the max speedup $S_{max} = w_|^{-1} = 10$ and the half
speedup point $N_P = w_|^{-1}$.

where $w_{||} = W_{||}/W_{tot}$ and $w_| = W_|/W_{tot}$. When $N_P$ is very large, the maximum
speedup achievable is

$$S_{max} = S_{comp}(N_P \rightarrow \infty) = w_|^{-1}$$

For example, if $w_1 = 0.1$, then the maximum speedup is 10 (see Figure 6.2).
This fundamental result is referred to as Amdahl's Law [Amdahl 1967], and the
value $w_|$ is often referred to as the "Amdahl fraction" of the application. Amdahl's
Law highlights the need to make every aspect of a code parallel. It also applies to
other overheads (e.g., communication) that cause no useful work to be done. Finally,
Amdahl's Law is also a useful tool for making trade-offs. Half the maximum speedup
is achieved at $N_P = w_|^{-1}$.

$$S_{comp}(N_P = w_|^{-1}) = w_|^{-1}/(w_{||} + 1) \approx \frac{1}{2}S_{max}$$

If $w_| = 0.1$, then using more than 10 processors will be of marginal utility. Likewise,
if an application needs a speedup of 100 to meet its performance goals, then the
implementation must be optimized to the point where $w_| < 0.01$.

## 6.2.7  Characterizing speedup

The speedup obtained by a parallel application is a fundamental measure of how effectively the application takes advantage of a parallel computing system. Speedup is usually characterized as a function of the number of processors $S(N_P)$. The shape of this curve generally falls into a number of different categories. Typically, speedup is measured in processor powers of two, $N_P = 1, 2, 4, 8, \ldots$, and is plotted logarithmically. Figure 6.3 depicts several different kinds of speedup curves that are commonly seen. The ideal is a linear speedup where $S(N_P) = N_P$. More typical is sublinear speedup where $S(N_P) = \alpha N_P$ and $0 < \alpha < 1$. Regrettably, even more typical for novice users is a speedup curve that saturates at some low number of processors. Rarest of all is superlinear speedup where $S(N_P) > N_P$. Superlinear speedup is even rarer and is occasionally achieved by experts.

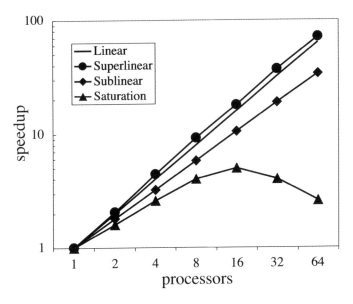

**Figure 6.3. Speedup curves.**
Plot showing different types of speedup.

The value of these curves is what they say about the parallel implementation. If linear speedup has been achieved, then typically there is no further performance optimization necessary. Linear speedup is easiest to achieve on embarrassingly parallel problems with little or no communication. In such problems, linear speedup should be the goal, and most programmers are eventually able to achieve this.

Sublinear performance is often acceptable and usually indicates that there is some constant overhead whose proportion remains constant as processors are added. For example, a program whose Amdahl fraction decreases with the number of processors $W_1(N_P) \propto N_P^{-1}$ will show sublinear behavior. If the application is embarrassingly parallel, then sublinear behavior can be an indication that some unnecessary overhead in the program exists that could potentially be avoided. If the program is not embarrassingly parallel and requires consistent communication, then sublinear performance is often the best that can be achieved.

Saturation is typical of many parallel programs early on in their development. It is characteristic of some bottleneck in the code where one processor is waiting for all the other processors to complete some task. Analysis of the program can usually uncover these bottlenecks and lead to their elimination.

Superlinear performance is typical of embarrassingly parallel programs with fixed problem sizes (i.e., problem sizes that do not grow as $N_P$). The serial performance of the program improves as $N_P$ increases because the problem size on each processor is getting smaller and results in better cache performance.

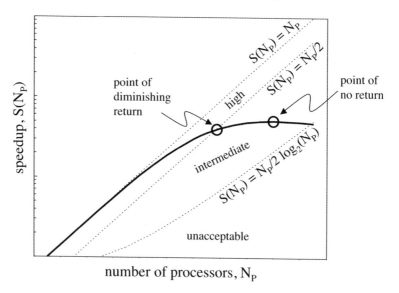

**Figure 6.4.  Speedup ranges.**
Plot showing different ranges of speedup.

Figure 6.3 shows speedup curves as a user measures them for a particular application. In reality, all applications have the same curve (see Figure 6.4) because all parallel programs do saturate for sufficiently large $N_P$ [Kuck 1996]. The goal of a good implementation is to push this point of no return to a sufficiently large value of $N_P$. Within this context, the speedup of an application can be divided into three ranges. In the high performance range, the speedup is linear to sublinear ($N_P/2 < S(N_P) < N_P$). As $N_P$ increases, the speedup starts decreasing and the benefit of adding processors is reduced. When $S(N_P) = N_P/2$, the program is getting only half the total performance: this point is referred to as the point of diminishing returns. In the intermediate performance range ($N_P/2 \log_2(N_P) < S(N_P) < N_P/2$), the program is getting a marginal benefit by adding processors. Eventually, the speedup peaks at the point of no return, at which point adding processors causes the program to slow down. In the unacceptable performance range ($S(N_P) < N_P/2 \log_2(N_P)$), there is little benefit to running the program in parallel.

So far, speedup has been discussed only as a function of $N_P$. However, another important variable is the problem size $N$ being solved by the program. Combining both of these results in a speedup surface $S(N_P, N)$. Figure 6.5 shows two slices through this surface. First, it is important to note that only a part of the whole range of $N_P$ and $N$ will physically fit into the memory of the computer. When measuring the speedup of an application, it is important to determine how $N$ changes as $N_P$ increases. There are two standard approaches. A speedup curve with a fixed problem size holds the total problem size $N$ constant as $N_P$ increases. In this case, the problem size per processors $N/N_P$ decreases. It may be the case that $N$ is sufficiently large that it may not fit on a small number of processors. For historical reasons, this speedup curve is often referred to as the "strong scaling" curve. A speedup curve with a scaled problem size increases the total problem size $N$ as $N_P$ increases. In this case, the problem size per processors $N/N_P$ remains fixed. For historical reasons, this speedup curve is often referred to as the "weak scaling" curve.

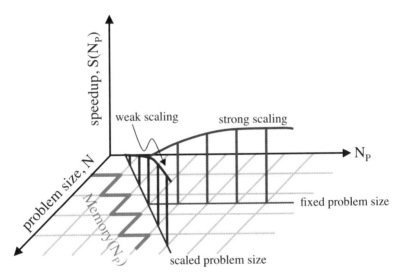

**Figure 6.5. Weak versus strong scaling.**
Plot showing speedup of scaled (weak) and fixed (strong) problem size.

## 6.2.8 Spatial and temporal locality

A more abstract view of a program can be obtained by examining it from the perspective of the computer running the program. To the computer, the program is simply a stream of memory references and corresponding operations. This view of a program is often referred to as the Von Neumann model [Von Neumann 1945]. In such a model, the memory references can be analyzed in terms of how close they are to each other (spatial locality) and how often a particular reference is reused (temporal locality) (see Figure 6.6). The spatial gap between memory references is referred to as the memory stride. Reuse is related to how often a piece of memory is used again.

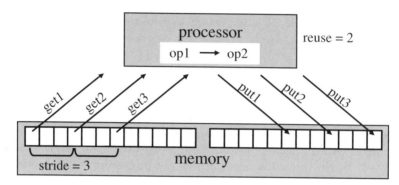

**Figure 6.6. Spatial/temporal locality model.**

The concepts of spatial/temporal locality are very powerful in that they allow an understanding of the program from the computer's point of view. Intuitively, applications with high spatial/temporal locality should be "easier" for a computer to execute than those with low spatial/temporal locality. Likewise, programs with high spatial/temporal locality should be easier to implement in parallel because the data accesses are regular and because each time a data element is brought in, it is likely to be used multiple times.

Spatial/temporal locality is not just an abstract concept. It can be measured (see [Weinberg et al. 2005]) by examining the statistics of the memory references of a program while it is running. With these statistics, it is possible to compute a spatial locality score by using the formula

$$Spatial \;\; Score = \sum \frac{Stride(i)}{i}$$

where $Stride(i)$ is the fraction of memory references with a stride of $i$. The spatial score is a weighted average of all these references. A program with only stride 1 references will have $Stride(1) = 1$ and zero otherwise, and will have a spatial score of 1. A program that has only very large strides will have a spatial locality score that approaches zero.

Similarly, a temporal score can be computed with the formula

$$Temporal \;\; Score = \sum \frac{Reuse(2^{i+1}) - Reuse(2^i)}{2^i}$$

where $Reuse(2^i)$ is the fraction of memory references that are revisited in less than $2^i$ memory references. Programs that revisit the same location often will have a temporal score approaching 1, while programs that never reuse data will have a temporal score approaching 0. Nominal spatial/temporal locality scores for the example programs are shown in Figure 6.7. In general, these example applications have high spatial locality scores because they tend to process data in a regular fashion. AddOne and ParallelIO have low temporal locality scores because they do very few operations per data element.

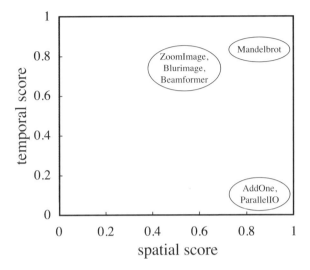

**Figure 6.7. Spatial/temporal scores of example programs.**
These applications have a high spatial locality score. AddOne and ParallelIO have low temporal locality scores because they do very few operations.

## 6.3   Standard parallel computer

The interpretation of the parallel application metrics presented in the previous sections is best done in the context of a model of the parallel computer hardware. Visualizing how a parallel program runs on a parallel computer is one of the most important and most challenging aspects of parallel programming. Typically, it is not necessary to understand the hardware in fine detail and a more abstract model is sufficient. This section presents a canonical parallel computer that will be sufficient for understanding the implementation implications of the parallel application metrics. For more detailed descriptions of computer architecture see [Hennessy & Paterson 2006].

The canonical multinode computer architecture consists of a number of nodes connected by a network. Each node consists of one or more processors and memory. If the node has more than one processor, it is a multicore node. The memory on the node may be further decomposed into various levels of cache, main memory, and disk storage (see Figure 6.8). There are many variations on this theme. A node may have multiple processors sharing various levels of cache, memory, and disk storage. In addition, there may be external global memory or disk storage that is visible to all nodes. An important implication of this canonical architecture is the "memory

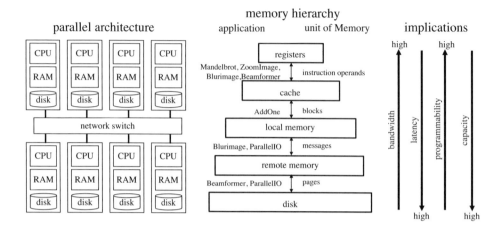

**Figure 6.8. Parallel architecture and memory hierarchy.**
A canonical parallel computer consists of nodes with processors and memory connected by a communication network (left). This architecture results in a canonical memory hierarchy (right).

hierarchy" (see Figure 6.8). The memory hierarchy concept refers to the fact that the memory "closer" to the processor is much faster (the bandwidth is higher and latency is lower). However, the price for this performance is capacity. The ranking of the memory hierarchy is typically as follows:

- Processor registers

- Cache L1, L2, ...

- Local main memory

- Remote main memory

- Local disk

- Remote disk

Typically, each level in the hierarchy exchanges a 10x performance increase for a 10x reduction in capacity. The "steepness" of the memory hierarchy refers to the magnitude of the performance reduction as one descends down the memory hierarchy. If these performance reductions are large, we say the system has a very steep memory hierarchy.

Different applications will stress different parts of this memory hierarchy. Figure 6.8 labels each part of the hierarchy with the different applications: AddOne (local memory), Mandelbrot (processor), ZoomImage (processor), ParallelIO (network and disk), Beamformer (processor and disk), and Blurimage (processor and network).

The concept of the memory hierarchy is probably the most important hardware idea to keep in mind when developing a parallel application. More specifically, a well-performing parallel application is one that best mitigates the performance impacts of the hardware memory hierarchy. This requires programmers to have a clear picture of the system in their minds so that they can understand the precise performance implications. The basic rule of thumb is to construct an implementation that minimizes both the total volume and the number of data movements up and down the hierarchy.

### 6.3.1 Network model

Within the memory hierarchy, the communication network that connects the processors in a parallel system is usually the most critical piece for the programmer to keep in mind because it raises issues that are unique to a parallel implementation (i.e., communication between processors). This is true whether the network is within the node or between the nodes or both. The other parts of the memory hierarchy are also important but are not unique to the parallel implementation. For example, how a program uses the registers or the local memory is fundamentally a serial programming issue. Likewise, how a program writes to its local disk is also primarily a serial programming issue. In general, it is best to address serial performance issues first and then proceed with the parallel implementation.

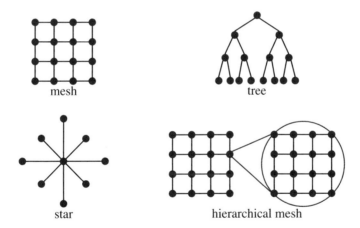

**Figure 6.9. Network topologies.**
How different processors are connected to each other with cabling and various intermediate points (e.g., routers) is referred to as the network topology.

Networks can come in many different shapes. How the various points in a network are connected is referred to as the topology of the network (see Figure 6.9). Designers of a parallel processing system spend a great deal of effort trying to design and build the best network topology. From a programmer perspective, the network topology can be abstracted away and approximated by the time it takes any one processor to send data to another processor. The starting point of modeling a communication network is this point-to-point performance. This can be effectively measured by timing how long it takes two processors to send messages of different sizes to each other. The result is a standard curve that can be characterized by a single function $T_{comm}(m)$, which is the time it takes to send a message of size $m$. The function $T_{comm}(m)$ is typically well described by the following simple two-parameter formula:

$$T_{comm}(m) = \text{Latency} + \frac{m}{\text{Bandwidth}}$$

Bandwidth (typically measured in bits, bytes, or words per second) is the maximum rate at which data can flow over a network. Bandwidth is typically measured by timing how long it takes to send a large message between two processors and dividing the message size by the total time:

$$\text{Bandwidth} = \lim_{m \to \infty} \frac{T(m)}{m} \tag{6.1}$$

Latency is how long it takes for a single bit to be sent from one processor to the next. It is usually measured by timing a very short message and is typically computed from the formula

$$\text{Latency} = \lim_{m \to 0} T(m) \tag{6.2}$$

These two parameters are important because some programs require sending a few very large messages (and are limited by bandwidth), and some programs require sending lots of very small messages (and are limited by latency).

Figure 6.10 shows the latency and instantaneous bandwidth for a typical cluster network as a function of message size. The important features of this curve, which are typical of most networks, are the leveling off in latency at small messages and the leveling off in bandwidth occurring at large messages. While knowing the bandwidth and latency of a system is helpful, what it is even more helpful is comparing these parameters with respect to the computing power of the processor. More specifically, dividing the processor speed (typically measured in floating-point operations per second—FLOPS) by the bandwidth (measured in 8-byte words per second) yields the number of FLOPS that can be performed in the time it takes to send a message of a given size (see Figure 6.10). This "inverse bandwidth" number provides a good guide to the minimum number of operations that need be performed on a value to amortize the cost of communicating that value.

In this case, for small messages, nearly 10,000 operations need to be performed on each 8-byte element. At large messages, only 100 operations need to be performed. These data clearly illustrate a key parallel programming design paradigm: it is better to send fewer large messages than many smaller messages.

What is particularly nice about describing the network relative to the processor performance is that these numbers are relatively constant for most of the systems of interest. For example, these values ($10^5$ for small messages and $10^2$ for large messages) are typical of many systems and do not vary much over time. The

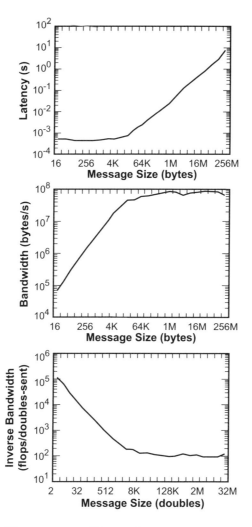

**Figure 6.10. Network performance.**
Latency, bandwidth, and "inverse bandwidth" as a function of message
size for a typical cluster network. Inverse bandwidth is shown in terms
of the number of FLOPS/doubles-sent.

absolute processor and network speeds can change dramatically over time, but these
ratios remain relatively constant. For example, while processor and networks speeds
have improved by almost $10^3$ over the last several decades, the relative performance
has changed by only a factor of 10.

These parameters suggest that if a parallel program uses large messages, it
should be performing >100 operations on each number before communicating the
number over the network. Likewise, if a program sends small messages, it should

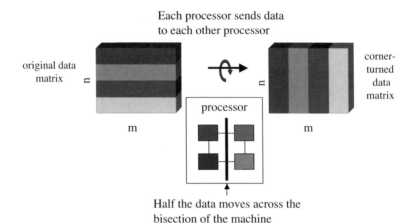

**Figure 6.11. Corner turn.**
The data movements required to redistribute data from a row distribution to a row distribution.

be performing >10,000 operations on each number before sending. Doing less than these amounts will tend to result in a parallel program that doesn't perform very well because most of the time will be spent sending messages instead of performing computations.

Using the simple point-to-point model, we can predict the time for a more complex operation such as a "corner turn" (see Figure 6.11). This requires all-to-all communication in which a set of processors $P_1$ sends a messages of size $m$ to each of a set of processors $P_2$,

$$T_{CornerTurn} = \frac{P_1 P_2 (\text{Latency} + m/\text{Bandwidth})}{Q}$$

where $B$ is the bytes per message and $Q$ is the number of simultaneous parallel paths from processors in $P_1$ to processors in $P_2$. The total amount of data moved in this operation is $m P_1 P_2$.

## 6.3.2 Kuck hierarchy

The memory hierarchy and network model described in the previous section are usually sufficient for programming most parallel systems. In other words, we view the computer as a set of processors connected by a network. The parallel programming paradigm that emerges from this model is to design a parallel algorithm so that the least amount of data and fewest number of messages are sent between processors.

Although this simple machine model is good for most purposes, there are times when a more sophisticated model is required that can handle hierarchical collections of processors, memories, and networks. Figure 6.12 presents such a model based on the terminology developed by Kuck in [Kuck 1996]. In this model there are processors, memories, and networks. At the lowest level (level 0), we have a set

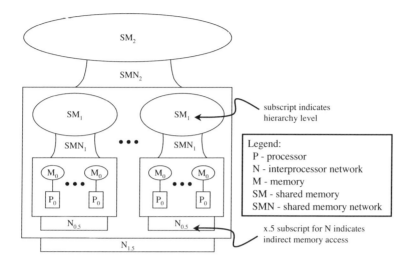

**Figure 6.12. Two-level hierarchy.**
Memory hierarchy terminology for a two-level hierarchy (adapted from [Kuck 1996]). $P_i$ = processor, $M_i$ = memory, $N_i$ = network, $SM_i$ = shared memory, $SMN_i$ = shared memory network.

of processors $P_0$ with their own local memory $M_0$. Messages can be sent between these processors using the network $N_{0.5}$. Processors at level 0 also have access to a shared memory at the next level, referred to as $SM_1$. Data from $SM_1$ is accessed by processors $P_0$ via the shared memory network $SMN_1$. This progression of networks and memory can be applied across any number of levels.

In a real system, it is unlikely that there will be networks and shared memory at every level. For example, consider a system consisting of nodes connected via a network (see Figure 6.13). Each node has processors with local cache and shared memory. In such a system, there would be $P_0$, $M_0$, $SM_1$, $SMN_1$, and $N_{1.5}$. Likewise, such a system would be missing $N_{0.5}$, $SM_2$, and $SMN_2$. The Kuck hierarchy is also useful for understanding more complex multicore processors. Before programming a parallel computer, it is usually worthwhile to take a moment to draw out a diagram like Figure 6.13. This usually provides valuable insight into the system and will highlight any gaps in understanding that need to be further investigated.

## 6.4   Parallel programming models

The parallel programming model describes how the software is going to implement the application on a parallel computer. A good software model allows the different types of parallelism to be exploited: data parallelism, task parallelism, pipeline parallelism, and round-robin. In addition, a good implementation of the parallel programming model allows the type of parallelism to be exploited to change as the system is built and the performance requirements evolve.

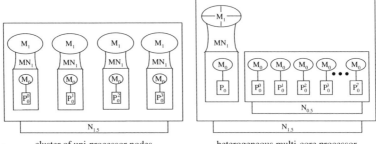

cluster of uni-processor nodes          heterogeneous multi-core processor

**Figure 6.13. Example Kuck hierarchies.**
Applying the Kuck hierarchy to a typical cluster of single-processor nodes results in the diagram on the left. Applying it to a more complex heterogeneous multicore processor consisting of a general-purpose processor and eight acceleration units results in the diagram on the right.

There are a number of different parallel programming models that are commonly used. We will discuss three in particular: manager/worker, messaging, and distributed arrays.

The manager/worker model is the simplest parallel programming model. It is used when a problem can be broken up into a set of relatively independent tasks that the workers can process without explicitly communicating with each other. The central constraint of the manager/worker model is that each worker communicates only by sending information to the manager. This constraint is very powerful and is enormously simplifying. Furthermore, it has proved very robust, and the vast majority of parallel programs with a small number of processors (i.e., workstations) use this approach. Unfortunately, this model can be used only in applications that require no interprocessor communications. In addition, the central manager prevents this approach from scaling to large numbers of processors.

The message passing model is in many respects the opposite of the manager/worker model. The message passing model requires that any processor be able to send and receive messages from any other processor. The infrastructure of the message passing model is fairly simple. This infrastructure is most typically instantiated in the parallel computing community via the Message Passing Interface (MPI) standard (http://www.mpi-forum.org). The message passing model requires that each processor have a unique identifier ($P_{ID}$ or Pid) and know how many other processors are working together on a problem ($N_P$ or Np). In MPI terminology, these are referred to as the processor "rank" and the "size" of the MPI world. Any parallel program can be implemented using the message passing model. The primary drawback of this model is that the programmer must manage every individual message in the system; therefore, this model often requires a great deal of additional code and may be extremely difficult to debug. Nevertheless, there are certain parallel programs that can be implemented only with a message passing model.

The distributed array model is a compromise between the two models. Distributed arrays impose additional constraints on the program, which allow complex programs to be written relatively simply. In many respects, the distributed array model is the most natural parallel programming model for MATLAB because it is implemented using arrays, which are the core data type of MATLAB algorithms. Briefly, the distributed array model creates arrays in which each processor stores or owns a piece of the whole array. Additional information is stored in the array so that every processor knows which parts of the array the other processors have. How the arrays are broken up among the processors is specified by a map [Lebak et al. 2005]. The different mappings are useful concepts to have even if the distributed array model is not being used. The concept of breaking up arrays in different ways is one of the key ideas in parallel computing. Computations on distributed arrays are usually performed using the "owner computes" rule, which means that each processor is responsible for doing a computation on the data it is storing locally. Maps can become quite complex and express virtually arbitrary distributions.

## 6.5 System metrics

Several ways of characterizing parallel applications have now been described along with a canonical parallel processor. The actual selection of a parallel mapping for an implementation is a constrained optimization process. The constraints are provided by the application, and the goal is usually to optimize a system level metric. This section presents a more formal description of some of the most common system metrics: performance, efficiency, form factor, and software cost.

### 6.5.1 Performance

Performance is the primary driver for using a parallel computing system and refers to the time it takes to process one dataset in a series of datasets. Performance is usually decomposed into latency and throughput.

Latency refers to the time it takes to get the first dataset through the processing chain. Latency is fundamentally constrained by how quickly the consumer of the data needs the information. Some typical latencies for different systems are

- microseconds: real-time control

- milliseconds: operator in the loop

- seconds: quality assurance systems

- minutes: monitoring systems

- hours: archival systems

The optimization process begins by selecting a latency target for a hypothetical application ($T_{latency}^{goal}$) and may be given in terms $T_{input}$. For this example, set an

arbitrary latency goal of
$$T_{latency}^{goal}/T_{input} \approx 10$$

Throughput is the rate at which the work units can be processed. Fundamentally, the data must be processed at the same rate it is coming into the system; otherwise, it will "pile up" at some stage in the processing. A key parameter here is the required throughput relative to what can be done on one processor. For this example, set an arbitrary throughput goal of

$$S_{comp}^{goal} = T_{comp}^{goal}/T_{comp}(1) \approx 100$$

## 6.5.2  Form factor

Ideally, an arbitrarily large computer with an infinite number of processors is available for the application. Unfortunately, the actual parallel computer available will be constrained in a number of ways:

**Size.** The physical volume of the parallel computer must fit in the room that has been allocated to it.

**Power.** Total power consumed by the parallel computer and its cooling system.

**Heat.** The total heat the parallel computer can produce that can be absorbed by the cooling system.

**IO Channels.** The number and speed of the data channels coming into and out of the system.

---

**Processor Selection.** How is a processor chosen for an application? Once it has been decided to go ahead and build a parallel processing system, then it is necessary to select the physical hardware. Often it is the case that the above form factor requirements entirely dictate this choice. For example, it may be that there is room for a total of five chassis with all the required power and cooling. Suppose each chassis has 14 slots. In each chassis, the application requires an input buffer board, one master control computer (and a spare), and a central storage device. This leaves ten slots, each capable of holding a dual processor node (see Figure 6.14). The result is

$$N_P^{real} = (5 \text{ chassis})\ (10 \text{ slots/chassis})\ (2 \text{ processors/slot})) = 100$$

At this point, the die is cast, and it will be up to the implementors of the application to make the required functionality "fit" on the selected processor. The procedure for doing this usually consists of first providing an initial software implementation with some optimization on the hardware. If this implementation is unable to meet the performance requirements, then usually a trade-off is done to see if scaling back some of the algorithm parameters (e.g., the amount of data to be processed) can meet the performance goals. Ultimately, a fundamentally different algorithm may be required, combined with heroic efforts by the programmers to get every last bit of performance out of the system.

---

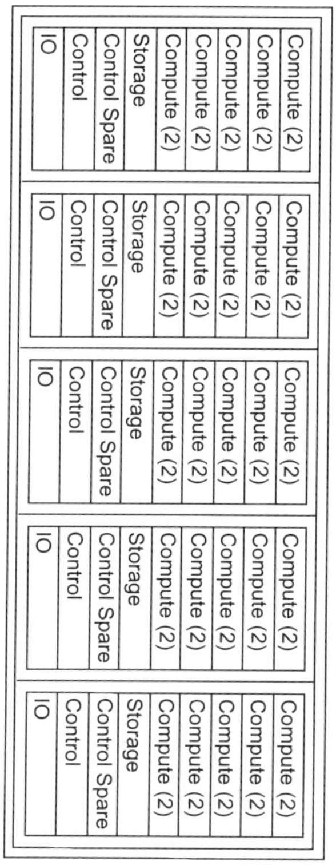

**Figure 6.14. Example computing rack.**
A canonical parallel processing rack. Each rack contains five chassis. Each chassis has 14 slots. Four of the slots may need to be reserved for IO, control (and spare), and storage. The result is that 100 processors can be fit into the entire rack.

## 6.5.3 Efficiency

Efficiency is the fraction of the peak capability of the system the application achieves. The value of $T_{comp}$ implies a certain efficiency factor on one processor relative to the theoretical peak performance (e.g., $\epsilon_{comp} \approx 0.2$). There are similar efficiencies associated with bandwidth (e.g., $\epsilon_{comm} \approx 0.5$) and memory (e.g., $\epsilon_{mem} \approx 0.5$). There are two principal implications of these efficiencies. If the required efficiency is much higher than these values, then it may mean that different hardware must be selected (e.g., nonprogrammable hardware, higher bandwidth networking, or higher density memory). If the required efficiency is well below these values, then it means that more flexible, higher-level programming environments can be used, thus greatly reducing schedule and cost.

The implementation of the software is usually factored into two pieces. First is how the code is implemented on each individual processor. Second is how the communication among the different processors is implemented. The typical categories for the serial implementation environments follow:

**Machine assembly.** Such as the instruction set of a specific processor. Assembly provides the highest performance but requires enormous effort and expertise and offers no software portability.

**Procedural languages with optimized libraries.** Such as C and Fortan used in conjunction with the Basic Linear Algebra Subroutine (BLAS). This approach still produces efficient code, with less effort and expertise, and is as portable as the underlying library.

**Object-oriented languages with optimized libraries.** Such as C++ used in conjunction with the C++ optimized libraries (e.g., VSIPL++ [Lebak et al. 2005]). This approach can produce performance comparable to procedural languages with comparable expertise and is usually significantly less effort. Object-oriented approaches may be more or less portable than procedural approaches and depend upon the availability of the compiler and libraries.

**MATLAB.** Performance is usually significantly less than procedural languages but generally requires far less effort. Portability is limited to the processors that support MATLAB.

The typical categories for the parallel implementation environment are the following:

**Direct Memory Access (DMA).** This is usually a processor and network-specific protocol for allowing one processor to write into the memory of another processor. It is similar to message passing but at a lower level. DMA delivers the highest performance, but requires enormous effort and expertise, and offers no software portability.

**Message passing.** Such as the Message Passing Interface (MPI). This is a protocol for sending messages between processors. It produces efficient code, with less effort and expertise, and is as portable as the underlying library.

**Manager/worker.** Using either a high-level approach such as a job scheduler or a low-level thread-based approach using OpenMP or pthreads.

**Distributed arrays.** Such as those found in Unified Parallel C (UPC), Co-Array Fortran (CAF), Parallel VSIPL++, and pMatlab. This approach creates parallel arrays, which allow complex data movements to be written succinctly. The performance is usually comparable to message passing.

Approximate estimates for the performance efficiencies of the above software approaches are given in Table 6.2 (see [Kepner 2004, Kepner 2006] for the specific data). The first column (labeled $\epsilon_{comp}$) gives a very rough relative performance efficiency of a single-processor implementation using the approach specified in the first column. The second row (labeled $\epsilon_{comm}$) gives a very rough relative bandwidth

**Table 6.2. Software implementation efficiency estimates.**
The first column lists the serial coding approach. The second column shows a rough estimate for the serial efficiency ($\epsilon_{comp}$) of the serial approach. The first row of columns 3, 4, 5, and 6 lists the different communication models for a parallel implementation. The second row of these columns is a rough estimate of the communication efficiency ($\epsilon_{comm}$) for these different models. The remaining entries in the table show the combined efficiencies ($\epsilon_{comp}\epsilon_{comm}$). Blank entries are given for serial coding and communication models that are rarely used together.

| Serial Code | Serial $\epsilon_{comp}$ | DMA | Comm Message Passing | Model Manager/ Worker | Distributed Arrays |
|---|---|---|---|---|---|
| $\epsilon_{comm}$ | - | 0.8 | 0.5 | 0.4 | 0.5 |
| Assembly | 0.4 | 0.36 | | | |
| C/Fortran | 0.2 | 0.16 | 0.1 | 0.08 | 0.1 |
| C++ | 0.18 | 0.14 | 0.09 | 0.07 | 0.09 |
| MATLAB | 0.04 | | 0.02 | 0.016 | 0.02 |

efficiency using the approach specified in the first row. The interior matrix of rows and columns shows the combined product of these two efficiencies and reflects the range of performance that can be impacted by the implementation of the software.

The significance of the product $\epsilon_{comp}\epsilon_{comm}$ can be illustrated as follows. The overall rate of work can be written as

$$R(N_P) = W/T = W/(T_{comp}(N_P) + T_{comm}(N_P))$$

Substituting $T_{comp}(N_P) = W/\epsilon_{comp}R_{peak}N_P$ and $T_{comm} = D/\epsilon_{comm}BW_{peak}N_P$ gives

$$R(N_P) = \frac{\epsilon_{comp}\epsilon_{comm}R_{peak}N_P}{\epsilon_{comm} + \epsilon_{comm}(D/W)(R_{peak}/BW_{peak})}$$

where $D/W$ is the inherent communication-to-computation ratio of the application and $R_{peak}/BW_{peak}$ is the computation-to-communication ratio of the computer. Both ratios are fixed for a given problem and architecture. Thus, the principal "knob" available to the programmer for effecting the overall rate of computation is the combined efficiency of the serial coding approach and the communication model.

## 6.5.4   Software cost

Software cost is typically the dominant cost in a parallel application. There are many approaches to implementing a parallel software system, and they differ in performance, effort, and portability. The most basic approach to modeling software cost is provided by the Code and Cost Modeling (CoCoMo) framework [Boehm et al. 1995]:

Programmer effort [Days] $\approx$

$$(\text{Total SLOC})\frac{(\text{New code fraction}) + 0.05(\text{Reused code fraction})}{\text{SLOC/Day}}$$

This formula says that the effort is approximately linear in the total number of software lines of code (SLOC) written. SLOC is typically defined as every noncomment, nonblank line in a program. It shows that there are three obvious ways to decrease the effort associated with implementing a program:

**Increased reuse.** Including code that has already been written is much cheaper than writing it from scratch. For example, using a MATLAB toolbox is cheaper than writing the same functionality from scratch.

**Higher abstraction.** If the same functionality can be written using fewer lines of code, this will cost less. In general, a higher-level language like MATLAB will require fewer lines of code than a lower-level language like C.

**Increased coding rate.** If the environment allows for more lines of code to be written in a given period of time, this will also reduce code cost. For example, a fully Integrated Development Environment (IDE) generally allows programmers to write code faster.

Approximate estimates for the programming impacts of the above approaches are given in Table 6.3 (see [Kepner 2004, Kepner 2006] for the specific data). The number of SLOC for a given program varies widely among programmers. However, SLOC normalized by programmer to a particular reference implementation is more accurate. Thus the data in Table 6.3 should be viewed as relative to a given programmer writing the same program many different ways. The first column gives the code size relative to the equivalent code written in a procedural language (e.g., C). The next column gives the typical rate (SLOC/day) at which lines are written in that environment. The column labeled "Serial" is the rate divided by the relative code size and gives the effective relative rate of work done normalized to a procedural environment. The row labeled "Code" gives the estimated increase in the size of the code when going from a serial code to a parallel code for the various parallel programming approaches. The row labeled "Effort" shows the relative increase in effort associated with each of these lines of parallel lines of code. The interior matrix combines all of these to give an effective rate of effort for each serial programming environment and each parallel programming environment. For example, in the case of an object-oriented environment, on average each line does the work of two lines in a procedural language. In addition, a typical programmer can code these lines in a serial environment at a rate of 25 lines per day. If a code written in this environment is made parallel using message passing, we would expect the total code size to increase by a factor of 1.5. Furthermore, the rate at which these additional lines are coded will be decreased by a factor of two because they are more difficult to write. The result is that the overall rate of the parallel implementation would be 25 effective procedural (i.e., C) lines per day.

Figure 6.15 notionally combines the data in Tables 6.2 and 6.3 for a hypothetical 100-processor system and illustrates the various performance and effort trade-offs associated with different programming models.

**Table 6.3. Software coding rate estimates.**
The first column gives the code size relative to the equivalent code written in a procedural language (e.g., C). The next column gives the typical rate (SLOC/day) at which lines are written in that environment. The column labeled "Serial" is the rate divided by the relative code size and gives the effective relative rate of work done normalized to a procedural environment. The row labeled "Code" gives the estimated increase in the size of the code when going from serial to parallel for the various parallel programming approaches. The row labeled "Effort" shows the relative increase in effort associated with each of these lines of parallel lines of code. The interior matrix combines all of these to give an effective rate of effort for each serial programming environment and each parallel programming environment given by (SLOC/day)/(Relative SLOC)/(1 + (Expansion Factor − 1)(Effort Factor)).

| Serial Code | Relative SLOC | SLOC /Day | Serial | DMA | Comm Message passing | Model Manager/ worker | Distributed arrays |
|---|---|---|---|---|---|---|---|
| Code | - | - | 1 | 2 | 1.5 | 1.05 | 1.05 |
| Effort | - | - | 1 | 2 | 2 | 2 | 1.5 |
| Assembly | 3 | 5 | 1.6 | 0.5 | | | |
| C/Fortran | 1 | 15 | 15 | 5 | 8 | 14 | 14 |
| C++ | 1/2 | 25 | 50 | 17 | 25 | 45 | 47 |
| MATLAB | 1/4 | 40 | 160 | | 80 | 140 | 148 |

## 6.5.5  Software productivity

Ultimately, the goal of any effort is to be productive. However, the defining productivity in any particular context requires some deeper analysis. The economic definition of productivity is

$$\Psi = \frac{\text{Utility}}{\text{Cost}}$$

where

$$\Psi = \text{Productivity}$$
$$U = \text{Utility}$$
$$C = \text{Cost}$$

In the case of software, cost is relatively easy to understand and proportional to programmer effort. If data on programmer effort isn't available, then code size can act as a reasonable approximation for effort [Boehm et al. 1995]. Utility is less straightforward, and economists define it as the relative benefit of a good or a service. Utility is employed to describe things that cannot be readily exchanged. For example, improvement made to a program generally benefit only that program. This improvement has utility for that program but not for another.

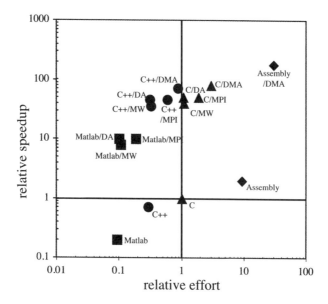

**Figure 6.15. Speedup versus effort.**
Estimated relative speedup (compared to serial C) on a hypothetical
100-processor system plotted against estimated relative effort (compared
to serial C). Languages plotted are Assembly, C (procedural), C++
(object-oriented), and MATLAB (high-level language). Communications
models included Direct Memory Access (DMA), Message Passing Interface (MPI), Manager/Worker (MW), and Distributed Arrays (DA).

Fortunately, in the specific context of this book, parallel programming in
MATLAB, utility is relatively easy to define. Utility is the speedup achieved by
applying parallel programming. Thus parallel productivity is

$$\Psi_{||} = \frac{\text{speedup}}{\text{parallel programming effort}}$$

Applying this definition, the hypothetical unaided and aided programmer mentioned
in the Preface results in productivity curves shown in Figure 6.16. In both cases,
each programmer maintains a constant productivity, but the aided programmer is
100x more productive than the unaided programmer.

The same ideas can be applied to parallel programming environments to obtain the relative productivity to a canonical programming environment such as serial
C. Using the data from Figure 6.15 it is possible to estimate the productivity by
taking the estimated speedup (relative to serial C) on a hypothetical 100-processor
system and dividing it by the relative programming effort. These results are shown
in Table 6.4. Not surprisingly, distributed array approaches appear to be the most
productive in any language. In addition, high-level languages such as C++ and
MATLAB appear to be the most productive. Interestingly, the differences between
MATLAB (less effort) and C++ (higher performance) offset when computing productivity.

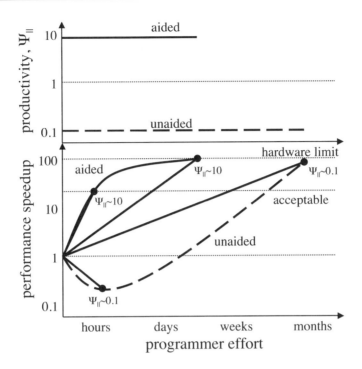

**Figure 6.16. Parallel productivity versus effort.**
Bottom plot shows the parallel speedup versus programmer effort for a programmer with expert assistance (aided) and without expert assistance (unaided). The parallel productivity $\Psi_{\parallel}$ is computed at various points. The top plot shows the aggregate parallel productivity over the course of the project.

**Table 6.4. Approximate relative productivity.**
Estimated relative productivity of different parallel programming approaches (compared to serial C) on a hypothetical 100-processor system. The first column lists the serial coding approach. The remaining columns show the combined effects of different serial and parallel programming environments. In general, distributed array approaches are the most productive.

| Serial Code | Serial | DMA | Comm Message Passing | Model Manager/ Worker | Distributed Arrays |
|---|---|---|---|---|---|
| Assembly | 0.2 | 5 | | | |
| C/Fortran | 1 | 25 | 25 | 35 | 50 |
| C++ | 2 | 75 | 75 | 100 | 150 |
| MATLAB | 2 | | 50 | 75 | 100 |

# References

[Amdahl 1967] G.M. Amdahl, Validity of the single-processor approach to achieving large scale computing capabilities, Proceedings of AFIPS Conference, 1967, pp. 483–485.

[Boehm et al. 1995] B. Boehm, B. Clark, E. Horowitz, R. Madachy, R. Shelby, and C. Westland, Cost Models for Future Software Life Cycle Processes: COCOMO 2.0, Annals of Software Engineering, 1995.

[DeLuca et al. 1997] Cecelia DeLuca, Curtis Heisey, Robert Bond, and James Daly, A portable object-based parallel library and layered framework for real-time radar signal processing. In Proc. 1st Conf. International Scientific Computing in Object-Oriented Parallel Environments (ISCOPE 97), pp. 241–248.

[Hennessy & Paterson 2006] John Hennessy and David Paterson, Computer Architecture: A Quantitative Approach, The Morgan Kaufmann Series in Computer Architecture and Design, 2006.

[Kepner 2004] Jeremy Kepner (editor), Special issue on HPC Productivity, International Journal of High Performance Computing Applications, Vol. 18, No. 4, 2004.

[Kepner 2006] Jeremy Kepner (editor), High Productivity Computing Systems and the Path Towards Usable Petascale Computing: User Productivity Challenges, CTWatch Quarterly, Vol. 2, No. 4A, November 2006.

[Kuck 1996] David Kuck, High Performance Computing: Challenges For Future Systems, Oxford, UK: Oxford University Press, 1996.

[Lebak et al. 2005] James Lebak, Jeremy Kepner, Henry Hoffmann, and Edward Rutledge, Parallel VSIPL++: An open standard software library for high-performance parallel signal processing. Proceedings of the IEEE 93(2), pp. 313–330.

[Loveman 1993] D.B. Loveman, High Performance Fortran. Parallel and Distributed Technology: Systems and Applications, IEEE 1(1), 1993.

[Luszczek et al. 2006] Piotr Luszczek, Jack Dongarra, and Jeremy Kepner, Design and Implementation of the HPC Challenge Benchmark Suite, CT Watch, Vol. 2, Number 4A, November 2006.

[Von Neumann 1945] John Von Neumann, First Draft of a Report on the EDVAC, 1945.

[Weinberg et al. 2005] J. Weinberg, M. O. McCracken, E. Strohmaier, and A. Snavely, Quantifying Locality in the Memory Access Patterns of HPC Applications, Supercomputing 2005.

[Zosel 1993] M.E. Zosel, High Performance Fortran: An Overview. Compcon Spring 93, Digest of Papers, San Francisco, CA, February 22–26, 1993.

# Part III

# Case Studies

# Chapter 7

# Parallel Application Analysis

### Summary

The breadth of applications that exploit parallel computing has expanded greatly over the past two decades. On the surface, the parallel implementations of these applications appear very diverse. Closer analysis reveals that it is possible to categorize these parallel applications by the types of parallelism they exploit, the spatial and temporal locality of their computations, and how they stress the memory hierarchy of the parallel computing system. Furthermore, these categories can be represented by relatively simple computations that capture the key parallel computing elements. The HPC Challenge benchmark suite is a collection of these representative computations. Comparing and contrasting these benchmarks highlights some of the important differences in real parallel applications. By identifying which category a parallel application belongs to, a programmer can more quickly make better parallel design decisions.

## 7.1 Historical overview

Surveying the world of parallel applications is a daunting task. Describing every parallel application is impossible, so how can a subset be selected? One way is to look at how this field has evolved over the past few decades.

Historically, the concept of "supercomputing" was born in government research labs at the onset of the computing era (see Figure 7.1). These mission-oriented labs focused on applications of high national interest: designing weapons, simulating ships and airplanes, and code breaking. Surprisingly, this "narrow" set of applications has very different computing requirements. The resulting programs use different mathematics (continuous versus discrete), different algorithms (physics versus number theory), and different languages (Fortran versus C).

These early systems typically consisted of just a small number of vector processors. Each vector processor would typically load a vector and then issue a sin-

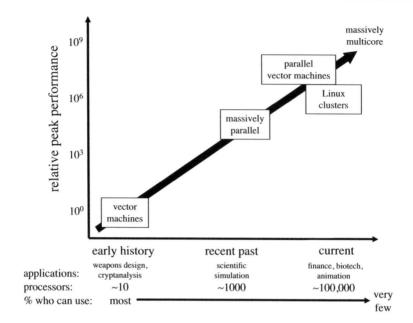

**Figure 7.1. Supercomputing evolution.**
Early history began with vector machines that were relatively easy to use. In the recent past, massively parallel computers have emerged. Currently, Linux clusters that are more difficult to program have become commonplace and massively multicore systems are the largest in the world.

gle instruction that would be applied to the entire vector at once. Such processors were often referred to as Single-Instruction Multiple-Data (SIMD) processors [Flynn 1972]. The key to effectively using these systems was to create large "for" loops that the vectorizing compiler could recognize and map onto the vector processors.

Although the use of parallel computing has expanded greatly since the early days, these first applications remain very important and are often the key drivers for the largest parallel computing systems in the world. In addition, much of the research into better ways to program parallel computers has been driven by these applications. Most notably the development of distributed array technologies such as POOMA [Cummings et al. 1998], GA++ [Nieplocha et al. 2002], and UPC [El-Ghazawi et al. 2005] all derive from these applications.

In the more recent past, parallel computing expanded out of national research labs and became a staple of scientific research across many disciplines. This led to the formal recognition of "computational science and engineering" or "simulation science" in many universities. Some of the scientific domains that benefited from the increased use of supercomputing included weather and climate simulation, materials science, chemistry, and astrophysics. Interestingly, although the use of parallel computing expanded to encompass the full range of academic inquiry, the requirements mainly still fall within those defined during the early days. The largest changes that occurred in this era were the adoption of massively parallel hardware and widespread use of the MPI programming model (along with its associated programming difficulties).

Currently, the diversity of applications in parallel computing has exploded beyond the research world into the full range of commercial activity. Bioinformatics, computational finance, computer animation, and data mining are just a few of the "new" applications driving parallel computing. Again, rather than broadening the space of computational requirements, these applications have narrowed the algorithm space (primarily embarrassingly parallel) and narrowed the hardware space (primarily commodity clusters and parallel desktops), but they have greatly expanded the software space (MATLAB, Java, Python) and increased the need for parallel programming environments that can be learned quickly.

The technology trends that marked this multidecade evolution of parallel computing have included the following:

- Over a billion-fold increase in peak performance.

- A change in focus from a few applications of high national interest (written in C and Fortran) to applications spanning the full range of science and industry (written in many different languages).

- An increase from a few to thousands of processors and a corresponding increase in the overall programming difficulty.

The final step in the expansion of parallel computing has been the development of multicore processors, which has made parallel computing ubiquitous. Now, every program is a parallel computing program. Fortunately, the distributed array approach, with its emphasis on data locality, works well from multicore processors to large commodity clusters.

## 7.2   Characterizing the application space

The quick historical overview of the previous section illustrates that while much has changed over the past few decades, much has also remained the same. In particular, what makes parallel applications "hard" or "easy" has been known since the early days. More specifically, easy applications tend to be embarrassingly parallel, access memory in a regular fashion, and perform many operations on each data element fetched from memory. Hard applications tend to require interprocessor communication, access memory in a irregular fashion, and perform few operations on each data element fetched from memory. Thus, from a parallel programming perspective, we are less concerned with the specifics of the application and more concerned with how much "easiness" or "hardness" is in the program. Assessing easiness or hardness can be done from three different perspectives. The first perspective is hardware centric and looks at how the program stresses the memory hierarchy of the hardware. The second perspective is algorithm centric and looks at the spatial and temporal locality of the memory access patterns of the algorithm. The third perspective is programmer centric and looks at the logical memory hierarchy of the computer and how the application's parallelism is matched to that hierarchy.

## 7.2.1  Physical memory hierarchy

The concept of a memory hierarchy has been around since the earliest days of computing. The most important features include processor registers/cache, local memory, remote memory, and storage. Typically, at any given time during the operation of the program, one part of the memory hierarchy will be most heavily used. In this respect, all programs run at 100% efficiency with respect to some part of the memory hierarchy. Ideally, this is the piece that is closest to the processor as the processor is the only part of the system that can perform useful work on the data. However, if some other part of the memory hierarchy is running at its maximum capability (e.g., access to remote memory), then it is most likely that the processor is running at a much lower efficiency.

A simple way to characterize a parallel computing system is to write a set of benchmark programs that target a specific piece of the memory hierarchy. Running these programs on a specific computer will measure the performance of that system. Comparing the performance of these benchmarks to that of a real application will provide insight into which part of the memory hierarchy the application most stresses. In other words, it is possible to determine which benchmark or benchmarks the application is most like.

Figure 7.2 shows the HPC Challenge benchmarks in relation to a canonical memory hierarchy. HPL (High Performance Linpack) tends to stress the processor (or processor to register). Stream focuses most on the bandwidth to main

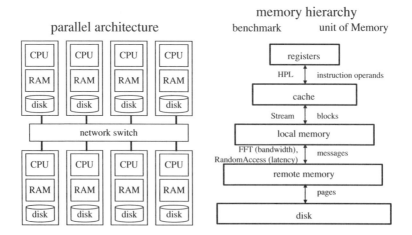

**Figure 7.2. Memory hierarchy and HPC Challenge.**
The HPC Challenge benchmarks are designed so that each benchmark stresses a particular part of the parallel computer's memory hierarchy.

memory. FFT (Fast Fourier Transform) stresses the bandwidth of the network, while RandomAccess measures the latency of the network. Measuring how these benchmarks perform over different values of $N_P$ and comparing with corresponding curves for a real parallel application can provide good insight into how HPL-like, Stream-like, FFT-like, or RandomAccess-like the application is. This comparison further indicates which parallel programming techniques will be most effective on the application.

## 7.2.2 Spatial/temporal locality

Another way to characterize parallel applications that is more intrinsic to their algorithms is in terms of the applications' spatial and temporal locality. Recall that spatial locality is a measure of how ordered the memory access patterns of a program are, and temporal locality is a measure of how many operations are done on a data element when it is fetched from memory. By profiling an application, it is possible to actually compute the spatial score and temporal score. Figure 7.3 shows these scores for several real applications [Weinberg et al. 2005]. These applications tend to occupy a region in the spatial/temporal space. The region bounded by the HPC Challenge benchmark suite tends to encompass all other applications. The precise location of any given application can be characterized by which HPC Challenge benchmark(s) it is closest to. Not surprisingly, scientific applications tend to lie closest to FFT and HPL. Likewise, data analysis applications tend to lie closest to Stream and RandomAccess. Furthermore, the spatial/temporal locality of an application can change as it executes and can become closer to different benchmarks at different times.

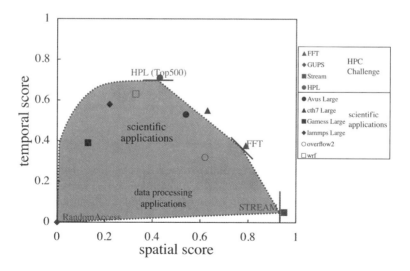

**Figure 7.3. Spatial versus temporal locality.**
Spatial/temporal scores of several applications and HPC Challenge as measured by MetaSim [Weinberg et al. 2005].

### 7.2.3   Logical memory hierarchy

How to most effectively program a parallel application is strongly dependent upon how the data needs to be moved across the logical memory hierarchy of the system. Certain data movement patterns are more difficult to code than others. Fortunately, there are a few main patterns.  By using benchmark applications that capture these patterns, it is possible to reason by analogy as to the ease or difficulty of programming a real application with similar data movement patterns. In particular, these patterns will shed light on the best parallel programming models to use for different applications.

The HPC Challenge benchmark suite uses a wide range of data movement patterns (see Figure 7.4). The simplest of these patterns is embarrassingly parallel and requires no movement of data across processors. This is the pattern of the Stream benchmark. The FFT benchmark exhibits a more regular all-to-all communication pattern. In this pattern, every process sends a regular predetermined amount of data to every other processor. The HPL pattern is similar to the FFT but usually involves one or more processors broadcasting data to one or more subsets of processors. Finally, the RandomAccess communication pattern is the most complicated because it randomly sends messages between processors.

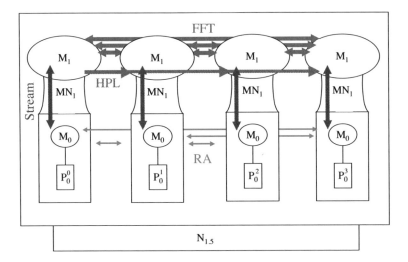

**Figure 7.4. Communication across the hierarchy.**
Communication patterns of the HPC Challenge benchmarks with respect to the Kuck memory hierarchy of a canonical computer.

## 7.3   HPC Challenge: Spanning the application space

The previous section has sought to motivate the idea that a small number of benchmark codes can represent the important parallel performance and parallel programming characteristics of a large space of applications. In particular, the HPC Challenge benchmark suite has been selected because it targets different points in the physical memory hierarchy, bounds the spatial/temporal locality of real applications, and employs a diversity of logical data movement patterns. In this section, the high-level details of these benchmarks are presented. Each of the benchmarks will be examined in closer detail in subsequent chapters.

## 7.3.1  Stream

The Stream benchmark is the simplest of the HPC Challenge benchmarks. It performs a number of simple operations on $N$ element vectors $\mathbf{a}$, $\mathbf{b}$, and $\mathbf{c}$. The most commonly reported operation is the Stream triadd operation:

$$\mathbf{a}(i) = \mathbf{b}(i) + q\mathbf{c}(i)$$

where $q$ is a constant. The goal of this benchmark is to measure the local memory bandwidth of all the processors in the system. Thus, each processor performs the above operation on its own local part of the above arrays without performing any communication with any other processor. The typical data distribution for this algorithm is $\mathbf{a} : \mathbb{R}^{P(N)}$ (see Figure 7.5).

Stream is representative of many embarrassingly parallel applications that access arrays of data in a regular fashion. Many data analysis problems (e.g., image processing) can be well represented by this benchmark. Stream is generally easy to implement in any parallel programming model.

## 7.3.2  FFT

The Fast Fourier Transform (FFT) is an important computation in many applications. It is the bedrock of signal processing because it allows time series $\mathbf{x}$ data to be efficiently converted into frequency data $\mathbf{z}$. The FFT is also important in the numerical solutions of partial differential equations that use pseudospectral methods.

The FFT is a fast method for computing the Discrete Fourier Transform (DFT):

$$\mathbf{z}(k) = \sum_{i=1}^{N} \mathbf{x}(i)e^{2\pi\sqrt{-1}k}$$

where $\mathbf{x}, \mathbf{z} : \mathbb{C}^N$. In general, this operation is given by

$$\mathbf{z} = \mathrm{FFT}(\mathbf{x})$$

The FFT is not an embarrassingly parallel operation. In fact, each element of the results $\mathbf{z}(i)$ depends upon every value of $\mathbf{x}$. Typically, a parallel FFT exploits the fact that a one-dimensional FFT can be computed by first transforming the input vector into a matrix, executing an FFT on the rows, multiplying by some constants, and then executing an FFT on the columns. The resulting matrix is then transformed back into a vector. Such an algorithm makes the parallelism

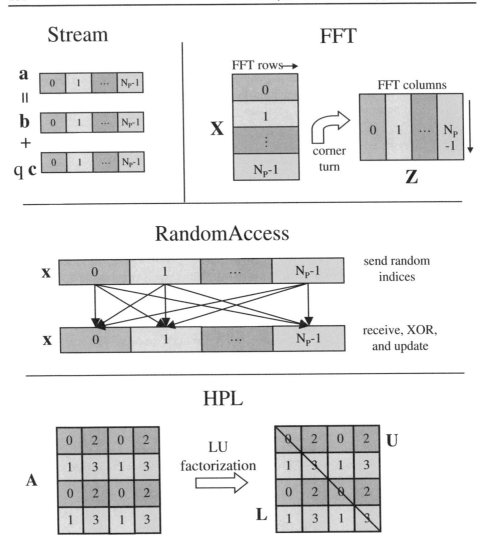

**Figure 7.5. Communication patterns of HPC Challenge.**

in the program fairly clear. Each FFT of a row or a column can be performed independently of each other. However, the data of the matrix will need to be redistributed between each step

$$\mathbf{Z} = \mathbf{X}$$

where $\mathbf{X} : \mathbb{C}^{P(M_1) \times M_2}$, $\mathbf{Z} : \mathbb{C}^{M_1 \times P(M_2)}$, and $N = M_1 M_2$. Such a redistribution requires every processor to send data to every other processor and typically stresses the bandwidth of the interprocessor communication network of a parallel computer (see Figure 7.5). This redistribution is a classic example of the kind of global communication operation that is readily represented using distributed arrays.

### 7.3.3 RandomAccess

While Stream is representative of many data analysis applications, there are others that have far more complex memory access patterns. For example, the simple operation of computing a histogram of a random number sequence essentially requires random updates to memory. The RandomAccess benchmark is designed to represent this class of operations found in databases, graph analysis, code analysis, and particle-based Monte Carlo simulation techniques. The core operation of the benchmark is

$$\mathbf{x}(i) = \text{XOR}(\mathbf{x}(i), r)$$

where $\mathbf{x} : \mathbb{Z}^N$ is a table of integers, $r : \mathbb{Z}$ is a random integer, and $i(r) = \text{AND}(r, N - 1)$ is the table location to update. Typically, the table is spread across processors $\mathbf{t} : \mathbb{Z}^P(N)$ (see Figure 7.5) with each processor generating a sequence of $r$. To perform the update requires that each processor look at the index $i(r)$, determine which processor owns the table entry $\mathbf{t}(i)$, and send the corresponding $r$ value to that processor to do the update. The implication of this parallel approach is that each processor is sending data to random subsets of processors. This communication pattern stresses the latency of the interconnect. In addition, this pattern is difficult to code in most parallel programming models.

### 7.3.4 HPL

The High Performance Linpack (HPL) benchmark has a long history and is most well known as the benchmark associated with the "Top 500" computing list. This list ranks the fastest 500 computers in the world according to how fast they perform the HPL benchmark. The core of the HPL benchmark is to compute $\mathbf{x} : \mathbb{R}^M$ that solves the system of linear equations

$$\mathbf{A}\mathbf{x} = \mathbf{b}$$

given randomly generated inputs $\mathbf{A} : \mathbb{R}^{M \times M}$ and $\mathbf{b} : \mathbb{R}^M$. The algorithm used to find $\mathbf{x}$ first factors the matrix into two matrices: a lower triangular matrix $\mathbf{L}$ and an upper triangular matrix $\mathbf{U}$. These matrices are then used to solve for $\mathbf{x}$ using Gaussian elimination. The computation is dominated by the numerous matrix-matrix multiplies found within the LU factorization step, which most stresses the processor in a parallel system.

The highest performance parallel implementations of HPL use a complex two-dimensional block-cyclic distribution to distribute the matrix $\mathbf{A} : \mathbb{R}^{P_{bc}(M) \times P_{bc}(M)}$ (see Figure 7.5). This distribution provides for optimal load balancing and allows each processor to do approximately the same amount of work as the computation progresses. A side effect of this distribution is that although the total amount of data moved is not large (compared to the computation), the communication patterns are quite complex and require each processor to compute a different subset of processors to talk to as the computation progresses. This pattern is difficult to code in most parallel programming models, but distributed arrays do help a lot. It is worth mentioning that it is possible to implement HPL using simpler data distributions (e.g., $\mathbf{A} : \mathbb{R}^{M \times P(M)}$), but these distributions will result in poorer parallel performance.

## 7.4 Intrinsic algorithm performance

By design, the HPC Challenge benchmarks represent vastly different algorithms and provide an excellent opportunity to highlight how different algorithms can have very different parallel implications. Assessing the different algorithms requires examining the following fundamental characteristics:

**Core data structures:** The array(s) at each stage that will consume the largest amount of memory and upon which most of the computations will be performed.

**Computational complexity** $(W)$**:** The total operations performed (or work done) and how they depend upon the algorithmic parameters.

**Operations per data element** $(W_{element})$**:** The number of operations performed (or work done) on each data element.

**Degrees of Parallelism** (DoP)**:** The parallelism inherent in the algorithm and how it relates to the core data structures.

**Communication complexity** $(D)$**:** The total number of data elements moved to execute the parallel algorithm.

**Computation-to-communication ratio** $(W/D)$**:** The amount of computation performed per data element moved.

A summary of the above values for each benchmark is given in Table 7.1.

### 7.4.1 Data structures

The core data structures for each benchmark were discussed in the previous section. Stream requires three $N$ element vectors. FFT also uses an $N$ element complex valued vector but reshapes this into an $M_1 \times M_2$ element matrix, where $N = M_1 M_2$. RandomAccess uses an $N$ element vector (or table) of integers. Finally, HPL uses an $M \times M$ matrix, where $N = M^2$ is the total number of elements in the matrix. All of the benchmarks are designed to run as a scaled problem so that $N$ is chosen to use a large fraction of the total memory of the computer. In general, this means that $N \propto N_P$. In practice, $N/N_P$ is held fixed and $N$ is determined by multiplying this value times $N_P$.

### 7.4.2 Computational complexity

The triadd portion of the Stream benchmark performs one multiply and one add per data element ($W_{element} = 2$), resulting in a total computational complexity of $W = 2N$. Similarly, RandomAccess performs only a single XOR operation per data element ($W_{element} = 1$ and $W = 2N$). The precise computational complexity of

## Table 7.1. HPC Challenge parallel algorithm characteristics.

Various computational characteristics of the HPC Challenge benchmarks.

| Program | Data Array | $W$ Compute Complexity (operations) | $W_{element}$ Operations/ Element | Degrees of Parallelism | $D$ Communication Complexity (Elements Sent) | $W/D$ Computation/ Communication (Ops/Element) |
|---|---|---|---|---|---|---|
| Stream | $\mathbf{a}, \mathbf{b}, \mathbf{c} : \mathbb{R}^{P(N)}$ | $2N$ | $2$ | $N$ | $0$ | $\infty$ |
| FFT | $\mathbf{X} : \mathbb{C}^{P(M_1) \times M_2}$, $\mathbf{Z} : \mathbb{C}^{M_1 \times P(M_2)}$ | $5N \log_2(N)$ | $5 \log_2(N)$ | $\min(M_1, M_2)$ | $N$ | $5 \log_2(N)$ |
| RandomAccess | $\mathbf{t} : \mathbb{Z}^{P(N)}$ | $N$ | $1$ | $N$ | $N$ | $1$ |
| HPL | $\mathbf{A} : \mathbb{R}^{P_{bc}(M) \times P_{bc}(M)}$ | $(2/3)M^3$ | $(2/3)M$ | $M$ | $M^2$ | $(2/3)M$ |

an FFT varies slightly from implementation to implementation. The canonical value for an FFT on complex data is $W = 5N \log_2(N)$ with a corresponding work per data element of $5 \log_2(N)$. While there are many algorithms for solving $\mathbf{Ax} = \mathbf{b}$, the HPL benchmarks dictate that the LU factorization followed by Gaussian elimination be used. In this case, the computational complexity is known to be $W = (2/3)M^3 = (2/3)N^{3/2}$, which results in a work per data element of $W_{element} = (2/3)\sqrt{N}$. The precise computational complexity of HPL is given in a subsequent chapter.

By design, the work per data element varies a lot among the different HPC Challenge benchmarks, from $W_{element} = 1$ for RandomAccess to $W_{element} = 2/3\sqrt{N}$ for HPL. These values fundamentally set how efficiently a single processor can perform these benchmarks. Given a canonical processor system with a canonical memory hierarchy, the expectation would be that HPL is the most efficient and Stream and RandomAccess are the least efficient.

## 7.4.3   Degrees of parallelism

The data structures and the computational complexity of the HPC Challenge benchmarks are intrinsic to the algorithms, independent of how they are mapped onto a parallel computer. To compute the degrees of parallelism requires assuming a particular parallel mapping. In this case, the parallel mappings discussed in the previous section will be used.

Stream uses a one-dimensional block parallel mapping for its three main vectors $\mathbf{a}, \mathbf{b}, \mathbf{c} : \mathbb{R}^{P(N)}$. In this case, each expression $\mathbf{a}(i) = \mathbf{b}(i) + q\mathbf{c}(i)$ can be performed independently, resulting in $N$ degrees of parallelism.

RandomAccess also uses a one-dimensional block parallel mapping of its main vector $\mathbf{t} : \mathbb{Z}^{P(N)}$. At first glance, because RandomAccess randomly updates $\mathbf{t}$, it might appear that there are no degrees of parallelism because it is possible that two processors might attempt to update the same $\mathbf{t}(i)$. However, because the XOR operation is commutative, the order in which these operations are performed does not matter. In this case, each expression $\mathbf{t}(i) = \text{XOR}(\mathbf{t}(i), r)$ can be performed independently, resulting in $N$ degrees of parallelism.

A parallel FFT typically requires two one-dimensional block distributions applied to the two matrices $\mathbf{X} : \mathbb{C}^{P(M_1) \times M_2}$, $\mathbf{Z} : \mathbb{C}^{M_1 \times P(M_2)}$. The degrees of parallelism at any given point in the algorithm depend upon which matrix is being used. In the first stage of the algorithm, where the operations are performed on $\mathbf{X}$, there are $M_1$ degrees of parallelism. In the second stage of the algorithm, where the operations are performed on $\mathbf{Z}$, there are $M_2$ degrees of parallelism. Typically, $N_P$ doesn't change from the first stage to the second so that the total degrees of parallelism are $\min(M_1, M_2)$.

The parallel HPL algorithm uses a two-dimensional block-cyclic distribution on its primary matrix $\mathbf{A} : \mathbb{R}^{P_{bc}(M) \times P_{bc}(M)}$. In theory, if the block size was set to 1 element, then this matrix could be split among $M^2 = N$ processors, resulting in $N$ degrees of parallelism. However, the underlying algorithm does have certain dependencies so that the effective maximum degrees of parallelism are typically $M = \sqrt{N}$.

The degrees of parallelism in the HPC Challenge benchmarks vary from $\sqrt{N}$ to $N$. Because HPC Challenge is meant to be run on large-scale problems in which $N \propto N_P$, it is almost always the case that $\sqrt{N} > N_P$. In other words, like many problems, there are ample degrees of parallelism to exploit and finding these is not difficult. The real challenge is creating an algorithm with sufficient locality that the parallel algorithm will run well on a given parallel computer.

### 7.4.4 Communication complexity

The amount of data moved is also dependent on the precise parallel mapping used. In the case of Stream, as long as its three vectors all use the same parallel mapping, there will be no data movement required ($D = 0$) and the resulting computation-to-communication ratio is $W/D \to \infty$. If, for some reason, any of the arrays had a parallel map that was different from the others, then an entire vector would need to be communicated to the other processors ($D = N$) and $W/D = 2$.

In the RandomAccess benchmark, the data communicated is similar to Stream with different mappings $D = N$. This might seem surprising since each processor is generating indices to update. However, these indices span the entire range from 1 to $N$, so the odds that a processor will generate indices that reside in its local memory is $1/N_P$. The result is that $W/D \to 1$ as $N_P$ gets large.

FFT requires a redistribution of data between its two matrices, which implies $D = M_1 M_2 = N$. The resulting computation-to-communication ratio is then $W/D = 5\log_2(N)$.

HPL also requires the entire matrix to be moved during the course of computation so that $D = M^2 = N$ and $W/D = (2/3)M = (2/3)\sqrt{N}$.

By design, the computation-to-communication ratio varies a lot among the different HPC Challenge benchmarks, from $W/D = 1$ for RandomAccess to $W_{element} = 2/3\sqrt{N}$ for HPL. These values give an indication of the locality of the computation and fundamentally set how efficiently a particular parallel computing system can perform these benchmarks. Given a canonical parallel computing system with a canonical memory hierarchy, it would be expected that HPL and Stream would be the most efficient and FFT and RandomAccess would be the least efficient. In many cases, the computation-to-communication ratio $W/D$ is the same as the work per data element $W_{element}$, except if the computation is embarrassingly parallel, as in the case of the Stream benchmark.

## 7.5  Hardware performance

The algorithm characteristics such as $W_{element}$ and $W/D$ provide good general guidelines as to the expected parallel performance of an application. In general, an algorithm with high $W_{element}$ and a high $W/D$ will perform better than an algorithm with low values.

To move beyond these general statements requires that patterns of data access and computation be probed in greater detail by looking at the spatial and temporal locality of these algorithms.

## 7.5.1   Spatial and temporal locality

As mentioned previously, spatial locality measures how close together the memory access patterns of a computation are to each other. Temporal locality measures how many operations are performed on each data element that is accessed. The measured spatial and temporal locality scores for the HPC Challenge benchmark suite are shown in Figure 7.3.

The Stream benchmark is the prototypical high spatial locality algorithm. It steps through each array in a highly sequential manner, so that each memory access is right next to the previous. It is difficult to imagine a program with a higher spatial locality. Stream is also a prototypical low temporal locality algorithm because it performs only two operations for every two values that are read in. Again, it is difficult to imagine an application with a lower temporal locality. As such, Stream defines the lower right corner of the spatial/temporal score plot.

The RandomAccess benchmark is the prototypical low spatial locality algorithm. It randomly reads data from memory so that each memory access is completely uncorrelated with the previous memory access. RandomAccess has a very low temporal locality similar to Stream. RandomAccess defines the lower left corner of the spatial/temporal score plot.

The spatial locality of FFT and HPL lies between Stream and RandomAccess. The temporal locality of HPL is very high because it performs $(2/3)\sqrt{N}$ operations per data element, which implies a lot of operations are performed for each memory access. The temporal locality of FFT is higher than that of Stream and RandomAccess but lower than that of HPL since it performs $5\log_2(N)$ operations per data element.

## 7.5.2   Performance efficiency

Knowing the operations per data element, the computation-to-communication ratio, and the spatial and temporal locality of an algorithm provides a lot of information about the applications that can be used to make general performance assessments. To make quantitative performance assessments requires knowledge of a specific parallel computing architecture. Here, a canonical parallel computer will be assumed (see Figure 7.2, which has a cache, local memory, and remote memory). In this canonical computer, each level of the memory hierarchy is characterized in terms of the latency and inverse bandwidth to that level of the memory hierarchy. Furthermore, the time units used will be processor clock cycles. Thus, the latency is measured in the number of processor clock cycles it takes to retrieve a single data element from that level in the hierarchy. Likewise, the inverse bandwidth is measured in terms of processor clock cycles per data element when a large amount of data is retrieved from that level in the memory hierarchy. Using these units, the parallel computer can be abstractly characterized as shown in Table 7.2. The performance of the HPC Challenge benchmarks can now be estimated.

**Table 7.2. Memory hierarchy parameters.**
Hypothetical memory hierarchy parameters for a canonical parallel computer.

| Memory Level | $L$ Latency (cycles) | $B^{-1}$ Bandwidth$^{-1}$ (cycles/element) |
|---|---|---|
| Processor $\rightarrow$ Local Cache (ca) | $10^1$ | $10^1$ |
| Processor $\rightarrow$ Local Memory (lm) | $10^3$ | $10^2$ |
| Processor $\rightarrow$ Remote Memory (rm) | $10^5$ | $10^3$ |
| All-to-all (aa) | - | $10^3$ |

## 7.5.3 Estimating performance

The first step in estimating the parallel performance is to estimate the performance on one processor. Performance is always measured relative to the peak performance on the processor. A baseline value of 1 will be considered the peak performance of our canonical processor. The peak performance of the parallel processor is then $N_P$.

The performance on one processor can be estimated by taking the ratio of the time it would take to perform the operations on a processor with no memory hierarchy to that on a processor with a memory hierarchy. In the case of Stream, this is

$$\text{Performance}(N_P = 1) = \frac{W}{W + 2B_{lm}^{-1}N}$$
$$= \frac{1}{1 + 2B_{lm}^{-1}W_{element}^{-1}}$$
$$\approx 1/B_{lm}^{-1} = 10^{-2}$$

where the denominator takes into account the time it takes to move the data into and out of memory. In this case, it is fairly clear that the local memory bandwidth is the determining factor in the performance. The parallel performance of Stream is easy to estimate since it is embarrassingly parallel:

$$\text{Performance}(N_P > 1) \approx N_P/B_{lm}^{-1}$$

Thus, although Stream has relatively poor serial performance, it scales up linearly with $N_P$.

The serial performance of RandomAccess can be estimated in a similar manner:

$$\text{Performance}(N_P = 1) = \frac{1}{1 + L_{lm}W_{element}^{-1}}$$
$$\approx 1/L_{lm} = 10^{-3}$$

In this case, it is fairly clear that the local memory latency is the determining factor in the performance. The parallel performance of RandomAccess is more complex to estimate because the rules of the benchmark specify each processor can generate sets of indices to update in groups of 1024. Thus, the number of messages sent by each processor will be the lesser of 1024 and $N_P$. Adding the additional time it takes to send the messages, the performance of parallel RandomAccess is

$$\text{Performance}(N_P > 1) = \frac{N_P}{1 + L_{lm}W_{element}^{-1} + L_{rm}\min(1024, N_P)(W/D)^{-1}}$$

$$= \frac{N_P}{1 + L_{lm} + L_{rm}\min(1024, N_P)}$$

$$\approx 1/L_{rm} = 10^{-5} \quad \text{for} \quad N_P < 1024$$

In this case, it is fairly clear that the remote memory latency is the determining factor in the performance.

The serial performance of the FFT is given by

$$\text{Performance}(N_P = 1) = \frac{1}{1 + 6B_{lm}^{-1}W_{element}^{-1}}$$

$$\approx 5\log_2(N)/6B_{lm}^{-1}$$

$$\approx 0.2 \quad \text{for} \quad N = 2^{24}$$

where the denominator accounts for the fact that in a serial FFT the data is read in and out of local memory three times. Unlike Stream and RandomAccess, the serial performance explicitly depends upon the problem size $N$. This is because as $N$ increases, $W_{element}$ increases in proportion to $\log_2(N)$. The parallel FFT performance is given by

$$\text{Performance}(N_P > 1) = \frac{N_P}{1 + 6B_{lm}^{-1}W_{element}^{-1} + 3B_{rm}^{-1}(W/D)^{-1}}$$

$$\approx 5N_P\log_2(N)/3B_{rm}^{-1}$$

$$\approx 0.02N_P[1 + 2\log_2(N_P)] \quad \text{for} \quad N/N_P = 2^{24}$$

where $N$ is scaled linearly with $N_P$. The above formula would suggest that the performance of the FFT scales superlinearly with $N_P$. However, there is an implicit assumption in the above formula that the communication network between remote memories can handle $N_P$ processors simultaneously communicating without any degradation in performance. This is an unrealistic assumption. A more realistic assumption is that $B_{rm}$ is fixed or grows logarithmically with $N_P$. Assuming $B_{rm}$ is fixed results in

$$\text{Performance}(N_P > 1) = \frac{N_P}{1 + 6B_{lm}^{-1}W_{element}^{-1} + 3N_P B_{rm}^{-1}(W/D)^{-1}}$$

$$\approx 5\log_2(N)/6B_{rm}^{-1}$$

$$\approx 0.02[1 + 2\log_2(N_P)] \quad \text{for} \quad N/N_P = 2^{24}$$

which is a more realistic model of parallel FFT performance.

The serial performance of HPL is

$$\text{Performance}(N_P = 1) = \frac{1}{1 + 2B_{lm}^{-1}W_{element}^{-1}}$$

$$= \frac{1}{1 + (4/3)B_{lm}^{-1}/\sqrt{N}}$$

$$\approx 1$$

That is, the operations per data element are sufficiently high so that time to move data into and out of the processor is negligible. A similar situation exists for the parallel case:

$$\text{Performance}(N_P > 1) = \frac{N_P}{1 + 2B_{lm}^{-1}W_{element}^{-1} + B_{rm}^{-1}(W/D)^{-1}}$$

$$= \frac{N_P}{1 + (4/3)B_{lm}^{-1}/\sqrt{N} + (2/3)B_{rm}^{-1}/\sqrt{N}}$$

$$\approx N_P$$

Even with a fixed network bandwidth,

$$\text{Performance}(N_P > 1) = \frac{N_P}{1 + 2B_{lm}^{-1}W_{element}^{-1} + N_P B_{rm}^{-1}(W/D)^{-1}}$$

$$= \frac{N_P}{1 + (4/3)B_{lm}^{-1}/\sqrt{N} + (2/3)N_P B_{rm}^{-1}/\sqrt{N}}$$

$$\approx N_P$$

## 7.5.4  Analysis results

The above performance estimates can be compared with the numerous HPC Challenge results. Using a system with performance characteristics similar to those shown in Table 7.2 produces the empirical results shown in Figure 7.6. These results indicate that the measured and predicted performance estimates agree. This level of agreement between theory and practice is the strongest form of evidence that the parallel designs have been implemented correctly and are achieving the maximum performance that the parallel computer can deliver.

## 7.5.5  Performance implications

The performance estimates set the fundamental limits of the parallel algorithms on a particular hardware system. The quality of the software implementation is measured relative to these performance limits. The power of having these limits is very valuable.

The first use of a performance estimate is to show if there is any potential benefit to using a parallel computer before one goes through the trouble of writing the parallel software. Stream and HPL substantially benefit from a parallel implementation. FFT will have a modest benefit. RandomAccess shows no performance benefit from using a canonical parallel computer.

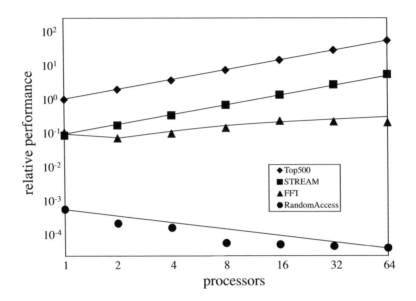

**Figure 7.6. HPC Challenge performance estimates.**
HPC Challenge performance versus processors. Dots denote measured
values. Solid lines denote performance predicted from performance estimates.

The second use of a performance estimate is that it highlights the part of
the software implementation that will most dramatically impact the performance.
For Stream, moving large blocks of data into and out of local memory at high
bandwidth is most important. For FFT, communicating large blocks of data between remote memories at high bandwidth is most important. For RandomAccess,
communicating small blocks of data with low latency is most important.

The third use of a performance estimate is as a way to judge how well the
implementation is proceeding. Specifically, if an implementation is achieving only a
small fraction of the estimated performance, further effort at optimizing the implementation will likely be worthwhile. In contrast, if an implementation is achieving a
high fraction of the estimated performance, further optimization may not be worthwhile.

## 7.6   Software performance

The performance analysis in the previous sections sets the upper bound on the
performance achievable for a specific algorithm on a specific parallel processor architecture. The goal of the software implementation is to strike a reasonable balance
between achieving this level of performance and the required effort. The choices in
the specific parallel MATLAB implementation include

> **Type of parallelism:** data, task, pipeline, and/or round-robin
>
> **Parallel programming model:** message passing, manager/worker, and
> distributed arrays

**Programming environment:** languages and/or libraries

Each of these choices will have specific implications on the software efficiency (processing, bandwidth, and memory) and software cost (code size and portability).

## 7.6.1 Stream

The performance analysis of the Stream benchmark indicates that a parallel implementation should perform well. The primary performance bottleneck for Stream is the bandwidth to the local memory of each processor. Thus, an implementation of the benchmark should manage local memory bandwidth carefully. Specifically, an implementation must avoid creating additional temporary copies of arrays, which might further increase the load on the local memory.

Stream is a sufficiently simple benchmark that can be implemented using different types of parallelism. However, it most naturally uses data parallelism in which each processor works on its local part of a large distributed array. The principal benefit of this approach is that the parallel version can be implemented with relatively minor changes to the serial code. Task, pipeline, and round-robin parallelism do exist within the Stream benchmark, but applying these would tend to result in an implementation with poor locality and correspondingly poor performance. For example, a pipeline implementation of Stream could perform the multiply step on one set of processors and the addition on another set, but this would require the whole array to be communicated. On a conventional parallel processor, this would be inefficient.

Given that data parallel is the optimal parallel model, the distributed array model using a distributed array library is the natural software technology to use for the implementation. Managing the memory bandwidth with this technology does require some care. First, using an explicit for loop to perform the computation usually incurs some overhead in a MATLAB implementation. Second, using a purely "vectorized" code of distributed arrays may incur some overhead from the distributed array library as it tries to determine which indices are local to which processor. Thus, an optimal implementation may work best using an explicitly local "vectorized" approach

$$\mathbf{a}.loc = \mathbf{b}.loc + q\mathbf{c}.loc$$

Using these techniques, a distributed array implementation of the Stream benchmark should be able to achieve a level of performance close to what the parallel processor can deliver. In addition, the parallel MATLAB code should be a relatively small change from the serial MATLAB code.

## 7.6.2 RandomAccess

At the other extreme is RandomAccess. The performance analysis indicates that a parallel implementation of RandomAccess will perform poorly on a conventional parallel computer. Normally, this would indicate that it may not be worthwhile to even attempt a parallel implementation. However, there are some circumstances for which a parallel implementation may still be desirable, for example, if the desired problem size is larger than what will fit in the memory of one computer. In these circumstances, it is important to measure the performance of the implementation against what the parallel processor is capable of delivering. A very good RandomAccess implementation may show no parallel speedup.

The primary performance bottleneck in RandomAccess is the ability to send small messages very quickly to lots of different processors. This performance is fundamentally set by the latency of the underlying parallel network, and the software implementation needs to take special care not to do anything that might add to this latency.

RandomAccess principally exhibits data parallelism, and the core data structure naturally maps onto a distributed array approach to parallelism. Unfortunately, the communication pattern tends to not run efficiently using a purely distributed array approach. Specifically, if the operation

$$\mathbf{t}(i) = \mathrm{XOR}(\mathbf{t}(i), r)$$

is performed directly on distributed arrays, there is likely to be additional overhead incurred while each processor tries to determine which processor owns each $i$. In addition, the distributed array library cannot know that the XOR operation is commutative and may try to enforce proper ordering on the update. All of these will have the effect of increasing the latency of the operation. Thus, a high performance implementation tends to use a hybrid approach that combines distributed arrays with message passing. Each processor generates a set of indices $i$, explicitly determines which processors own each index, and then sends the indices to those processors to perform the update.

Using these techniques, a hybrid distributed array and message passing implementation of the RandomAccess benchmark should be able to achieve a level of performance close to what the parallel processor can deliver. Unfortunately, on most parallel processors, this performance will not be good. In addition, because the parallel MATLAB code requires message passing, this code will be a relatively large change from the serial MATLAB code.

## 7.6.3   FFT

The performance analysis of the FFT benchmark indicates that moderate speedup can be achieved on a parallel processor. This application falls in the gray area between a clear win and not worth it. Undertaking a parallel implementation is, as with RandomAccess, most likely driven by the need to perform an FFT on a very large problem that will not fit in the memory of one processor. Again, it is important to compare the performance of the implementation with what is achievable on the parallel processor. The performance bottleneck of FFT is the all-to-all communication pattern required in redistributing the data in the step

$$\mathbf{Z} = \mathbf{X}$$

where $\mathbf{X} : \mathbb{C}^{P(M_1) \times M_2}$ and $\mathbf{Z} : \mathbb{C}^{M_1 \times P(M_2)}$. The performance of this step is fundamentally set by the bandwidth of the communication networks. A parallel implementation must take care not to degrade this bandwidth.

FFT exhibits both data and pipeline parallelism, which can naturally be expressed with distributed arrays. The redistribution mentioned above is a classic example of the coding benefits of distributed arrays. Writing the equivalent expression with message passing results in a large expansion of code. However, a generic redistribution, which must work for any possible map, will incur certain overheads that a message passing implementation will not. In addition, a message passing implementation can more tightly manage data buffers and the order the messages are sent around the network so that a particular processor is not inundated with messages. Thus, it is common for data redistributions, such as this one, to be special-cased into their own function that can take advantage of these map-specific optimizations.

Using these techniques, a distributed array implementation of the FFT benchmark should be able to achieve a level of performance close to what the parallel processor can deliver (i.e., a modest amount of parallel speedup). In addition, the parallel MATLAB code should be a relatively small change from the serial MATLAB code.

## 7.6.4   HPL

The performance analysis of the HPL benchmark indicates that a parallel implementation should perform well. The primary performance bottleneck for HPL is the rate at which the processor can do floating-point operations found in many matrix multiply operations. Thus, an implementation of the benchmark should ensure that these operations are preserved and not broken up into many smaller matrix multiplies.

HPL principally exhibits data parallelism, and the core data structure naturally maps onto a distributed array approach to parallelism. If a simple parallel distribution is used, such as $\mathbf{A} : \mathbb{C}^{P(M) \times M}$, then the resulting communications are simple to code with distributed arrays. Unfortunately, such a distribution will result in an uneven distribution of work as the computation progresses. A more load-balanced approach employs a two-dimensional block-cyclic distribution $\mathbf{A} : \mathbb{C}^{P_{bc}(M) \times P_{bc}(M)}$. The communication patterns resulting from such a distribution are quite complex and can be difficult to orchestrate in a purely distributed array approach. Typically, a hybrid distributed array message passing approach is used to achieve optimal performance.

Using these techniques, a distributed array implementation of the HPL benchmark should be able to achieve a level of performance close to what the parallel processor can deliver. However, the parallel MATLAB code will be a large change from the serial MATLAB code.

## 7.7   Performance versus effort

The previous section applied the performance analysis to the HPC Challenge benchmark suite and made a series of predictions about the performance and software effort associated with implementing these benchmarks. Figure 7.6 already showed that the performance of the benchmarks written in C using message passing agreed with the performance model. What about the parallel MATLAB versions written using distributed arrays? Details of these implementations are given in subsequent chapters.

There are two comparisons that are of interest. First is the performance of parallel MATLAB relative to serial MATLAB since this is what most users care about. Second is the performance of parallel MATLAB relative to C+MPI as a way of gauging the quality of the distributed array implementation and as a guide to future performance enhancements.

The four primary benchmarks were implemented using parallel MATLAB and run on a commodity cluster system (see the end of the chapter for a precise description of the hardware). Both the parallel MATLAB and C+MPI reference implementations of the benchmarks were run on 1, 2, 4, 8, 16, 32, 64, and 128 processors. At each processor count, the largest problem size that would fit in the main memory was run. The collected data measures the relative compute performance and memory overhead of parallel MATLAB with respect to C+MPI. The relative memory, performance, and code sizes are summarized in Table 7.3.

**Table 7.3. HPC Challenge implementation results.**
(Top) Maximum problem size relative to the C+MPI single-processor case on 128 processors. (Middle) Benchmark performance relative to the C+MPI single-processor case on 128 processors. (Bottom) Code size is measured in terms of source lines of code (SLOC). The parallel code sizes of the HPC Challenge C+MPI reference code are taken from the HPC Challenge FAQ. FFT code size includes code used to create random waves and does not include code for initial and final all-to-all operations. Combined these should roughly offset each other.

| Implementation | Stream | FFT | RandomAccess | HPL(32) |
|---|---|---|---|---|
| Maximum Problem Size | | | | |
| C+MPI/C serial | 63.9 | 72.7 | 48 | 32.6 |
| pMatlab/C serial | 42.8 | 21.3 | 32 | 9.3 |
| C+MPI/pMatlab | 1.5 | 3.4 | 1.5 | 3.5 |
| Relative Performance | | | | |
| C+MPI/C serial | 62.4 | 4.6 | 0.074 | 28.2 |
| pMatlab/C serial | 63.4 | 4.3 | 0.0016 | 6.8 |
| C+MPI/pMatlab | 1 | 1 | 46 | 4 |
| Code Size | | | | |
| C+MPI | 347 | 787 | 938 | 8800 |
| pMatlab | 119 | 78 | 157 | 190 |
| C+MPI/pMatlab | 3 | 10 | 6 | 40 |

In general, the parallel MATLAB implementations can run problems that are typically 1/2 the size of the C+MPI implementation problem size. This is due to the need to create temporary arrays when using high-level expressions. The parallel MATLAB performance ranges from being comparable to the C+MPI code (FFT and Stream), to somewhat slower (Top 500), to a lot slower (RandomAccess). In contrast, the parallel MATLAB code is typically 3x to 40x smaller than the equivalent C+MPI code.

Relative to serial MATLAB, all of the parallel MATLAB codes allow problem sizes to scale linearly with the number of processors. Likewise, they all experience significant performance improvements (with the exception of RandomAccess). RandomAccess performance is limited by the underlying communication mechanism. Relative to C+MPI, the parallel MATLAB problem sizes are smaller by a factor of 2, and the performance of parallel MATLAB on both Stream and FFT is comparable.

In the Stream benchmark, the maximum problem size of the parallel MATLAB code is 1.5x smaller than that of the C+MPI code because of the need to create intermediate temporary arrays. The need for temporaries is a side effect of most high-level programming environments. The performance of the parallel MATLAB code is the same as that of the C+MPI code. This is because the MATLAB interpreter recognizes the scale and add statement and replaces it with a call to the appropriate optimized Basic Linear Algebra Subroutine (BLAS). The parallel MATLAB code is 3x smaller than the C+MPI code due to the elimination of various for loops and the use of built-in MATLAB functions.

For the RandomAccess benchmark, the maximum problem size of the parallel MATLAB code is 1.5x smaller than that of the C+MPI code because of the need to create intermediate temporary arrays. On one processor, the parallel MATLAB RandomAccess performance is comparable to the performance of the C+MPI code. However, on a larger number of processors, the parallel MATLAB code is 45x slower than the C+MPI code. This performance difference is due to the large latency of the underlying communication mechanism, which can be potentially alleviated if a lower latency communication mechanism were employed. The parallel MATLAB code is 6x smaller than the C+MPI code.

For the FFT benchmark, the maximum problem size of the parallel MATLAB code is 3.5x smaller than that of the C+MPI code because of the need to create intermediate temporary arrays. In addition, MATLAB internally uses a split representation for complex data types, while the underlying serial FFT library being called uses an interleaved representation. The result is that the data needs to be transformed between these representations. On one processor, the MATLAB FFT performance is 5x slower than the that of the C code due to the time overhead required to perform the conversion between complex data storage formats. As the problem grows, the FFT time becomes dominated by the time to perform the all-to-all communication necessary between computation stages. Since these are primarily large messages, the performance of parallel MATLAB becomes the same as the performance of the C+MPI code at large numbers of processors. The parallel MATLAB code is 10x smaller than the C+MPI code due to the use of built-in local FFT calls and the elimination of MPI messaging code.

In the HPL benchmark, the maximum problem size of the parallel MATLAB code is 3.5x smaller than that of the C+MPI code because of the need to create intermediate temporary arrays. In particular, the lower and upper triangular matrices are returned as full matrices; in contrast, in the C+MPI code, these matrices can be merged into a single array. The parallel MATLAB code provides a 10x speedup on 32 processors, which is about 4x slower than the speedup using the C+MPI code. Improving the network of this hardware should significantly improve the parallel

MATLAB code performance, relative to the C+MPI code. The parallel MATLAB code is 40x smaller than the C+MPI code. About 10x of this code reduction is due to the higher-level abstractions from parallel MATLAB and about 4x is due to using the simpler algorithm.

One approach to depicting the performance of the HPC Challenge benchmarks is shown in Figure 7.7. The speedup and relative code size for each implementation were calculated with respect to a serial C/Fortran implementation. In this plot, we see that with the exception of Random Access, the C+MPI implementations all fall into the upper right quadrant of the graph, indicating that they deliver some level of parallel speedup, while requiring more code than the serial code. As expected, the serial MATLAB implementations do not deliver any speedup but do all require less code than do implementations in the serial C/Fortran code. The parallel MATLAB implementations (except RandomAccess) fall into the upper left quadrant of the graph, delivering parallel speedup while requiring fewer lines of code.

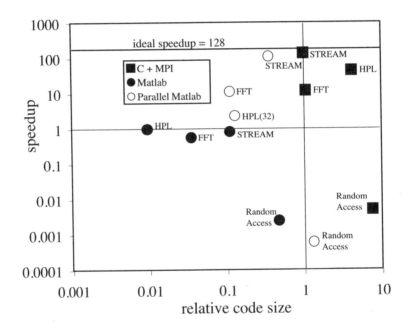

**Figure 7.7. Speedup versus relative code size.**
Speedup (relative to serial C) versus code size (relative to serial C). The upper right quadrant is the traditional HPC regime: more coding is required to give more performance and most of the C+MPI codes fall here. The lower left quadrant is the traditional regime of serial high-level languages that produce much smaller codes but are slower. RandomAccess lies in the lower right and represents algorithms that are simply a poor match to the underlying hardware and communication mechanism. The upper left quadrant is where most of the parallel MATLAB implementations are found and represents smaller codes that are delivering some speedup.

This trade-off between performance and effort is summarized by looking at the relative productivity of the environments (see Chapter 6). Using the speedup and relative code size data, the productivity of each approach on each benchmark is shown in Figure 7.8. Not surprisingly, where parallel MATLAB obtains good speedup, it is highly productive.

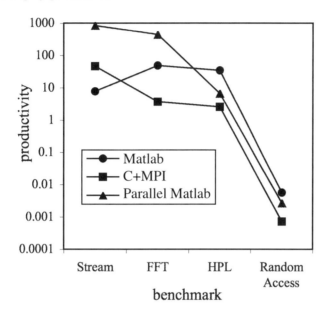

**Figure 7.8. HPC Challenge productivity.**
Relative productivity of each of the benchmarks in each of the different coding environments.

# References

[Bliss & Kepner 2007] N. Bliss and J. Kepner, pMATLAB parallel MATLAB library, Special issue on high productivity programming languages and models, International Journal of High Performance Computing Applications, Vol. 21, No. 3, pp. 336–359, 2007.

[Cummings et al. 1998] J.C. Cummings, J.A. Crotinger, S.W. Haney, W.F. Humphrey, S.R. Karmesin, J.V. Reynders, S.A. Smith, and T.J. Williams, Rapid application development and enhanced code interoperability using the POOMA framework, Proceedings of the SIAM Workshop on Object-Oriented Methods and Code Interoperability in Scientific and Engineering Computing (OO98), 1998.

[Dongarra and Luszczek 2005] Jack Dongarra and Piotr Luszczek, Introduction to the HPC Challenge Benchmark Suite, Technical Report UT-CS-05-544, University of Tennessee, 2005.

[El-Ghazawi et al. 2005] Tariq El-Ghazawi, William Carlson, Thomas Sterling, and Kathy Yelick, UPC: Distributed Shared Memory Programming, Hoboken, NJ: John Wiley & Sons, 2005.

[Flynn 1972] Michael Flynn, Some computer organizations and their effectiveness, IEEE Transactions on Computers, Vol. C-21, No. 9, p. 948, 1972.

[Nieplocha et al. 2002] J. Nieplocha, R. Harrison, M. Krishnan, B. Palmer, and V. Tipparaju, Combining shared and distributed memory models: Evolution and recent advancements of the Global Array Toolkit, Proceedings of the POHLL-02 Workshop of the International Conference on Supercomputing, New York, 2002.

[Reuther et al. 2004] Albert Reuther, Tim Currie, Jeremy Kepner, Hahn Kim, Andrew McCabe, Michael Moore, and Nadya Travinin, LLGrid: Enabling on-demand grid computing with gridMatlab and pMatlab, Proceedings of the Eighth Annual High Performance Embedded Computing Workshop (HPEC2004), Lexington, MA, 2004.

[Weinberg et al. 2005] J. Weinberg, M.O. McCracken, E. Strohmaier, and A. Snavely, Quantifying locality in the memory access patterns of HPC applications, Conference on High Performance Networking and Computing, Proceedings of the ACM/IEEE Conference on Supercomputing, 2005.

# Chapter 8

# Stream

**Summary**

The Stream benchmark is a simple program that is very useful for illustrating several important parallel programming concepts. Stream is representative of a wide class of embarrassingly parallel programs. Stream highlights the importance of data locality and how to extract concurrency from data locality. Stream also shows performance implications of different data-parallel access approaches. Finally, Stream sheds light on the performance trade-offs of multicore processors.

Stream was introduced in Chapter 7 as a benchmark for measuring bandwidth between a processor and its main memory [McCalpin 2005]. Stream is also a good example of a wide range of embarrassingly parallel applications and will allow the demonstration of a number of useful parallel coding techniques, in particular, how to write a data-parallel program that extracts parallelism from distributed arrays.

Stream creates several large $N$ element vectors and repeatedly performs basic operations on these vectors. Because the number of operations performed on each element of a vector is small, Stream performance is limited by the bandwidth to main memory. Stream provides an excellent illustration of the performance trade-offs of multicore processors that all share the same access to memory.

## 8.1 Getting started

To run the program, start MATLAB and go to the Examples/Stream directory (i.e., type `cd Examples/Stream`). Edit the file `pStream.m` and set `PARALLEL=0`. At the prompt, type

```
pStream
```

Because Stream is a benchmark, it will produce a large volume of performance data similar to

169

```
Allocation Time (sec)                   = 1.4523
Launch Time (sec)                       = 0.094735
A, B, C errors                          = 0    1.819e-12    3.638e-12
Np                                      = 1
Pid                                     = 0
Global Array size (elem)                = 33554432
Global Array size (bytes)               = 268435456
Global memory required (bytes)          = 805306368
Local Array size (elem)                 = 33554432
Local Array size (bytes)                = 268435456
Local memory required (bytes)           = 805306368
Number of trials                        = 4
Local Copy Bandwidth (MB/sec)           = 2338.2472
Local Scale Bandwidth (MB/sec)          = 710.2395
Local Add Bandwidth (MB/sec)            = 994.2772
Local Triadd Bandwidth (MB/sec)          = 798.4208
Global Copy Bandwidth (MB/sec)          = 2338.2472
Global Scale Bandwidth (MB/sec)         = 710.2395
Global Add Bandwidth (MB/sec)           = 994.2772
Global Triadd Bandwidth (MB/sec)         = 798.4208
```

The above information can be broken up into four categories. First are the program parameters that describe the size of the problem $N$, the number of bytes required, the number of trials, the number of processors $N_P$, and the $P_{ID}$ of the output. The second category includes the array initialization times and launch times, which describe how long it takes before the program starts running. The third category is the local and global bandwidth values. The fourth category is the validation values. These outputs will be discussed further in the Test subsection. For now, edit the file pStream.m, set PARALLEL=1, and run Stream again using each of the following commands:

```
eval(pRUN('pStream',1,{}))
eval(pRUN('pStream',2,{}))
eval(pRUN('pStream',4,{}))
```

These commands run the Stream program on one, two, and four processors. Running on a parallel computer will produce performance values that look similar to those in Table 8.1. These results will be reviewed later in the Test subsection.

**Important Note**: The last argument to the pRUN command determines which parallel computer the program will be run on. You may need to obtain the proper setting from your system administrator; see the book website (http://www.siam.org/KepnerBook) for details. Setting the last argument to {} runs multiple copies of the program on your local machine and will result in different performance values from those shown in Table 8.1.

## 8.2  Parallel design

The specification of the stream benchmark consists of three $N$ element vectors $\mathbf{a}, \mathbf{b}, \mathbf{c} : \mathbb{R}^N$ such that the total memory occupied is a significant fraction of the processor memory. A specific series of operations is performed on these vectors in the following order:

$$
\begin{aligned}
\text{Copy}: & \quad \mathbf{c} = \mathbf{a} \\
\text{Scale}: & \quad \mathbf{b} = q\,\mathbf{c} \\
\text{Add}: & \quad \mathbf{c} = \mathbf{a} + \mathbf{b} \\
\text{Triadd}: & \quad \mathbf{a} = \mathbf{b} + q\,\mathbf{c}
\end{aligned}
$$

The above operations are repeated $n$ times. The basic algorithm for Stream is shown in Algorithm 8.1 (see caption for details).

**Algorithm 8.1. Serial Stream.**
The algorithm creates three $N$ element vectors and performs a series of operations on those vectors. Each operation is timed using the TIC and TOC commands.

$\text{STREAM}(\mathbf{a}, \mathbf{b}, \mathbf{c} : \mathbb{R}^N, q : \mathbb{R}, n : \mathbb{Z})$

```
1    t_copy, t_scale, t_add, t_copy : R
2    for i = 1 : n
3        do
4            TIC
5                c = a
6            t_copy  += TOC
7            TIC
8                b = q c
9            t_scale += TOC
10           TIC
11               c = a + b
12           t_add   += TOC
13           TIC
14               a = b + q c
15           t_triadd += TOC
```

The goal of Stream is to measure memory bandwidth in bytes per second. The benchmark requires the vectors to be 8-byte double-precision floating point values resulting in the following bandwidths formulas:

$$\begin{aligned}
\text{Copy Bandwidth} &: \quad 16 \ n \ N/t_{copy} \\
\text{Scale Bandwidth} &: \quad 16 \ n \ N/t_{scale} \\
\text{Add Bandwidth} &: \quad 24 \ n \ N/t_{add} \\
\text{Triadd Bandwidth} &: \quad 24 \ n \ N/t_{triadd}
\end{aligned}$$

Validation is a critical part of any benchmark program. If the values of the vector **a** are initialized to $a_0$, then the final results can be checked against the formulas

$$\begin{aligned}
a_{n-1} &= (2q + q^2)^{n-1} \ a_0 \\
\mathbf{a}_n(:) &= (2q + q^2)^n \ a_0 \\
\mathbf{b}_n(:) &= q \ a_{n-1} \\
\mathbf{b}_n(:) &= (1 + q) \ a_{n-1}
\end{aligned}$$

Although Stream is very simple, it contains the essence of many programs. Specifically, it operates on a series of vectors, with defined initial values. It repeats a sequence of standard vector operations and produces answers that can be checked for correctness.

The parallel Stream program can be implemented quite easily using distributed arrays. As long as all the vectors use the same distributed mapping, the resulting program will require no interprocessor communication. The no communication requirement can be strictly enforced by making the program use the *.loc* construct. This approach is generally recommended as it guarantees that no communication will take place. If a mapping that required communication were accidentally used, then the resulting program will either produce an error or will fail to validate. This mapping results in the parallel algorithm shown using P notation in Algorithm 8.2. A visual representation of the design for the parallel Stream algorithm is shown in Figure 8.1.

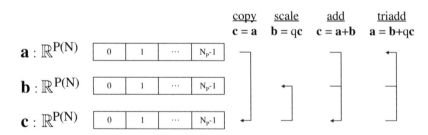

**Figure 8.1. Parallel Stream design.**
Each vector is a distributed array. If each vector has the same parallel map, then the resulting program will require no communication.

**Algorithm 8.2. Parallel Stream.**
The parallel algorithm creates three $N$ element distributed vectors and performs a series of operations on just the local part of those vectors. The resulting times can be averaged to obtain overall parallel bandwidths.

PARALLELSTREAM($\mathbf{a}, \mathbf{b}, \mathbf{c} : \mathbb{R}^{P(N)}, q : \mathbb{R}, n : \mathbb{Z}$)

```
 1   t_copy, t_scale, t_add, t_copy : ℝ
 2   for i = 1 : n
 3        do
 4            TIC
 5                c.loc = a.loc
 6            t_copy += TOC
 7            TIC
 8                b.loc = q c.loc
 9            t_scale += TOC
10            TIC
11                c.loc = a + b.loc
12            t_add += TOC
13            TIC
14                a.loc = b + q c.loc
15            t_triadd += TOC
```

## 8.3  Code

The next step is to write the Stream program. The parallel code can be implemented by simply converting the vectors from regular arrays to distributed arrays. The core of the parallel code is shown below (see `Examples/Stream/pStream.m` for a complete listing). Keep in mind that this same code is run by every MATLAB instance. The only difference between these instances is that each has a unique $P_{ID}$ (i.e., `Pid`) that is used to determine which parts of a distributed array belong to each MATLAB instance (i.e., $\mathbf{a}.loc$, $\mathbf{b}.loc$, and $\mathbf{c}.loc$).

**Code Listing 8.1.   Parallel Stream MATLAB program.**

```
 1  PARALLEL = 1;
 2  NTRIALS = 4; lgN = 25; N = 2.^lgN;
 3  A0 = 1.0; B0 =2.0; C0 = 0.0; q = 3.14;
 4
 5  ABCmap = 1; SyncMap = 1;     % Serial maps.
 6  if (PARALLEL)                % Parallel maps.
 7     ABCmap = map([1 Np], ,0:Np-1);
 8     SyncMap = map([Np 1], ,0:Np-1);
 9  end
10  tic;                         % Allocate vectors.
11     Aloc = local(zeros(1, N, ABCmap)) + A0;
12     Bloc = local(zeros(1, N, ABCmap)) + B0;
13     Cloc = local(zeros(1, N, ABCmap)) + C0;
14  Talloc = toc;
15  tic;                         % Synch launch.
16     sync = agg(zeros(1, Np, SyncMap));
17  Tlaunch = toc;
18
19  TsumCopy=0.0; TsumScale =0.0; TsumAdd=0.0; TsumTriad=0.0;
20  for i = 1:NTRIALS
21     tic;
22         Cloc(:,:)  = Aloc;           % Copy.
23     TsumCopy = TsumCopy + toc;
24     tic;
25         Bloc(:,:)  = q*Cloc;         % Scale.
26     TsumScale = TsumScale + toc;
27     tic;
28         Cloc(:,:)  = Aloc + Bloc;    % Add.
29     TsumAdd = TsumAdd + toc;
30     tic;
31         Aloc(:,:)  = Bloc + q*Cloc; % Triadd.
32     TsumTriad = TsumTriad + toc;
33  end
```

In the above program,

**Lines 5–9** create the parallel maps ABCmap and SyncMap. The PARALLEL flag is an additional debugging tool that allows the distributed arrays A, B, and C to be turned on and off.

**Lines 11–13** create the distributed vectors A, B, and C; extract their local parts; and then initialize them to A0, B0, and C0. Because the program requires no communication, the distributed arrays A, B, and C are never actually allocated. Instead, only their local parts Aloc, Bloc, and Cloc are created. This simplifies the program and reduces the total memory required to run the program by eliminating unnecessary duplication.

**Line 14** stores the time it took to allocate these arrays.

**Line 16** shows how a synchronization point or a barrier can be created across all the $P_{ID}$s of the program. In this case, a simple $N_P$ element distributed vector is created and then aggregated across all the processors. Aggregating this vector forces all $P_{ID} > 0$ to reach this point before $P_{ID} = 0$ can proceed. This synchronization point is required to obtain a true measure of the performance of the system. Synchronization points like this are often inserted in parallel programs when all the $P_{ID}$s need to be roughly at the same point of execution. Using `agg()` for this synchronization synchronizes all $P_{ID} > 0$ with the $P_{ID} = 0$. A more aggressive synchronization can be achieved using `agg_all()`, which requires every $P_{ID}$ to send its value to every other processor.

**Lines 20–33** execute the copy, scale, add, and triadd operations on `Aloc`, `Bloc`, and `Cloc`. The time for each of these operations is summed for each trial.

The above code is a good example of the map-based programming approach. After the maps `ABCmap` and `SyncMap` are created, they are used to extract local distributed vectors `Aloc`, `Bloc`, and `Cloc`.

There are a number of properties of the map-based approach that can be observed in this code example:

- Low Code Impact. The program has been converted from a serial program to a parallel program with approximately 10 additional lines of code.

- Serial code is preserved. By setting `PARALLEL=0`, there is no use of distributed arrays, and the program can be run in serial without any supporting parallel libraries.

- Small parallel library footprint. Only three parallel library functions were required: `map`, `local`, and `agg`.

- Scalable. The code can be run on any problem size or number of processors such that $N > N_P$, provided the vectors all have identical maps.

- Bounded communication. Because local variables are used, there is strict control on when communication takes place.

- Map independence. As long as the same map is used for all three vectors, the program will work for any distribution in the second dimension (i.e., block, cyclic, or block-cyclic). To make the program map independent for any combination of maps would require replacing the local operations with global operations. For example, if scale was implemented using `C(:,:)` `= A`, then it would run correctly regardless of the map. However, if `A` and `C` had different maps, then significant communication would be required.

- Performance guarantee. Because the copy, scale, add, and triadd operations commands are working local variables that are regular MATLAB numeric arrays, there is a guarantee that there is no hidden performance penalty when running these lines of code.

## 8.4  Debug

As mentioned earlier, parallel debugging brings up many challenges. The primary benefit of the map-based approach is that it lends itself to a well-defined code-debug-test process. The specific steps are listed in Table 2.2.

Step 1 runs the program in serial on the local machine with the array vectors `Aloc`, `Bloc`, and `Cloc` constructed as ordinary arrays (i.e., `PARALLEL=0`). This ensures that basic serial code is still correct after the `local` function is applied. Step 2 runs the program in serial on the local machine with `Aloc`, `Bloc`, and `Cloc` derived from distributed arrays (i.e., `PARALLEL=1`) and ensures the program works properly with distributed arrays as inputs. Step 3 runs the program in parallel on the local machine. This step will detect if the parallel maps that generate `Aloc`, `Bloc`, and `Cloc` are correct. Of all the steps, this is probably the most important and will catch the most errors. Step 4 runs the program in parallel on the remote machine. Step 5 runs the program in parallel on the remote machine but with a problem size of interest. Up to this point, all the testing should have been done on a small problem size. This step allows the performance on a real problem to be measured.

These steps essentially mirror those that were done during the "getting started" section, and each step tests something very specific about the parallel code. In addition to functionally debugging the program, the above process also can be used to optimize the performance of the code (see next section). The Stream benchmark uses some additional coding practices to assist with debugging beyond the above steps.

The Stream program prints the program parameters that describe the size of the problem $N$, the number of bytes required, the number of trials, the number of processors $N_P$, and the $P_{ID}$ of the output. This process is done on every $P_{ID}$ of the program. Comparing the resulting values by looking at the different output files from each $P_{ID}$ (i.e., MatMPI/*.out) is a powerful way to catch bugs.

Stream also displays the initialization times and launch times for every program $P_{ID}$. These times describe how long it takes before the program starts running. A signal that something is wrong early in the program is if these values differ significantly across $P_{ID}$s.

Because Stream is a benchmark, the performance of the execution is measured and reported in terms that relate back to the processor. However, this is also a good practice on general programs. Performance values that differ significantly across instances can be an indication of a deeper problem in the program (e.g., very different array sizes being created).

Finally, the Stream program has a correctness check that ensures the program is giving the proper results. In a real application, this check is usually not possible, but more approximate checks can be performed and these are very useful. For example, often the sign of the values in an array can be checked or the sum of the values in an array can be checked. Again, displaying these from every instance can highlight errors that are dependent on the $P_{ID}$.

# 8.5  Test

Stream is a very good program for exploring the performance implications of a number of coding approaches. Testing a parallel program—assuming that it has been debugged and is giving the right answers—mainly involves looking at how long it took to run and seeing if it is performing as expected. Most of the performance data necessary to conduct this analysis was collected in the "getting started" section (see Table 8.1).

The first test is to compare the performance of running the program using $N_P = 1$ with distributed arrays turned off (`PARALLEL=0`) and distributed arrays turned on (`PARALLEL=1`). Columns 2 and 3 in Table 8.1 provide this data. In this case, the performance differences are small and indicate that distributed arrays do not incur a performance penalty. If using distributed arrays with $N_P = 1$ slows things down significantly, then this must be addressed. It is very difficult to get any benefit with $N_P > 1$ if the $N_P = 1$ is slower than the base serial code. Working only on the local parts of distributed arrays almost guarantees the performance will be the same as when distributed arrays are not being used.

Looking more closely at the values in either column 2 or 3 reveals that these are broken up into three categories. Rows 2, 3, 7 and 8 contain the allocation time and launch time. Rows 4 and 5 contain the local bandwidth reported by $P_{ID} = 0$ on the various operations. Rows 9 and 10 contain the global bandwidth, which can be estimated by multiplying the local bandwidth by $N_P$ and can be computed exactly by averaging the values across all instances. In columns 2 and 3, where $N_P = 1$, the local and global bandwidths are identical. In general, *copy* has the highest bandwidth, while *scale*, *add*, and *triadd* are fairly similar. The precise reasons for these differences are a function of the details of the processor architecture. In Table 8.1, the bandwidths are consistent with the peak main memory bandwidth for the specific processor. Thus, it can be inferred that the program is performing close to the peak of what the underlying hardware will support. This kind of performance data is invaluable in optimizing a program. It allows for a quantitative determination of whether additional effort optimizing the program will be worthwhile. If a program is performing at less than 1% of peak, then it is likely that additional effort will be worthwhile. If a program is performing at greater than 10% of peak, then this effort may not be as fruitful. Finally, in this instance, the peak is not the processor peak but the peak memory bandwidth. Stream is representative of many programs that do not do a lot of operations on each data element and are limited by the memory bandwidth and not the processor speed.

The data in Table 8.1 were collected on an eight-core system where all the cores shared the same memory. Columns 3–7 show the effect of increasing the number of program instances. First, the allocation time remains roughly the same. Second, the launch time increases as it takes more time to launch four instances than to launch two. This can become significant when $N_P$ becomes large, and care must be taken to use efficient launching mechanisms. Third, and most importantly, the local bandwidths across all the operations decrease some with $N_P$. In other words, the global bandwidth increases some with $N_P$. Even though additional processing cores are available, adding program instances will not result in a speedup in performance.

In this situation, the only way to improve performance is by adding processors that have separate memories.

Adding more instances of a program within a shared-memory processing node (denoted here a $1*N_P$) is sometimes referred to as "scaling up." Adding more instances of a program across a shared-memory processing node (denoted here a $N_P*1$) is sometimes referred to as "scaling out." The relative performance of scaling up and scaling out for Stream triadd is shown in Table 8.1. These results indicate that Stream benefits from scaling up but will scale very well when scaling out. This phenomenon is common across many memory-intensive applications and has obvious implications for how to run the program and even for which types of parallel computers these kinds of programs will run on most efficiently.

**Table 8.1. Multicore and multinode Stream triadd performance.**
Relative allocation time, absolute launch time, and relative local and global bandwidth for Stream triadd on multicore and multinode computing systems for different values of $N_P$. Performance data are shown for a fixed problem size ($N$ constant). All values are normalized to column 2 in which $N_P = 1$ with the distributed arrays turned off (`PARALLEL=0`). Columns 3–7 are the values with distributed arrays turned on (`PARALLEL=1`). The notation 1*8 means that $N_P = 8$, and all $P_{ID}$s were run on the same processing node with the same shared memory. The notation 16*1 means that $N_P = 16$, and each $P_{ID}$ was run on a separate processing node with a separate memory.

| Multicore processors:      | 1   | 1*1 | 1*2  | 1*4  | 1*8  |      |
|----------------------------|-----|-----|------|------|------|------|
| Relative allocation time   | 1   | 1.0 | 1.0  | 0.8  | 0.55 |      |
| Launch time (sec)          | 0.0 | 0.0 | 0.5  | 1.2  | 1.8  |      |
| Relative local bandwidth   | 1   | 1.0 | 0.89 | 0.86 | 0.64 |      |
| Relative global bandwidth  | 1   | 1.0 | 1.8  | 3.4  | 5.1  |      |
| Multinode processors:      | 1   | 1*1 | 2*1  | 4*1  | 8*1  | 16*1 |
| Relative allocation time   | 1   | 1.0 | 1.0  | 1.0  | 1.0  | 1.0  |
| Launch time (sec)          | 0.0 | 0.0 | 1.7  | 2.2  | 2.4  | 2.5  |
| Relative local bandwidth   | 1   | 1.0 | 1.0  | 1.0  | 1.0  | 1.0  |
| Relative global bandwidth  | 1   | 1.0 | 2.0  | 4.0  | 8.0  | 16.0 |

Another important dimension to test is how the performance of the application scales with problem size $N$. Table 8.1 indicates that if the problem size is scaled with $N_P$ while scaling out, then a linear performance increase should be expected. This increase raises the question of what is the optimal problem size to run on a single node, since this will determine the overall performance as the application is scaled out. Figure 8.2 shows the relative performance of Stream triadd as a function of relative problem size. The performance is very flat over a 1000x range in problem size and then increases by 50% for very small problem sizes. This increase is due to the problem being able to fit in the cache of the processor, which has higher memory bandwidth.

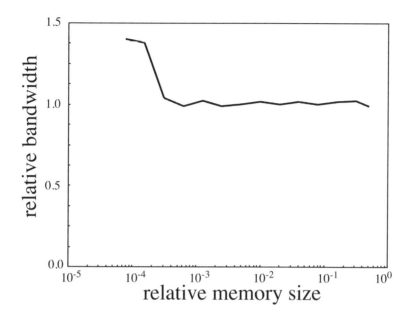

**Figure 8.2. Stream performance versus size.**
The relative bandwidth of Stream triadd as a function of the relative size of the problem run. The performance remains the same over a large range and then increases by 50% for very small problems due to cache effects.

Integrating all the Stream performance data together allows the following conclusions to be drawn for running applications of this kind on clusters of multicore processing nodes. First, running multiple program instances ($1^*N_P$) on a single processing may give some benefit. Second, the single node performance does not change much with problem size $N$. Third, performance should increase linearly when the program is run across multiple nodes ($N_P^*1$).

# References

[McCalpin 2005] John McCalpin, 2005, STREAM: Sustainable Memory Bandwidth in High Performance Computers, http://www.cs.virginia.edu/stream/

# Chapter 9

# RandomAccess

**Summary**

The RandomAccess benchmark is a simple program that is designed to stress the communication network of a parallel computer. It is typical of a class of problems that typically do not perform well on canonical parallel computers. RandomAccess is useful for illustrating a number of advanced parallel programming concepts. The communication pattern of this benchmark is difficult to implement with purely distributed arrays and requires a hybrid parallel programming that combines distributed array programming with message passing. The chapter discusses two versions of the benchmark using different communication patterns that show how fewer larger messages can perform better than many small messages.

RandomAccess was introduced in Chapter 7 as a benchmark for measuring the latency between processors on a network [Dongarra and Luszczek 2005]. RandomAccess is also a good example of a challenging parallel application with a complex communication pattern and allows the demonstration of a number of useful parallel coding techniques, in particular, how to write a hybrid program that uses distributed arrays for organizing communication but uses message passing to actually send the messages.

RandomAccess creates a large $N$ element table and repeatedly performs a simple update operation on this table. The location of the updates is determined by randomly generating locations over the entire range of the table. Thus, no two successive updates are likely to be near each other in the table. Because the number of operations performed on each element of a vector is small and the updates can be done only a few at a time, RandomAccess performance is limited by the latency of the communication network of the parallel computing system. RandomAccess provides an excellent illustration of the kinds of applications that typically do not perform well on canonical parallel computers. It is not uncommon for a large parallel application to have a portion with similarities to RandomAccess. This chapter illustrates both coding and algorithmic approaches to minimizing the performance impact of a RandomAccess-like part of a program.

## 9.1   Getting started

To run the program, start MATLAB and go to the Examples/RandomAccess directory (i.e., type `cd Examples/RandomAccess`). Edit the file `pRandomAccess.m` and set `PARALLEL=0`. At the prompt, type

    pRandomAccess

Because RandomAccess is a benchmark, it will produce a large volume of performance data similar to

```
Allocation Time (sec)                = 1.5989
Distributed table size               = 2^25 = 33554432 words
Distributed table size (bytes)       = 268435456
Local table size (bytes)             = 268435456
Number of updates                    = 8388608
Block size (should be 1024)          = 1024
Launch Time (sec)                    = 0.005367
Run time (sec)                       = 3.2708
Giga Updates Per Sec                 = 0.0025647
Validating results...
Validate time (sec)                  = 120.7053
Error rate                           = 0.001209
Validation Passed
```

The above information can be broken up into four categories. First are the program parameters that describe the size of the problem $N$, the number of bytes required, the number of updates performed, and the block size of these updates. The second category contains the array initialization times and launch times, which describe how long it takes before the program starts running. The third category is execution time and the performance in Giga Updates Per Second (GUPS). The fourth category is the validation values. These outputs will be discussed further in the Test subsection. For now, edit the file `pRandomAccess.m` and set `PARALLEL=1` (to turn on the parallel parts of the code) and `VALIDATE = 0` (to shorten the execution time). Run RandomAccess again using each of the following commands:

    eval(pRUN('pRandomAccess',1,{}))
    eval(pRUN('pRandomAccess',2,{}))
    eval(pRUN('pRandomAccess',4,{}))

These commands run the RandomAccess program with $N_P = 1$, 2, and 4. Running on a parallel computer will produce performance values that look similar to Table 9.1 (see Test subsection). These results will be reviewed later in the Test subsection.

**Important Note**: The last argument to the `pRUN` command determines which parallel computer the program will be run on. You may need to obtain the proper setting from your system administrator; see the book website (http://www.siam.org/KepnerBook) for details. Setting the last argument to {} runs multiple copies of the program on your local machine and may result in different performance values from those shown in Table 9.1.

## 9.2 Parallel design

The specification of the RandomAccess benchmark consists of creating an $N$ element table of unsigned 64-bit integers $\mathbf{x} : \mathbb{Z}^N$ such that the memory occupied by $\mathbf{x}$ is a significant fraction of the total available memory. An update is performed on this table as follows:

$$\mathbf{x(i)} = \text{XOR}(\mathbf{x(i)}, \mathbf{r})$$

where $\mathbf{r} : \mathbb{Z}^{1024}$ is a 1024-element vector of random integers, and $\mathbf{i} = \text{AND}(\mathbf{r}, N-1)$ is vector of table locations to update. The above operations are repeated $4N/1024$ times (although accurate performance results can generally be achieved with fewer iterations). The basic algorithm for RandomAccess is shown in Algorithm 9.1 (see caption for details).

**Algorithm 9.1. Serial RandomAccess.**
The algorithm creates an $N$ element table and performs updates to random locations in the table. Lines 2–4 initialize the values and compute the number of updates and blocks to use. Line 7 gets the next set of 1024 random numbers. Line 8 computes the table index derived from these random values. Line 9 performs the update on table $\mathbf{x}$.

RANDOMACCESS($\mathbf{x} : \mathbb{Z}^N$)

```
 1   r, i : Z^1024
 2   N_up = 4N        N_b = N_up/1024
 3   r = RANDSTART( 0 : 1023 )
 4   TIC
 5   for b = 1 : N_b
 6       do
 7            r = RAND(r)
 8            i = AND(r, N − 1)
 9            x(i) = XOR(x(i), r)
10   t_up = TOC
```

The goal of RandomAccess is to measure the ability of the computer to perform small updates to memory. Performance is measured in GUPS and is computed via

$$\text{Giga Updates Per Second} : \quad N_{up}/t_{up}/10^9$$

Validation is a critical part of any benchmark program. If the values of the table $\mathbf{x}$ are initialized so that $\mathbf{x}(i) = i - 1$, then resetting the random-number generator and rerunning the benchmark will return $\mathbf{x}$ to its initial values. Comparing with the correct initial values, it is possible to compute how many errors occurred in the update process:

$$N_{err} = \sum_{i=1}^{N} \text{NOT}(\ \mathbf{x}(i) == (i-1)\ )$$

Unlike many benchmarks, RandomAccess allows an error rate of

$$N_{err}/N_{up} < 0.1\%$$

Errors can occur in a number of ways. In Algorithm 9.1, the primary source of errors will occur when $\mathbf{i}$ has duplicate values. Only one of the duplicate updates will be performed when all the updates are being performed as a block (this is typically done for performance purposes). During validation, the program must be run in a manner that is error free, so Line 10 is replaced with the following loop:

> **for** $j = 1 : 1024$
>     **do**     $\mathbf{x}(\mathbf{i}(j)) = \text{XOR}(\mathbf{x}(\mathbf{i}(j)), \mathbf{r}(j))$

The above loop will not generate errors but will tend to run much more slowly as seen in the previous section.

Although RandomAccess is very simple, it contains the essence of many programs. Specifically, it operates on a table with defined initial values. It repeats a sequence of standard updates to unpredictable locations in memory and produces answers that can be checked for correctness.

In the parallel RandomAccess program, each $P_{ID}$ generates a block of 1024 random numbers, resulting in $1024N_P$ updates during each iteration of the program. If the values $\mathbf{i}$ generated by each $P_{ID}$ were confined to the local range of $\mathbf{x}$, then RandomAccess would be an embarrassingly parallel benchmark. However, this is not the case. Each $P_{ID}$ generates a set of $i \in [1, N]$ that spans the whole range of the table $\mathbf{x}$. Thus, each $P_{ID}$ must determine which of its indices need to be sent to the other $P_{ID}$s.

## 9.2.1  Spray algorithm

Because of this dynamic behavior, parallel RandomAccess is difficult to implement using only distributed arrays. A hybrid distributed array and message passing approach is one effective model for programming this benchmark. The hybrid approach uses a distributed array to distribute $\mathbf{x}$ combined with message passing to send the updates to the different $P_{ID}$s (see Algorithm 9.2). This algorithm essentially "sprays" the updates across the computer.

**Algorithm 9.2. Parallel RandomAccess spray.**

The algorithm uses an $N$ element distributed table. Each $P_{ID}$ generates a set of 1024 random locations, determines which $P_{ID}$ each location belongs to, and then sends the updates to the correct $P_{ID}$. Line 3 initializes the random-number sequence to the appropriate point for each $P_{ID}$. Line 4 computes the $P_{ID}$s each $P_{ID}$ will send to and receive from. Line 10 sets the message tag, which is useful for debugging the message flows. Line 11 loops over the send $P_{ID}$s. Lines 12 and 13 determine which updates belong to $p$ and send them in a message. Line 14 initializes the received updates to those local to the $P_{ID}$. Lines 15 and 16 loop over the receive $P_{ID}$s and append their messages to the values to be updated. Lines 19 and 20 perform the update on the local part of $\mathbf{x}$.

$\text{PARALLELRANDOMACCESSSPRAY}(\mathbf{x} : \mathbb{Z}^{P(N)})$

1    $\mathbf{r}, \mathbf{i} : \mathbb{Z}^{1024}$
2    $N_{up} = 4N \qquad N_b = N_{up}/1024$
3    $\mathbf{r} = \text{RANDSTART}( \ (N_b/N_P)(1024P_{ID} + 0 : 1023) \ )$
4    $P_{ID}^{send} = P_{ID}^{recv} = \{0, \dots, N_P - 1\}\backslash P_{ID}$
5    TIC
6    **for** $b = 1 : N_b$
7        **do**
8           $\mathbf{r} = \text{RAND}(\mathbf{r})$
9           $\mathbf{i} = \text{AND}(\mathbf{r}, N - 1)$
10         $tag = b \mod 32$
11         **for** $p \in P_{ID}^{send}$
12            **do**
13               $\mathbf{r}_{send} = \mathbf{r}( \ \mathbf{x}.loc_p\langle 1\rangle \leq \mathbf{i} \leq \mathbf{x}.loc_p\langle end\rangle \ )$
14               $\text{SENDMSG}(p, tag, \mathbf{r}_{send})$
15           $\mathbf{r}_{recv} = \mathbf{r}( \ \mathbf{x}.loc_{P_{ID}}\langle 1\rangle \leq \mathbf{i} \leq \mathbf{x}.loc_{P_{ID}}\langle end\rangle \ )$
16           **for** $p \in P_{ID}^{recv}$
17            **do**
18               $\mathbf{r}_{recv} = \text{APPEND}(\mathbf{r}_{recv}, \text{RECVMSG}(p, tag))$
19           $\mathbf{i} = \text{AND}(\mathbf{r}_{recv}, N - 1) - \mathbf{x}.loc_{P_{ID}}\langle 1\rangle - 1$
20           $\mathbf{x}.loc(\mathbf{i}) = \text{XOR}(\mathbf{x}.loc(\mathbf{i}), \mathbf{r}_{recv})$
21   $t_{up} = \text{TOC}$

Algorithm 9.2 shows how distributed arrays and message passing can be used together. Specifically, the distributed array $\mathbf{x}$ is used to split data across the $P_{ID}$s. The information in $\mathbf{x}$ is also used to select the values to be sent by comparing the index locations in $\mathbf{i}$ with the maximum and minimum global index on each $P_{ID}$. Notationally, lines 13 and 15 use the angle bracket notation to retrieve this global index. Recall that referencing a particular index in the local part is done in the usual way: $\mathbf{x}.loc(i)$. In general, the global index $\mathbf{x}(i)$ is a different element in the array from the local index $\mathbf{x}.loc(i)$. If the local part from a particular $P_{ID}$ is desired, then this can be further denoted $\mathbf{x}.loc_p$. When the global index of a particular local value is needed, this is denoted using $\mathbf{x}.loc\langle i\rangle$. Obviously, $i = \mathbf{x}\langle i\rangle$. More generally, the following identity will hold:

$$\mathbf{x}(\mathbf{x}.loc\langle i\rangle) = \mathbf{x}.loc(i)$$

The minimum and maximum global indices on a particular $P_{ID}$ are thus given by $\mathbf{x}.loc_p\langle 1\rangle$ and $\mathbf{x}.loc_p\langle end\rangle$.

The spray algorithm depicted in Algorithm 9.2 is the canonical approach to implementing parallel RandomAccess and will send $N_P^2$ messages with approximately $1024/N_P$ updates in each message. As written, all $P_{ID}$s will first send in the same order, likely resulting in bottlenecks because every $P_{ID}$ will first try to send to $P_{ID} = 0$, then $P_{ID} = 1$, etc. A simple improvement is to change the order of $P_{ID}^{send}$ so that no two $P_{ID}$s are sending to the same place at the same time. Likewise, the order of $P_{ID}^{recv}$ can be set so that each $P_{ID}$ receives the messages in the order that the messages were sent to that $P_{ID}$. The communication pattern of this modified spray algorithm is shown in Figure 9.1.

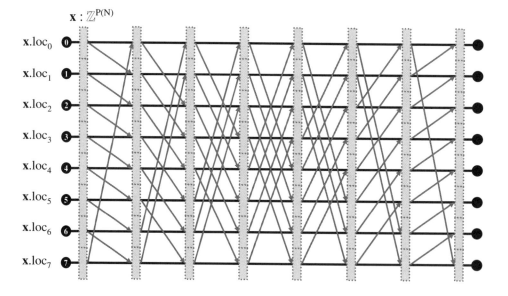

**Figure 9.1. RandomAccess spray communication pattern.**
Each $P_{ID}$ sends a message to all other $P_{ID}$s, resulting in $N_P^2$ messages with $1024/N_P$ updates per message. The pattern shown is constructed so that no two $P_{ID}$s are sending to the same destination at the same time.

## 9.2.2   Tree algorithm

The RandomAccess spray algorithm is the most straightforward parallel approach to implementing this benchmark. However, it has a number of limitations that require modifications. First, as $N_P$ approaches 1024, it will become increasingly likely that some $P_{ID}$s will have no updates to send to other $P_{ID}$s. This approach requires a more dynamic algorithm in which each $P_{ID}$ checks to see if any messages have arrived, thus allowing the algorithm to run for any value of $N_P$. Unfortunately, even with these changes, the spray algorithm runs slowly because it sends $N_P^2$ very small messages per iteration. Thus, all competitive versions of RandomAccess use a different algorithm that sends fewer larger messages.

The RandomAccess tree algorithm turns each $P_{ID}$ into a "software router" to reduce the total number of messages sent. In this approach, each $P_{ID}$ splits its updates into a set of high values and a set of low values, and either keeps or sends these to another $P_{ID}$. After one step, each $P_{ID}$ will have a set of updates whose range has been reduced from $N$ to $N/2$. After two steps, the range of values on each $P_{ID}$ has been reduced to $N/4$. Repeating this step for a total of $\lg(N_P)$ steps reduces the range values to the point that they all lie within the **x**.*loc* of each $P_{ID}$. The tree algorithm is depicted in Algorithm 9.3, and the corresponding communication pattern is shown in Figure 9.2. The version shown works if $N_P$ is an exact power of 2. A simple modification of the algorithm allows it to work for any $N_P$ that can be factored.

The advantage of the tree algorithm is that only $N_P \lg(N_P)$ messages with 512 updates per message are sent during each iteration of the tree RandomAccess algorithm, which is $N_P/\lg(N_P)$ fewer messages than the spray algorithm. The trade-off is that while the spray algorithm sends $8192 N_P$ bytes per iteration, the tree algorithm sends $4096 N_P \lg(N_P)$ updates per iteration. Thus, while the tree sends fewer messages, it has to send $2/\lg(N_P)$ more bytes of data. Normally, sending more data should take longer. However, if the messages are small, the time to send is dominated by the latency of the network. In this instance, the time to send a 1-byte message will be nearly the same as sending a 4096-byte message, resulting in a significant performance advantage for the tree algorithm.

**Algorithm 9.3. Parallel RandomAccess tree.**
Line 9 initializes values that will be used in the tree algorithm. Line 10 starts the while loop that will proceed until all the updates have been routed to their correct $P_{ID}$. Line 12 computes the $P_{ID}$ to swap data with. Line 13 computes the $P_{ID}$ used to split $\mathbf{r}$ into high and low values in lines 15 and 16. Lines 17–24 send and receive the high and low values based on whether $P_{ID}$ is greater than or less than $P_{pair}$. Lines 26 and 27 perform the update on the local part of $\mathbf{x}$.

PARALLELRANDOMACCESSTREE($\mathbf{x} : \mathbb{Z}^{P(N)}$)

1  $\mathbf{r}_0, \mathbf{r}, \mathbf{i} : \mathbb{Z}^{1024}$
2  $N_{up} = 4N \qquad N_b = N_{up}/1024$
3  $\mathbf{r}_0 = \text{RANDSTART}(\ (N_b/N_P)(1024 P_{ID} + 0 : 1023)\ )$
4  TIC
5  **for** $b = 1 : N_b$
6     **do**
7        $\mathbf{r}_0 = \text{RAND}(\mathbf{r}_0) \qquad \mathbf{r} = \mathbf{r}_0$
8        $tag = b \mod 32$
9        $P_{mid} = N_P/2 \qquad P_{mod} = N_P$
10       **while** $P_{mod} > 1$
11          **do**
12             $P_{pair} = (P_{ID} + P_{mid}) \mod P_{mod} + \lfloor P_{ID}/P_{mod} \rfloor P_{mod}$
13             $P_{split} = P_{mid} + \lfloor P_{ID}/P_{mod} \rfloor P_{mod}$
14             $\mathbf{i} = \text{AND}(\mathbf{r}, N - 1)$
15             $\mathbf{r}_{hi} = \mathbf{r}(\ \mathbf{i} \geq \mathbf{x}.loc_{P_{split}} < \langle 1 \rangle\ )$
16             $\mathbf{r}_{lo} = \mathbf{r}(\ \mathbf{i} < \mathbf{x}.loc_{P_{split}} < \langle 1 \rangle\ )$
17             **if** $P_{ID} < P_{pair}$
18                **do**
19                   SENDMSG($P_{pair}, tag, \mathbf{r}_{hi}$)
20                   $\mathbf{r} = \text{APPEND}(\mathbf{r}_{lo}, \text{RECVMSG}(P_{pair}, tag))$
21             **if** $P_{ID} > P_{pair}$
22                **do**
23                   SENDMSG($P_{pair}, tag, \mathbf{r}_{lo}$)
24                   $\mathbf{r} = \text{APPEND}(\mathbf{r}_{hi}, \text{RECVMSG}(P_{pair}, tag))$
25             $P_{mid} = P_{mid}/2 \qquad P_{mod} = P_{mod}/2$
26          $\mathbf{i} = \text{AND}(\mathbf{r}, N - 1) - \mathbf{x}.loc_{P_{ID}}\langle 1 \rangle - 1$
27          $\mathbf{x}.loc(\mathbf{i}) = \text{XOR}(\mathbf{x}.loc(\mathbf{i}), \mathbf{r})$
28  $t_{up} = \text{TOC}$

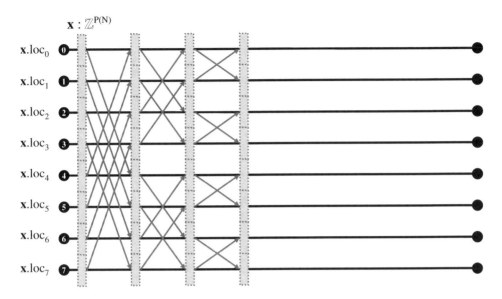

**Figure 9.2. RandomAccess tree communication pattern.**
Each $P_{ID}$ sends its upper or lower half updates to one $P_{ID}$. This process
is repeated until the updates are migrated to their appropriate $P_{ID}$,
resulting in $N_P \lg(N_P)$ messages with 512 updates per message.

## 9.3  Code

The next step is to write the RandomAccess program. The implementation consists
of two main parts. First is the control part of the code that sets the parameters,
initializes the data structures, and executes the core parallel algorithm. Second is
the core parallel algorithm, which can be either the spray algorithm or the tree
algorithm. The control portion of the parallel code is shown in Code Listing 9.1
(see `Examples/RandomAccess/pRandomAccess.m` for a complete listing). Keep in
mind that this same code is run by every MATLAB instance. The only difference
between these instances is that each has a unique $P_{ID}$ (i.e., `Pid`) that is used to
determine which parts of a distributed array belong to each MATLAB instance (i.e.,
$\mathbf{x}.loc$).

**Code Listing 9.1.  Parallel RandomAccess MATLAB program.**

```
 1  PARALLEL = 1;              .      % Turn distributed arrays on.
 2  VALIDATE = 1;                     % Turn verification on.
 3  ErrorRate = 0.01;                 % Set allowed error rate.
 4  lgN = 25; N = 2^lgN;              % Size main table X.
 5  lgNb = 10; Nb = 2^lgNb;           % Size of block.
 6  Nup = 4*N; Nblocks = Nup/Nb;      % Number of updates and blocks.
 7  mask = uint64(N-1);               % Mask that selects low bits.
 8  Xmap = 1;                         % Serial map.
 9  if PARALLEL
10     Xmap = map([1 Np],{},0:Np-1); % Map for table.
11  end
12  tic;
13     X = zeros(1,N,Xmap);                   % Allocate main table.
14     Xloc = uint64(global_ind(X,2)-1);      % Init local part.
15  Talloc = toc;
16  myX = global_block_range(X,2);            % Local index range.
17  allX = global_block_ranges(X,2);          % All index ranges.
18  myBLOCK = global_ind(zeros(1,Nblocks,Xmap),2); % Local blocks.
19  ranStarts = RandomAccessStarts((myBLOCK(1)-1)*Nb + ...
20     (0:(Nb-1))*length(myBLOCK) );          % Init random sequence.
21  tic;
22     sync = agg(zeros(1, Np, Xmap));        % Synchronize start.
23  Tlaunch = toc;
24  tempVALIDATE = VALIDATE; VALIDATE = 0; % Cache flag.
25  tic;
26     pRandomAccessSpray;       % Run spray algorithm.
27     %pRandomAccessTree;       % Run tree algorithm.
28  Trun = toc;
29  VALIDATE = tempVALIDATE;     % Put flag back.
30  if VALIDATE
31     tic;
32       pRandomAccessSpray;       % Run spray algorithm.
33       %pRandomAccessTree;       % Run tree algorithm.
34       Xloc0 = uint64(global_ind(X,2)-1); % True values.
35       Nerrors = length(find(Xloc ~= Xloc0)); % Compute errors.
36     Tvalidate = toc;
37  end
```

In the above program,

**Line 1** sets the `PARALLEL` flag, which turns on and off the distributed arrays.

**Line 2** sets the `VALIDATE` flag, which turns on and off the validation portion of the program. This flag is present because validation can significantly increase the run time of the program.

**Lines 3–7** set various parameters of the RandomAccess program.

**Lines 8–15** create the parallel map `Xmap`, allocate the distributed table `X`, and initialize the local part `Xloc` so that `X(i)=i-1`. This initialization is done using the `global_ind` function that returns the global index of each local element and is equivalent to setting $\mathbf{x}.loc(i) = \mathbf{x}.loc\langle i \rangle - 1$.

**Line 16** uses the `global_block_range` function to return the global indices of the first $(\mathbf{x}.loc\langle 1 \rangle)$ and last $(\mathbf{x}.loc\langle end \rangle)$ elements in the local part of `X`.

**Line 17** uses the `global_block_ranges` function to return an array containing the global indices of the first $(\mathbf{x}.loc\langle 1 \rangle)$ and last $(\mathbf{x}.loc\langle end \rangle)$ elements of all the local parts of `X` for all $P_{ID}$s. These indices will be used to determine which updates to send to which $P_{ID}$s.

**Lines 18–19** distribute the blocks of updates among the $P_{ID}$s so that each starts at the correct point in the random-number sequence.

**Line 22** uses the `agg` function to synchronize the $P_{ID}$s so that they start at approximately the same time. `agg` has each $P_{ID}$ send its part of a distributed array to $P_{ID} = 0$. A more aggressive `synch` can be performed using `agg_all`, which has each $P_{ID}$ send its part of a distributed array to all the other $P_{ID}$s.

**Lines 25–28** run and time the RandomAccess benchmark using either the spray algorithm or the tree algorithm.

**Lines 30–37** rerun the RandomAccess benchmark using either the spray algorithm or the tree algorithm with an error-free update mechanism, compare the results with correct values, and tally the number of errors.

The above code is a good example of how the distributed array programming environment can help with message passing. Specifically, operations like `global_block_range` and `global_block_ranges` can be very useful for determining which data to send where when one is using a hybrid programming model.

## 9.3.1 Spray code

The spray algorithm implementation is shown in Code Listing 9.2 (see `Examples/RandomAccess/pRandomAccessSpray.m` for a complete listing).

**Code Listing 9.2.  RandomAccess MATLAB spray algorithm.**

```
 1  ran = ranStarts;              % Init random sequence.
 2  tag = 0;                      % Init message tag.
 3  % Set optimal send and receive order.
 4  mySendOrder = circshift(
      [0:(Pid-1) (Pid+1):(Np-1)],[0,-Pid]);
 5  myRecvOrder = fliplr(
      circshift([0:(Pid-1) (Pid+1):(Np-1)], [0,-Pid]));
 6  for ib = myBLOCK              % Loop over my blocks.
 7     tag = mod(tag+1,32);       % Increment message tag.
 8     ran = RandomAccessRand(ran);   % Next random numbers.
 9     Xi = double(bitand(ran,mask))+1; % Compute global index.
10     for p = mySendOrder       % Find and send updates.
11       ranSend = ran((Xi>=allX(p+1,2))& (Xi<=allX(p+1,3)));
12       SendMsg(p,tag,ranSend );
13     end
14     ranRecv = ran( (Xi >= myX(1)) & (Xi <= myX(2)) );
15     for p = myRecvOrder       % Receive updates.
16       ranRecv = [ranRecv RecvMsg(p,tag)]; % Append.
17     end
18     Xi = double(bitand(ranRecv,mask))+1-(myX(1)-1); % Local Xi.
19     if (not(VALIDATE))        % Fast update.
20       Xloc(Xi) = bitxor(Xloc(i),ranRecv);
21     else                      % Slow error-free update.
22       for j=1:length(ranRecv)
23         Xloc(Xi(j)) = bitxor(Xloc(Xi(j)), ranRecv(j));
24       end
25     end
26  end
```

In the above program,

**Lines 4 and 5** compute the message send order and receive order so that each $P_{ID}$ is sending to a different destination in accordance with Figure 9.1.

**Lines 10–13** loop over each destination $P_{ID}$ and determine which updates to send to that $P_{ID}$ using the information in allX.

**Line 14** determines the updates to keep on the local $P_{ID}$ using the information in myX.

**Lines 15–17** loop over each source $P_{ID}$, receive the updates from that $P_{ID}$, and append them to ranRecv.

**Line 18** computes the global indices of the received updates and converts them to their corresponding local index in Xloc by subtracting the global index of the first element myX(1).

**Lines 19–26** perform the updates to Xloc using either a fast update scheme that may produce some errors or a slow update scheme that is error free.

The above code shows how to use the output of `global_block_range` and `global_block_ranges` to select data to send to processors. This is a fairly common function in a message passing program. In a pure message passing program, all the information in `allX` and `myX` would need to be computed by hand, based on $N$ and $N_P$. This is often complex and error-prone code. Using the distributed array support functions allows this information to be computed automatically in an error-free way while still allowing control of the message pattern.

### 9.3.2 Tree code

The tree algorithm implementation is shown in Code Listing 9.3 (see `Examples/RandomAccess/pRandomAccessTree.m` for a complete listing). The tree program mirrors the spray code in many respects. The primary differences are the following:

**Line 3** factors $N_P$ into a list of prime factors that are then used in each iteration of the tree algorithm.

**Line 9** initializes several values used for determining where to split the data into high and low sets of updates.

**Line 10** loops until the tree has been traversed.

**Line 14** computes the corresponding pair $P_{ID}$ so that this $P_{ID}$ will exchange data.

**Lines 17 and 18** split the updates into high and low sets.

**Lines 19–25** send the high/low set of updates to the pair $P_{ID}$ and then receive and append the low/high set updates.

Similar to the spray code, the tree code shows how to use the output of `global_block_range` and `global_block_ranges` to select data to send to various $P_{ID}$s.

**Code Listing 9.3.   RandomAccess MATLAB tree algorithm.**

```
1   ran = ranStarts;              % Init random sequence.
2   tag = 0;                      % Init message tag.
3   tree = factor(Np);            % Factor processors into a tree.
4   for ib = myBLOCK              % Loop over all update blocks.
5     tag = mod(tag+1,32);        % Increment message tag.
6     ran = RandomAccessRand(ran);   % Next random numbers.
7     ranRecv = ran;              % Init input.
8     % Initialize values for computing splits.
9     midP = Np ./ tree(1); modP = Np; k = 0;
10    while (modP > 1)
11      % Compute Pid to exchange info with.
12      pairPid = mod((Pid+midP),modP)+floor(Pid./modP).*modP;
13      % Compute Pid for splitting data.
14      splitPid = midP + floor(Pid./modP).*modP;
15      Xi = double(bitand(ranRecv,mask))+1; % Global index.
16      % Find values above and below split.
17      hi = ranRecv(Xi >= allX(splitPid+1,2));
18      lo = ranRecv(Xi < allX(splitPid+1,2));
19      if (Pid < pairPid)        % Exchange hi/lo data.
20        SendMsg(pairPid,tag,hi);
21        ranRecv = [lo RecvMsg(pairPid,tag)];
22      elseif (Pid > pairPid)
23        SendMsg(pairPid,tag,lo);
24        ranRecv = [hi RecvMsg(pairPid,tag)];
25      end
26      % Update values for computing splits.
27      midP = midP./tree(k+1); modP = modP./tree(k+1); k=k+1;
28    end
29    Xi = double(bitand(ranRecv,mask))+1-(myX(1)-1); % Local Xi.
30    if (not(VALIDATE))          % Fast update.
31      Xloc(i) = bitxor(Xloc(i),ranRecv);
32    else                        % Slow error-free update.
33      for j=1:length(ranRecv)
34        Xloc(Xi(j)) = bitxor(Xloc(Xi(j)), ranRecv(j));
35      end
36  end
```

### 9.3.3   Coding summary

Both the spray and tree implementations are good examples of how a hybrid distributed array and message passing program can be facilitated with the map-based programming approach. After the map Xmap is created, it is used to allocate the distributed array X and initialize its local part Xloc.

There are a number of properties of the map-based approach that can be observed in this code example:

- Code Impact. Converting the program from a serial to a parallel program using a hybrid approach results in a code that is significantly larger than the serial code. However, the hybrid code is significantly smaller than a purely message passing approach because all the array indexing information is provided by the distributed arrays.

- Serial code is preserved. By setting `PARALLEL=0`, there is no use of distributed arrays and the program can be run in serial without any supporting parallel libraries.

- Modest parallel library footprint. In addition to the usual distributed array functions `Np`, `Pid`, and `agg`, the program also uses the distributed array index functions `global_ind`, `global_block_range`, and `global_block_ranges`, as well as the core message passing functions `SendMsg` and `RecvMsg`. Eight parallel library functions are used in all, which is a higher number than used in a pure distributed array program.

- Scalable. The code can be run on any problem size such that $N$ is a power of 2 and for any values of $N_P$.

- Bounded communication. Because local variables and direct message passing are used, there is strict control of when communication takes place. In addition, the hybrid approach allows communication patterns that are far more complex than can be typically supported using only distributed arrays.

- Map dependence. A byproduct of the hybrid approach is that the code will run only using a block distributed map.

- Serial performance guarantee. Because the update operation is applied to local variables that are regular MATLAB numeric arrays, there is a guarantee that there is no hidden performance penalty when running these lines of code.

## 9.4 Debug

As mentioned earlier, parallel debugging brings up many challenges. The primary benefit of the map-based approach is that it lends itself to a well-defined code-debug-test process (see Table 2.2). A hybrid coding approach requires that this process be modified.

Step 1 runs the program in serial on the local machine with the table `X` constructed as an ordinary array (i.e., `PARALLEL=0`). This step ensures that the basic serial code is still correct. For this serial code to work, additional steps need to be taken with a pure distributed array code. First, all the array indexing functions need to provide valid results on nondistributed arrays. Second, all messaging code is written such that for $N_P = 1$ it will not be executed. In Code Listing 9.3, the variables `mySendOrder` and `myRecvOrder` are constructed so that they will be empty if $N_P = 1$, so their corresponding `for` loops will not be executed. Likewise, in Code Listing 9.3, the conditional statements `Pid < pairPid` and `Pid > pairPid` prevent messages from being sent when `Pid = pairPid`, which occurs when $N_P = 1$.

Step 2 runs the program in serial on the local machine with X as a distributed array (i.e., `PARALLEL=1`) and ensures the program works properly with distributed arrays as inputs. As in step 1, the code must be written so that no messaging is invoked when $N_P = 1$.

Step 3 runs the program in parallel on the local machine. This step will detect if the parallel maps that generate X and Xloc are correct. More importantly, this step will be the first time the messaging code is exercised. Of all the steps, this is the most important since message passing can easily produce many errors. The most common error occurs when a $P_{ID}$ fails to properly calculate correct send $P_{ID}$ or corresponding receive $P_{ID}$ for a message. Such an error typically results in a hung program because a $P_{ID}$ is waiting for a message that has never been sent. Another common error occurs if the contents of the message are incorrect. Using distributed array indexing functions applied to X for determining the message contents greatly reduces this class of errors.

Step 4 runs the program in parallel on the remote machine.

Step 5 runs the program in parallel on the remote machine but with a problem size of interest. Up to this point, all the testing should have been done on a small problem size. This step allows the performance on a real problem to be measured.

These steps essentially mirror those that were done during the "getting started" section, and each step tests something very specific about the parallel code. In addition to functionally debugging the program, the above process also can be used to optimize the performance of the code (see next section). The RandomAccess benchmark uses some additional coding practices to assist with debugging beyond the above steps.

The RandomAccess program prints the program parameters that describe the size of the problem $N$, the number of bytes required, and the number of updates performed. This step is done on every $P_{ID}$ of the program. Comparing these values by looking at the different output files from each $P_{ID}$ (i.e., MatMPI/*.out) is a powerful way to catch bugs.

RandomAccess also displays the allocation time and launch time for every $P_{ID}$. These times describe how long it takes before the program starts running. A signal that something is wrong early in the program is these values differing significantly across $P_{ID}$s.

Because RandomAccess is a benchmark, the performance of the execution is measured and reported in terms that relate back to the processor. If the performance values differ significantly across $P_{ID}$s, it can be an indication of a deeper problem in the program (e.g., very different array sizes being created).

Finally, the RandomAccess program has a correctness check that ensures the program is giving the proper results. In a real application, this check is usually not possible, but more approximate checks can be performed and these are very useful. For example, often the sign of the values in an array can be checked or the sum of the values in an array can be checked. Again, displaying these from every $P_{ID}$ is useful because it can highlight errors that are dependent on the $P_{ID}$.

## 9.5  Test

As will become apparent, RandomAccess is a good example of a program whose performance does not increase with increasing $N_P$. In fact, RandomAccess is designed to highlight communication limitations in a wide range of computing architectures. For these reasons, RandomAccess is worthwhile to study because it highlights computations that are fundamentally difficult to run well in parallel. In addition, RandomAccess is a very good program for exploring the performance implications of different messaging algorithms, specifically, how to trade off message size versus the number of messages.

### 9.5.1  Multicore performance

Testing a parallel program—assuming that it has been debugged and is giving the right answers—mainly involves looking at how long it took to run and seeing if it is performing as expected. Most of the performance data necessary to conduct this analysis was collected in the "getting started" section (see Table 9.1). In addition, Table 9.1 includes the multicore performance on an eight-core system for both the spray and tree algorithms.

**Table 9.1. Multicore RandomAccess performance.**
Relative allocation time, absolute launch time, relative execution, and relative performance for the RandomAccess benchmark using the spray and tree algorithms on an eight-core processor. All values are normalized to column 2 in which $N_P = 1$ with the distributed arrays turned off (`PARALLEL=0`). Columns 3–6 are the values with distributed arrays turned on (`PARALLEL=1`). The notation 1*8 means that $N_P = 8$, and all $P_{ID}$s were run on the same processing node with the same shared memory.

| Multicore processors: | 1 | 1*1 | 1*2 | 1*4 | 1*8 |
|---|---|---|---|---|---|
| **Spray algorithm** | | | | | |
| Relative allocation time | 1 | 1.0 | 0.88 | 0.58 | 0.41 |
| Launch time (sec) | 0 | 0 | 1.28 | 1.34 | 1.66 |
| Relative execution time | 1 | 1.0 | 11 | 24 | 48 |
| Relative GUPS | 1 | 1.0 | 1/11 | 1/24 | 1/48 |
| **Tree algorithm** | | | | | |
| Relative allocation time | 1 | 1.0 | 0.57 | 0.52 | 0.30 |
| Launch time (sec) | 0 | 0 | 1.75 | 1.94 | 1.65 |
| Relative execution time | 1 | 1.0 | 10 | 17 | 17 |
| Relative GUPS | 1 | 1.0 | 1/10 | 1/17 | 1/17 |

The first test is to compare the performance of running the program using $N_P = 1$ with distributed arrays turned off (`PARALLEL=0`) and distributed arrays turned on (`PARALLEL=1`). Columns 2 and 3 in Table 9.1 provide this data. In this case, the performance differences are negligible and indicate that distributed arrays do not incur a performance penalty. If using distributed arrays with $N_P = 1$ slows things down significantly, then this must be addressed. It is very difficult to get any benefit with $N_P > 1$ if the $N_P = 1$ case is slower than the base serial code. Working only on the local parts of distributed arrays almost guarantees the performance will be the same as for the case in which distributed arrays are not being used.

Columns 3–5 of Table 9.1 show the parallel performance of the code on a multicore system. The relative allocation time rows show that allocation generally decreases with increasing $N_P$ because each $P_{ID}$ need only allocate $N/N_P$ data elements. The measured decrease in allocation time is not linear with $N_P$ because there are some overheads associated with allocation. Typically, allocation time will not be a large fraction of the overall computation. However, in cases in which $N_P$ is large, these overheads can become important; so it is always good to measure allocation time and make sure it is reasonable.

The launch time row shows a generally increasing launch time with $N_P$. Ideally, it would be a constant value that is independent of $N_P$. However, depending upon the underlying launch mechanism, this time can be an increasing function of $N_P$. Typically, launch time will not be a large fraction of the overall computation, but it can easily become significant when $N_P$ is large. For example, suppose launch time was proportional to $N_P$ and each additional $P_{ID}$ added 1 second. If $N_P = 100$, then the launch time would be 100 seconds. If this is the Amdahl fraction of the program, then the program will need to run for at least $N_P^2$ seconds in order to achieve a 50x speedup over the serial case.

The most interesting rows are the relative execution time and relative GUPS rows. Since $N$ and the number of updates performed are the same, these two rows are simply inverses of each other; i.e., the relative performance is inversely proportional to the relative execution time. The first thing to note is the large drops in performance when going from $N_P = 1$ to $N_P = 2$. This is typical of the RandomAccess benchmark when it is run in parallel using a message passing system. Recall that RandomAccess sends small messages, and the time to send these messages can easily dominate the calculation. Thus, RandomAccess is a very good example of the kind of application that is very difficult to speed up on a parallel system and that typically requires special communication hardware to do so.

Although the RandomAccess benchmark does not scale well, its performance can be improved. Specifically, the spray algorithm shows performance that decreases linearly with $N_P$. The tree algorithm, which sends fewer larger messages, does not slow down as much. In fact, for $N_P = 8$, the tree algorithm delivers nearly 2.8x the performance as the spray algorithm delivers. Recall that the predicted relative performance increase of the tree algorithm was $N_P/\lg(N_P) = 2.7$.

## 9.5.2   Multinode performance

The results for running both the spray and tree algorithms on a multinode system are shown in Table 9.2.

The relative allocation time is similar for both the spray and tree algorithms and decreases with $N_P$. The decrease in allocation is larger and more consistent than in the multicore case. In the multicore case, allocation is coming out of the

**Table 9.2. Multinode RandomAccess performance.**
Relative allocation time, absolute launch time, relative execution time, and relative performance for the RandomAccess benchmark using the spray and tree algorithms on a 16-node system. All values are normalized to column 2 in which $N_P = 1$ with the distributed arrays turned off (PARALLEL=0). Columns 3–7 are the values with distributed arrays turned on (PARALLEL=1). The notation 16*1 means that $N_P = 16$, and each $P_{ID}$ was run on a separate processing node with a separate memory.

| Multinode processors: | 1 | 1*1 | 2*1 | 4*1 | 8*1 | 16*1 |
|---|---|---|---|---|---|---|
| **Spray algorithm** | | | | | | |
| Relative allocation time | 1 | 1.0 | 0.79 | 0.43 | 0.25 | 0.16 |
| Launch time (sec) | 0 | 0 | 7.89 | 11.8 | 9.9 | 12.3 |
| Relative execution time | 1 | 1.0 | 14 | 16 | 18 | 19 |
| Relative GUPS | 1 | 1.0 | 1/14 | 1/16 | 1/18 | 1/19 |
| **Tree algorithm** | | | | | | |
| Relative allocation time | 1 | 1.0 | 0.79 | 0.42 | 0.25 | 0.17 |
| Launch time (sec) | 0 | 0 | 7.77 | 11.8 | 9.85 | 9.91 |
| Relative execution time | 1 | 1.0 | 12 | 11 | 8.6 | 5.5 |
| Relative GUPS | 1 | 1.0 | 1/12 | 1/11 | 1/8.6 | 1/5.5 |

same memory system, and contention for this resource can increase the allocation time and result in greater variation. Allocation on a multinode system is completely independent and is faster and more deterministic than on one node.

The launch time on a multinode system tends to increase with $N_P$ and shows a lot of variation. Furthermore, the launch time is much longer than in the multicore case because separate systems must be contacted over a network to start each $P_{ID}$.

Relative execution time and relative performance for both the spray and tree algorithm do not show any improvement for $N_P > 1$. As in the multicore case, this low performance is fundamental to the RandomAccess benchmark. However, the multinode system's spray and tree performances are better than those for the multicore system. This is because on a multicore system there is some contention for the communication system, while in the multinode case the communication systems are separate. The overall performance of all cases is shown in Figure 9.3. The performance can be broken into three categories. The multicore spray algorithm shows a steady decrease in performance with $N_P$, and it is unlikely that this approach will result in any performance benefit. The multicore tree and multinode spray show flat performance with $N_P$. This performance is better than the multicore spray performance, but is also unlikely to result in any performance benefit, except that on a multinode system it is possible to run with larger values of $N$ than on a single node system. Finally, the multinode tree algorithm shows increasing performance with $N_P$, and for a sufficient value of $N_P$, it will be faster than the $N_P = 1$ case. These factors explain why all competitive implementations of the RandomAccess benchmark use a variation of the tree algorithm and are run on very large multinode systems.

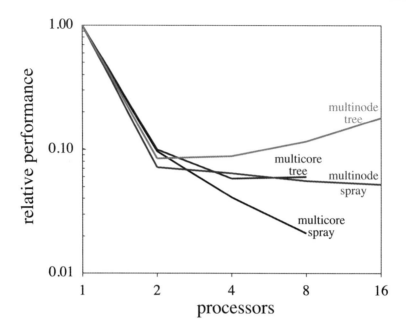

**Figure 9.3. Parallel RandomAccess relative performance.**
Relative performance of the spray and tree algorithms on multicore and
multinode systems.


Integrating all the RandomAccess performance data together allows the following conclusions to be drawn for running applications of this kind on clusters of
multicore processing nodes. First, RandomAccess is fundamentally limited by the
latency of the underlying hardware system, and the $N_P > 1$ will tend to run slower
than the $N_P = 1$. Second, running multiple $P_{ID}$s $(1*N_P)$ on a single processing
node may not give much benefit. Thus, "scaling up" may not be the best approach.
Third, performance may increase and eventually pass the $N_P = 1$ when using the
tree algorithm on multiple nodes $(N_P*1)$. Thus, "scaling out" appears to be the
most beneficial approach.

# References

[Dongarra and Luszczek 2005] Jack Dongarra and Piotr Luszczek, Introduction to
    the HPC Challenge Benchmark Suite, Technical Report UT-CS-05-544, Uni-
    versity of Tennessee, 2005.

# Chapter 10

# Fast Fourier Transform

## Summary

The Fast Fourier Transform (FFT) is important to a wide range of applications, from signal processing to spectral methods for solving partial differential equations. The computationally challenging nature of the FFT has made it a staple of benchmarks for decades. The FFT benchmark is a simple program that stresses both the local memory bandwidth and the network bandwidth of a parallel computer. It is typical of a class of problems that can perform well on canonical parallel computers, provided there is sufficient network bandwidth. The communication pattern of this benchmark is complicated, but it is well matched to distributed arrays and can be implemented succinctly and efficiently.

The FFT was introduced in Chapter 7 as a benchmark for measuring the bandwidth between processors on a network [Dongarra and Luszczek 2005]. FFT is also a good example of a communication-intensive parallel application with complex communication patterns and allows the demonstration of a number of useful parallel coding techniques, in particular, how to write a distributed array program that succinctly and efficiently implements these complicated patterns.

The FFT benchmark creates a complex valued vector $\mathbf{x} : \mathbb{C}^N$ and performs the FFT algorithm on this vector to produce another complex valued vector $\mathbf{z} : \mathbb{C}^N$. The FFT is an efficient way to implement the Discrete Fourier Transform (DFT), which is given by the formula

$$\mathbf{z}(k) = \sum_{j=1}^{N} \mathbf{x}(j) \exp[-2\pi\sqrt{-1}(k-1)(j-1)/N]$$

The DFT "tests" the vector $\mathbf{x}$ for its "closeness" to the wave "$k$" by multiplying $\mathbf{x}$ by the wave given by $\exp[-2\pi\sqrt{-1}(k-1)(j-1)/N]$. The resulting product is then summed and the value is stored in $\mathbf{z}(k)$. As written, the DFT performs $5N^2$ operations. The FFT accelerates the DFT by recognizing that certain products can be reused for calculating multiple values $\mathbf{z}$, reducing the total number of operations to $5N \lg(N)$.

The dramatic reduction in operations provided by the FFT comes at the cost of creating a complex data movement pattern. A serial FFT algorithm is usually limited by the memory bandwidth. Likewise, a parallel FFT algorithm is usually limited by the aggregate bandwidth or bisection bandwidth of the communication network. The FFT provides an excellent illustration of the kinds of complex communication patterns that can perform well on canonical parallel computers, provided there is sufficient network bandwidth. This chapter illustrates both coding and optimization approaches for efficiently implementing the FFT algorithm.

## 10.1  Getting started

To run the program, start MATLAB and go to the Examples/FFT directory (i.e., type cd Examples/FFT). Edit the file pFFT.m and set PARALLEL=0. At the prompt, type

        pRandomAccess

Because FFT is a benchmark, it will produce a large volume of performance data similar to

        Np                                      = 1
        Pid                                     = 0
        Distributed vector size                 = 33554432 words
        Distributed vector size (bytes)         = 536870912
        Local vector size (bytes)               = 536870912
        Allocation Time (sec)                   = 26.3669
        Launch Time (sec)                       = 0.025377
        Compute time (sec)                      = 16.0619
        Communication time (sec)                = 0.035599
        Run time (sec)                          = 16.0975
        Performance (Gigaflops)                 = 0.26056
        Bandwidth (Gigabytes/sec)               = 45.2432
        Max local error                         = 3.5046e-17
        Max error                               = 3.5046e-17
        Validation Passed

The above information can be broken up into four categories. First are the program parameters that describe the problem: $N_P$, $P_{ID}$, size of the problem $N$, and number of bytes required. The second category contains the array initialization times and launch times, which describe how long it takes before the program starts running. The third category contains the compute, communication, and run times and the resulting performance derived from these times. The fourth category is the validation values. These outputs will be discussed further in the Test subsection. For now, edit the file pFFT.m and set PARALLEL=1 (to turn on the parallel parts of the code) and VALIDATE = 0 (to shorten the execution time). Run pFTT again using each of the following commands:

```
eval(pRUN('pFFT',1,{}))
eval(pRUN('pFFT',2,{}))
eval(pRUN('pFFT',4,{}))
```

These commands run the FFT program with $N_P = 1$, 2, and 4. Running on a parallel computer will produce performance values that look similar to those in Table 10.1 (see Test subsection).

**Important Note**: The last argument to the pRUN command determines which parallel computer the program will be run on. You may need to obtain the proper setting from your system administrator; see the book website (http://www.siam.org/ KepnerBook) for details. Setting the last argument to {} runs multiple copies of the program on your local machine and may result in different performance values from those shown in Table 9.1.

## 10.2   Parallel design

The specification of a parallel FFT benchmark uses the property that a lower-dimensional FFT can be computed using a combination of higher-dimensional FFTs. For example, the FFT of a one-dimensional vector can be computed using the FFT of a two-dimensional matrix. Likewise, the FFT of a matrix consists of performing an FFT of the rows followed by an FFT of the columns (or vice versa). Thus, the two-dimensional FFT of an $N_P \times M$ matrix can be computed as follows:

$\mathbf{X} : \mathbb{C}^{N_P \times M}$
**for** $i = 1 : N_P$
$\qquad$ **do** $\qquad \mathbf{X}(i, :) = \text{FFT}(\mathbf{X}(i, :))$
**for** $j = 1 : M$
$\qquad$ **do** $\qquad \mathbf{X}(:, j) = \text{FFT}(\mathbf{X}(:, j))$

A parallel two-dimensional FFT can be implemented fairly simply with distributed arrays as follows:

$\mathbf{X} : \mathbb{C}^{P(N_P) \times M}, \mathbf{Z} : \mathbb{C}^{N_P \times P(M)}$
$\mathbf{X}.loc(1, :) = \text{FFT}(\mathbf{X}.loc(1, :))$
$\mathbf{Z} = \mathbf{X}$
**for** $j = 1 : size(\mathbf{Z}.loc(1, :))$
$\qquad$ **do** $\qquad \mathbf{Z}.loc(:, j) = \text{FFT}(\mathbf{Z}.loc(:, j))$

In the above algorithm fragment, the input is a distributed matrix $\mathbf{X}$ distributed in the second dimension, and the output is a distributed matrix $\mathbf{Z}$ distributed in the first dimension. The row and the column FFTs are thus local operations and can simply leverage an existing serial one-dimensional FFT. Transforming the data between these two distributions is done via the assignment statement: $\mathbf{Z} = \mathbf{X}$.

A parallel one-dimensional FFT algorithm follows a similar form to the parallel two-dimensional FFT algorithm with a few additions. First, the order of the input and the output must be rearranged. Second, the output of the row FFTs must be multiplied by a set of "twiddle" factors prior to performing the column FFTs. The

parallel one-dimensional FFT algorithm is shown in Algorithm 10.1 (see caption
for details). Note: A constraint of this particular parallel one-dimensional FFT
algorithm is that $N$ be evenly divisible by $N_P^2$.

**Algorithm 10.1. Parallel FFT.**
Computes the FFT of an $N$ element complex vector using a parallel
two-dimensional FFT. Line 1 computes the second dimension of the
corresponding matrix. Line 2 allocates two distributed matrices. Line 3
computes the local twiddle factors based on $P_{ID}$. Line 4 copies the local
part of the vector into the local part of the distributed matrix. Line 5
redistributes the matrix. Line 6 FFTs the rows and multiplies by the
twiddle factors. Line 7 redistributes the data. Lines 8 and 9 FFT the
columns. Line 10 redistributes the data and Line 11 copies the local
part of the matrix to the local part of the vector.

$\mathbf{z} : \mathbb{C}^{P(N)} = \mathrm{PARALLELFFT1D}(\mathbf{x} : \mathbb{C}^{P(N)})$

$\quad 1 \quad M = N/N_P$
$\quad 2 \quad \mathbf{X} : \mathbb{C}^{P(N_P) \times M}, \mathbf{Z} : \mathbb{C}^{N_P \times P(M)}$
$\quad 3 \quad \mathbf{w} = \exp[-2\pi\sqrt{-1}P_{ID}/N \, (1:M)]$
$\quad 4 \quad \mathbf{Z}.loc = \mathbf{x}.loc$
$\quad 5 \quad \mathbf{X} = \mathbf{Z}$
$\quad 6 \quad \mathbf{X}.loc(1,:) = \mathbf{w} \, .* \, \mathrm{FFT}(\mathbf{X}.loc(1,:))$
$\quad 7 \quad \mathbf{Z} = \mathbf{X}$
$\quad 8 \quad \mathbf{for} \; j = 1 : size(\mathbf{Z}.loc(1,:))$
$\quad 9 \qquad \mathbf{do} \quad \mathbf{Z}.loc(:,j) = \mathrm{FFT}(\mathbf{Z}.loc(:,j))$
$\quad 10 \quad \mathbf{X} = \mathbf{Z}$
$\quad 11 \quad \mathbf{z}.loc = \mathbf{X}.loc$

The parallel FFT is a good example of an algorithm with complicated data
movements that are a good match to distributed arrays. This data movement
pattern consists of five steps illustrated in Figure 10.1. First, the input data is
reshaped into a matrix by copying the local part of the distributed vector $\mathbf{x} : \mathbb{C}^{P(N)}$
to the local part of the distributed matrix $\mathbf{Z} : \mathbb{C}^{N_P \times P(M)}$. Second, the data is
redistributed across $P_{ID}$s by assigning $\mathbf{Z}$ to the distributed matrix $\mathbf{X} : \mathbb{C}^{P(N_P) \times M}$.
Now each row is local to a $P_{ID}$ and the row FFT can be performed using a serial
FFT call. Third, the data is redistributed back to $\mathbf{Z}$ so that each column is local
to a $P_{ID}$ and the column FFT can be performed. Fourth, data is redistributed a
third time into $\mathbf{X}$. Fifth, the data is reshaped by copying the local part of $\mathbf{X}$ to the
local part of the distributed vector $\mathbf{z} : \mathbb{C}^{P(N)}$.

The goal of the FFT benchmark is to measure the ability of the computer to
perform a large FFT. The performance is measured in gigaflops, which is computed
via

$$\text{Gigaflops}: \quad 5N\lg(N)/t_{run}/10^9$$

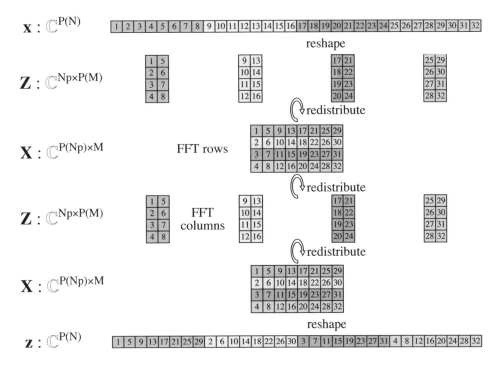

**Figure 10.1. Parallel FFT design.**
The FFT of a 32-element vector with $N_P = 4$ is shown. Values inside
each vector or matrix indicate the index of that value relative to the
input vector. The one-dimensional parallel FFT performs a number of
reshape and redistribute operations so that the data elements are in the
proper order to use a parallel two-dimensional FFT.

where $t_{run} = t_{comp} + t_{comm}$ is the sum of the computation and communication
time. $t_{comp}$ is computed by timing lines 6, 8, and 9 in Algorithm 10.1. $t_{comm}$ is
computed by timing lines 5, 7, and 10 in Algorithm 10.1. The parallel FFT requires
a lot of communication. In fact, the entire vector is redistributed three times during
the course of the algorithm. Thus, the FFT is also a good measure of the overall
bandwidth of the system, which can be measured in gigabytes/sec via

$$\text{Gigabytes/sec}: \quad 48N/t_{comm}/10^9$$

Validation is a critical part of any benchmark program. If the values of the
vector $\mathbf{x}$ are initialized to a wave with integer frequency $k$,

$$\mathbf{x} = \exp[-2\pi\sqrt{-1}k/N \ (1:M)]$$

then the FFT of $\mathbf{x}$ can be approximated as $\tilde{\mathbf{z}}(k) = N$ and zero everywhere else. The
expected error rate will be a function of the machine precision and accuracy of the

approximation $\tilde{\mathbf{z}}$ and can be computed as

$$err = \max(|\mathbf{z} - \tilde{\mathbf{z}}|)/N^{3/2}$$

The factor of $N^{3/2}$ is composed of two factors: first, a factor of $N$ to scale the result to a relative error since the maximum value is $N$, and second, a factor of $N^{1/2}$ to account for the error of the approximation to the true result because the FFT of a sine wave will have very small peaks around the central peak (sometimes called sidelobes) that are approximately $N^{1/2}$. For a typical machine precision, $err < 10^{-10}$ is acceptable.

## 10.3   Code

The next step is to write the FFT program. The key lines of the code are shown in Code Listing 10.1 (see `Examples/FFT/pFFT.m` for a complete listing). Keep in mind that this same code is run by every MATLAB instance. The only difference between these instances is that each has a unique $P_{ID}$ (i.e., `Pid`) used to determine which parts of a distributed array belong to each MATLAB instance (i.e., x.*loc*). In the FFT program,

   **Line 1** sets the `PARALLEL` flag, which turns on and off the distributed arrays.

   **Line 2** sets the vector size and computes the size of the corresponding matrix. This implementation requires that the vector size $N$ be evenly divisible by $N_P^2$.

   **Lines 3–8** create the parallel map `Xmap`, allocate the distributed vector `X`, and initialize `X` to a set of random complex numbers. The local part is then retrieved. In validation mode (not shown), the vector can be initialized to a known input.

   **Line 9** creates an empty distributed `Xshell` array by using `put_local` to assign a constant to `X`. `Xshell` contains all the parallel information of an $N$ element vector but does not take up the storage for the elements.

   **Lines 10, 13, 16, 20, 23, 26, and 30** start and stop the timers for the computation and communication sections of the program.

   **Line 11** reshapes the local $M$ element vector into an $N_P \times M/N_P$ matrix.

   **Line 12** inserts the matrix into the corresponding $N_P \times M$ distributed matrix.

   **Line 14** redistributes the data using the `transpose_grid` function by transposing the processor grid in the map of the distributed matrix. For example, it would take a matrix with the map `map([1 Np],{},0:Np-1)` and convert it to a matrix with the map `map([Np 1],{},0:Np-1)`. Using this command is more efficient than using the more general assignment statement between distributed arrays.

   **Lines 17–19** FFT the rows of the matrix, multiply by the twiddle factors, and insert the results back into the distributed matrix.

   **Line 21** redistributes a second time using the `transpose_grid` function.

   **Lines 24–25** FFT the columns of the matrix and insert the results back into the distributed matrix `X`.

   **Line 27** redistributes the data a third time using the `transpose_grid` function.

   **Line 29** inserts the $1 \times M$ local part of the distributed matrix `X` into the local part of the $1 \times N$ distributed vector `Xshell` to create an output vector `X` with the same size and distribution as the input vector.

**Code Listing 10.1.   Parallel FFT MATLAB program.**

```
1   PARALLEL=1;                    % Turn parallelism on and off.
2   N = 2^24; M = N/Np;            % Set vector/matrix dimensions.
3   Xmap = 1;                      % Serial map.
4   if PARALLEL
5     Xmap = map([1 Np],{},0:Np-1);% Parallel map.
6   end
7   X = complex(rand(1,N,Xmap),rand(1,N,Xmap));   % Create X.
8   Xloc = local(X);               % Get local part.
9   Xshell = put_local(X,0);       % Create an empty X.
10  tic;
11    Xloc = reshape(Xloc,Np,M/Np);   % Reshape local part.
12    X = put_local(zeros(Np,M,Xmap),Xloc);
13  Tcomp = toc; tic;
14    X = transpose_grid(X);       % Redistribute.
15    Xloc = local(X);
16  Tcomm = toc; tic;
17    Xloc = fft(Xloc,[],2);       % FFT rows.
18    Xloc = omega .* Xloc;        % Multiply by twiddle factors.
19    X = put_local(X,Xloc);
20  Tcomp = Tcomp + toc; tic;
21    X = transpose_grid(X);       % Redistribute.
22    Xloc = local(X);
23  Tcomm = Tcomm + toc; tic;
24    Xloc = fft(Xloc,[],1);       % FFT columns.
25    X = put_local(X,Xloc);
26  Tcomp = Tcomp + toc; tic;
27    X = transpose_grid(X);       % Redistribute.
28    Xloc = local(X);
29    X = put_local(Xshell,Xloc);% Insert into vector.
30  Tcomm = Tcomm + toc;
```

The above code is a good example of how the distributed array programming environment can implement complicated data-movement patterns. Specifically, operations like transpose_grid combined with reshape and put_local allow data redistribution to occur in an efficient manner with a clear understanding of when an operation is strictly local and when communication will take place.

A number of properties of the map-based approach can be observed in this code example:

- Code Impact. Converting the program from a serial to a parallel program results in a code that is somewhat larger than the serial code. The majority of this code increase is from using a two-dimensional FFT-based approach that allows the row and column FFTs to be performed locally. Converting the two-dimensional FFT-based serial program to a parallel program requires only a nominal increase in code.

- Serial code is preserved. By setting `PARALLEL=0`, there is no use of distributed arrays and the program can be run in serial without any supporting parallel libraries.

- Modest parallel library footprint. In addition to the usual distributed array functions `Np`, `local`, and `put_local`, the program uses only the special `transpose_grid` redistribution function for performance reasons. Four parallel library functions are used in all, which is typical of a distributed array program.

- Scalable. The code can be run on any problem size such that $N$ is evenly divisible by $N_P^2$. This constraint can be relaxed with some additional code to handle the boundary conditions.

- Bounded communication. Distributed arrays are used directly only when communication is required. Otherwise, all operations are performed on local variables.

- Map dependence. This particular algorithm requires that the input and output have $\times P()$ map.

- Serial performance guarantee. The FFT operation is applied to local variables that are regular MATLAB numeric arrays; there is a guarantee that there is no hidden performance penalty when running these lines of code.

## 10.4  Debug

As mentioned earlier, parallel debugging brings up many challenges. The primary benefit of the map-based approach is that it lends itself to a well-defined code-debug-test process (see Table 2.2).

Step 1 runs the program in serial on the local machine with the vector `X` constructed as an ordinary array (i.e., `PARALLEL=0`). This ensures that the basic serial code is still correct. For this serial code to work, the parallel library provides serial versions of `local`, `put_local`, and `transpose_grid`. For example, the statement `Xloc = local(X)` simply assigns X to Xloc when X is a nondistributed array.

Step 2 runs the program in serial on the local machine with `X` as a distributed array (i.e., `PARALLEL=1`) and ensures the program works properly with distributed arrays as inputs.

Step 3 runs the program in parallel on the local machine. This step will detect if the parallel maps that generate `X` and `Xloc` are correct. More importantly, this step will be the first time the communication is exercised. Of all the steps, this is the most important since communication can easily produce many errors. The most common error occurs when the map of an array is different from what it is assumed to be. This situation can often be detected by looking at the sizes of the local parts and recognizing that the sizes are not consistent with the desired mapping.

Step 4 runs the program in parallel on the remote machine.

Step 5 runs the program in parallel on the remote machine but with a problem size of interest. Up to this point, all the testing should have been done on a small problem size. This step allows the performance on a real problem to be measured.

These steps essentially mirror those that were done during the "getting started" section, and each step tests something very specific about the parallel code. In addition to functionally debugging the program, the above process also can be used to optimize the performance of the code (see next section). The FFT benchmark uses some additional coding practices to assist with debugging beyond the above steps.

The FFT program prints the program parameters that describe the size of the problem $N$, the number of bytes required, and the size of Xloc. This step is done on every $P_{ID}$ of the program. Comparing these values by looking at the different output files from each $P_{ID}$ (i.e., MatMPI/*.out) is a powerful way to catch bugs. FFT also displays the allocation time and launch time for every $P_{ID}$. These times describe how long it takes before the program starts running. A signal that something is wrong early in the program is these values differing significantly across $P_{ID}$s.

Because FFT is a benchmark, the performance of the execution is measured and reported in terms that relate back to the processor. FFT further breaks these times up into computation time and communication time. If the performance values differ significantly across $P_{ID}$s, there may be a deeper problem in the program (e.g., very different array sizes being created).

Finally, the FFT program has a correctness check that ensures the program is giving the proper results. In a real application, this check is usually not possible, but more approximate checks can be performed and these are very useful. For example, often either the sign of the values in an array can be checked or the sum of the values in an array can be checked. Again, displaying these from every $P_{ID}$ is useful because it can highlight errors that are dependent on the $P_{ID}$.

## 10.5   Test

FFT is a good example of a program whose performance does increase with increasing $N_P$, provided there is sufficient communication bandwidth. FFT is frequently used as measure of the bandwidth capability of a parallel computing system.

### 10.5.1   Multicore performance

Testing a parallel program—assuming that it has been debugged and is giving the right answers—mainly involves looking at how long it took to run and seeing if it is performing as expected. Most of the performance data necessary to conduct this analysis was collected in the "getting started" section. Table 10.1 shows the multicore performance on an eight-core system.

The first test is to compare the performance of running the program using $N_P = 1$ with distributed arrays turned off (PARALLEL=0) and distributed arrays turned on (PARALLEL=1). Columns 2 and 3 in Table 10.1 provide this data. In this case, the performance differences are negligible and indicate that distributed arrays

**Table 10.1. Multicore FFT performance.**
Absolute launch time, relative allocation, computation, communication, and run times, as well as the relative performance for the FFT benchmark using an eight-core processor.  All values are normalized to column 2 in which $N_P = 1$ with the distributed arrays turned off (`PARALLEL=0`).  Columns 3–6 are the values with distributed arrays turned on (`PARALLEL=1`).  The notation 1*8 means that $N_P = 8$, and all $P_{ID}$s were run on the same processing node with the same shared memory.

| Multicore processors: | 1 | 1*1 | 1*2 | 1*4 | 1*8 |
|---|---|---|---|---|---|
| Launch time (sec) | 0 | 0.0 | 1.23 | 1.80 | 1.57 |
| Relative allocation time | 1 | 1.0 | 0.79 | 0.54 | 0.42 |
| Relative compute time | 1 | 1.0 | 0.41 | 0.25 | 0.07 |
| Relative comm time | | | 0.99 | 0.33 | 0.30 |
| Relative execution time | 1 | 1.0 | 1.41 | 0.58 | 0.37 |
| Relative performance | 1 | 1.0 | 0.71 | 1.72 | 2.70 |
| Relative bandwidth | | | 1 | 3.00 | 3.30 |

do not incur a performance penalty. If using distributed arrays with $N_P = 1$ slows things down significantly, then this must be addressed. It is very difficult to get any benefit with $N_P > 1$ if the $N_P = 1$ case is slower than the base serial code. Working only on the local parts of distributed arrays almost guarantees the performance will be the same as when distributed arrays are not being used.

Columns 3–5 of Table 10.1 show the parallel performance of the code on a multicore system. The launch time row shows a generally increasing launch time with $N_P$. Ideally, it would be a constant value that is independent of $N_P$. However, depending upon the underlying launch mechanism, this time can be an increasing function of $N_P$. Typically, launch time will not be a large fraction of the overall computation, but it can easily become significant when $N_P$ is large. For example, suppose launch time was proportional to $N_P$ and each additional $P_{ID}$ added 1 second. If $N_P = 100$, then the launch time would be 100 seconds. If this is the Amdahl fraction of the program, then the program will need to run for at least $N_P^2$ seconds in order to achieve a 50x speedup over the serial case.

The relative allocation time row shows that allocation generally decreases with increasing $N_P$ because each $P_{ID}$ need only allocate $N/N_P$ data elements. The measured decrease in allocation time is not linear with $N_P$ because there are some overheads associated with allocation. Typically, allocation time will not be a large fraction of the overall computation. However, for cases in which $N_P$ is large, these overheads can become important, and so it is always good to measure allocation time and make sure it is reasonable.

The relative compute time generally decreases linearly with $N_P$ because each core is working on a smaller problem. The relative communication time is computed with respect to the $N_P = 1$ compute time. Thus, for $N_P = 2$, the relative communication time is equal to the compute time, resulting in a net decrease in overall performance compared to the $N_P = 1$ case. As $N_P$ increases, the communication time decreases and a net decrease in the relative compute time is observed.

The relative performance row indicates that a speedup of 2.7 with $N_P = 8$ is achieved. This is not unexpected given the large amount of communication that is incurred. In some instances, this performance improvement might be advantageous; in other circumstances, it may not be worth the added programming complexity. In general, the parallel FFT often falls in this middle performance regime.

The relative bandwidth row shows that as $N_P$ increases, the bandwidth among the processors increases. In fact, increasing the $N_P$ by a factor of 4 (i.e., going from $N_P = 2$ to $N_P$) results in a bandwidth increase of 3.3. This increase in bandwidth with $N_P$ is the only reason that the FFT achieves any parallel performance. If the bandwidth did not improve, then the overall communication time would remain nearly the same as the $N_P = 1$ computation time.

### 10.5.2   Multinode performance

The results for running the parallel FFT on a multinode system are shown in Table 10.2. Results are shown for both a fixed problem size ($N$ constant) and a scaled problem size ($N \propto N_P$). The fixed problem size is the same as in the multicore case. The scaled problem size is the same as in the multicore case for $N_P = 1$ but increases by 16 when $N_P = 16$. Increasing the overall problem size is often one of the advantages of a multinode system over a multicore system.

**Table 10.2. Multinode FFT performance.**
Absolute launch time, relative allocation, computation, communication, and run times, as well as the relative performance for the FFT benchmark using a 16-node system. Performance data are shown for a fixed problem size ($N$ constant) and a scaled problem size ($N \propto N_P$). All values are normalized to column 2 in which $N_P = 1$ with the distributed arrays turned off (PARALLEL=0). Columns 3–7 are the values with distributed arrays turned on (PARALLEL=1). The notation 16*1 means that $N_P = 16$, and each $P_{ID}$ was run on a separate processing node with a separate memory.

| Multinode processors: | 1 | 1*1 | 2*1 | 4*1 | 8*1 | 16*1 |
|---|---|---|---|---|---|---|
| **Fixed problem size** | | | | | | |
| Launch time (sec) | 0 | 0.0 | 10.21 | 9.57 | 11.36 | 10.03 |
| Relative allocation time | 1 | 1.0 | 0.82 | 0.61 | 0.51 | 0.39 |
| Relative compute time | 1 | 1.0 | 0.56 | 0.27 | 0.088 | 0.044 |
| Relative comm time | | | 1.01 | 0.63 | 0.41 | 0.29 |
| Relative execution time | 1 | 1.0 | 1.57 | 0.90 | 0.50 | 0.33 |
| Relative performance | 1 | 1.0 | 0.64 | 1.11 | 2.00 | 3.03 |
| Relative bandwidth | | | 1 | 1.51 | 2.42 | 3.53 |
| **Scaled problem size** | | | | | | |
| Relative performance | 1 | 1.0 | 0.62 | 1.08 | 2.08 | 3.92 |
| Relative bandwidth | | | 1 | 1.43 | 2.86 | 4.83 |

The launch time on a multinode system tends to increase with $N_P$ and shows a lot of variation. Furthermore, the launch time is much larger than in the multicore case because separate systems must be contacted over a network to start each $P_{ID}$. The relative allocation and compute times are similar for the multicore and multinode systems.

The communication time for $N_P = 8$ is higher on the multinode system than on the multicore system, resulting in slightly lower performance. The multinode system has a performance speedup of 2.02 versus 2.7 on the multicore system. However, the multinode system can be further scaled to $N_P = 16$, at which point the overall performance speedup is 3.03.

The multinode system also allows scaling the problem size. Interestingly, the performance increases with a scaled problem so that a speedup of 3.92 is seen with $N_P = 16$. This is primarily due to the operation count increasing more rapidly with problem size $O(N \lg(N))$ than the data communicated $O(N)$. In addition, the overall bandwidth increases because the messages being sent are larger and relatively less time is spent on communication latency. Thus, as the problem size grows, the overall performance will increase.

The performance of the multicore (fixed), multinode (fixed), and multinode (scaled) are shown in Figure 10.2. In all cases, the addition of communication re-

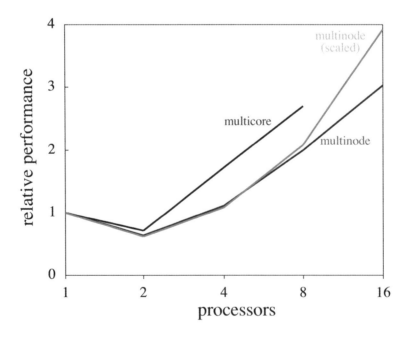

**Figure 10.2. Parallel FFT relative performance.**
Relative performance of the parallel FFT on multicore and multinode systems. The multinode performance for a scaled problem $(N \propto N_P)$ is also shown.

sults in a net decrease in performance for $N_P = 2$. As $N_P$ increases, the bandwidth increases and a net performance improvement is seen. In both the multicore (fixed) and multinode (fixed) cases, the slope of the performance suggests that increasing $N_P$ would provide additional performance. The multinode (scaled) shows an increasing performance slope with $N_P$.

Integrating all the FFT performance data together allows the following conclusions to be drawn for running applications of this kind on clusters of multicore processing nodes. First, FFT is fundamentally limited by the bandwidth of the underlying hardware system, and the $N_P > 1$ will tend to run slower than $N_P = 1$. Some performance benefit is seen for both multicore and multinode systems with fixed problem sizes. It would appear that greater performance benefit can be realized for multinode systems on scaled problems.

# References

[Dongarra and Luszczek 2005] Jack Dongarra and Piotr Luszczek, Introduction to the HPC Challenge benchmark suite, Technical Report UT-CS-05-544, University of Tennessee, 2005.

# Chapter 11

# High Performance Linpack

**Summary**

The HPL benchmark solves a dense linear system $\mathbf{Ax} = \mathbf{b}$ and is representative of a wide class of problems in computational linear algebra. The specification of HPL is simple, and serial implementations can be quite short. Efficient parallel HPL algorithms require complex two-dimensional block-cyclic data distributions that result in lengthy implementations. Furthermore, the communication pattern of HPL is difficult to implement with purely distributed arrays and requires a hybrid approach that combines distributed array programming with message passing. A simpler one-dimensional block algorithm is shown that is readily applied to a wide class of parallel linear algebra problems. HPL is useful for illustrating a number of advanced parallel programming concepts, such as overlapping computation with communication and critical path analysis.

High Performance Linpack (HPL) was introduced in Chapter 7 as a benchmark for measuring core processor performance [Dongarra and Luszczek 2005]. Fundamentally, it tests the ability of each processor in a parallel system to perform dense matrix multiplies. Most processors have dedicated hardware for supporting the vector dot products that are used in matrix multiply. An efficient HPL implementation can often achieve close to the theoretical peak performance of the system. In fact, HPL is often used to define the peak performance of the system and is the basis of the Top500 list (http://www.Top500.org) used to rate the largest computing systems in the world.

HPL is also a good example of a challenging parallel application with a complex communication pattern and allows the demonstration of a number of useful parallel coding techniques, in particular, how to write a hybrid program that uses distributed arrays for organizing communication but uses message passing to actually send the messages.

HPL creates a large random matrix $\mathbf{A} : \mathbb{R}^{N \times N}$ and corresponding random vector $\mathbf{b} : \mathbb{R}^N$ and solves for the vector $\mathbf{x} : \mathbb{R}^N$ in the linear system of equations

$$\mathbf{Ax} = \mathbf{b}$$

The HPL algorithm has a number of steps. First, the **A** is factored into a lower triangular matrix **L** and an upper triangular matrix **U** such that

$$\mathbf{LU} = \mathbf{A}$$

This common linear algebraic operation is referred to as "LU factorization" and is the heart of HPL. After **L** and **U** are obtained, **x** is solved for by using Gaussian elimination.

HPL typically performs $O(N^3)$ operations and communicates $O(N^2)$ data elements. Because the number of operations performed on each element is large and the operations can be done many at a time, HPL performance is limited by the speed of the processors. The speed of the communication network is typically less important for competitive parallel HPL implementations. However, competitive HPL implementations require block-cyclic distributions for $\mathbf{A} : \mathbb{R}^{P_{c(n)}(N \times N)}$, $\mathbf{b} : \mathbb{R}^{P_{c(n)}(N)}$, and $\mathbf{x} : \mathbb{R}^{P_{c(n)}(N)}$. Distributed array programming naturally supports these distributions. The coding required to coordinate the index bookkeeping in a hybrid implementation is beyond the scope of this chapter.

One-dimensional block distributions are the starting point of most parallel linear algebra algorithms. Typically, simpler one-dimensional block algorithms are implemented first and improved upon if additional performance is required. This chapter illustrates both coding and algorithmic approaches for implementing efficient one-dimensional block parallel algorithms by overlapping computation and communication. In addition, the technique of critical path analysis is introduced to show how the parallel performance of complex algorithms can be assessed.

## 11.1  Getting started

To run the program, start MATLAB and go to the Examples/HPL directory (i.e., type `cd Examples/HPL`). Edit the file `pHPL.m` and set `PARALLEL=0`. At the prompt, type

    pHPL

Because HPL is a benchmark, it will produce a large volume of performance data similar to

```
Np                                      = 1
Pid                                     = 0
Distributed matrix size                 = 5000^2 words
Distributed matrix size (bytes)         = 200000000
Local matrix size (bytes)               = 200000000
Allocation Time (sec)                   = 1.8742
Launch Time (sec)                       = 0.002242
0
Run time (sec)                          = 58.3743
Performance (Gigaflops)                 = 1.4282
Verification Passed
```

The above information can be broken up into five categories. First are the program parameters that list $N_P$, $P_{ID}$, the size of the problem $N$, the total number of bytes required, and the bytes required on each $P_{ID}$. The second category contains the array allocation times and launch times, which describe how long it takes before the program starts running. The third category is the run time iteration, which counts from 0 to $N_P - 1$. In the case of $N_P = 1$, only 0 is shown. The fourth category is execution time and the performance in gigaflops. The fourth category is the validation status. These outputs will be discussed further in the Test subsection. For now, edit the file pHPL.m and set PARALLEL=1 (to turn on the parallel parts of the code) and VALIDATE = 0 (to shorten the execution time). Run pHPL again using each of the following commands:

```
eval(pRUN('pHPL',1,{}))
eval(pRUN('pHPL',2,{}))
eval(pRUN('pHPL',4,{}))
```

These commands run the HPL program with $N_P = 1$, 2, and 4. Running on a parallel computer will produce performance values that look similar to Table 11.1 (see Test subsection). These results will be reviewed later in the Test subsection.

**Important Note**: The last argument to the pRUN command determines which parallel computer the program will be run on. You may need to obtain the proper setting from your system administrator; see the book website (http://www.siam.org/KepnerBook) for details. Setting the last argument to {} runs multiple copies of the program on your local machine and may result in different performance values from those shown in Table 11.1.

## 11.2   Parallel design

The core of the HPL benchmark consists of performing an LU factorization on a double precision random matrix. A simple three-line LU algorithm is as follows [Demmel 2001]:

> **for** $i = 1 : N - 1$
> > **do**
> > > $\mathbf{A}(i+1 : N, i) = \mathbf{A}(i+1 : N, i)/\mathbf{A}(i,i)$
> > > $\mathbf{A}(i+1 : N, i+1 : N) = \mathbf{A}(i+1 : N, i+1 : N)$
> > > $\quad -\mathbf{A}(i+1 : N, i) * \mathbf{A}(i, i+1 : N)$

The algorithm proceeds as follows: for each column $i$, the entries below the diagonal $\mathbf{A}(i+1 : N, i)$ are divided by the diagonal element $\mathbf{A}(i,i)$. The outer product of this column is then taken with the corresponding row $\mathbf{A}(i+1 : N, i) * \mathbf{A}(i, i+1 : N)$ and the resulting matrix is subtracted. The result of the above algorithm is to transform $\mathbf{A}$ such that its upper part holds upper triangular matrix $\mathbf{U}$ and its lower part holds the lower triangular matrix $\mathbf{L} - \mathbf{I}$, where $\mathbf{I}$ is the identity matrix.

The basic LU algorithm is simple but will tend to produce errors if the values of $\mathbf{A}(i,i)$ are close to zero. A modification of the algorithm that alleviates this problem is referred to as LU factorization with partial pivoting and is shown in Algorithm 11.1 (see caption for details).

Algorithm 11.2 shows how distributed arrays and message passing can be used together. Specifically, the distributed array $\mathbf{A}$ is used to split data across the

$P_{ID}$s. The information in $\mathbf{A}$ is also used to determine the global indices $\mathbf{i}$ owned by each $P_{ID}$ as well as the global indices of $\mathbf{i}p$ (the current columns being factored). Notationally, lines 1 and 6 use the angle bracket notation to retrieve these global indices. Recall that referencing a particular index in the local part is done in the usual way: $\mathbf{A}.loc(i,j)$. In general, the global index $\mathbf{A}(i,j)$ is a different element in the array from the local index $\mathbf{A}.loc(i,j)$. If the local part from a particular $P_{ID}$ is desired, then this can be further denoted $\mathbf{A}.loc_p$. When the global index of a particular local value is needed, this is denoted using $\mathbf{A}.loc\langle i,j\rangle$. Obviously, $i = \mathbf{A}\langle i, 1\rangle$. More generally, the following identity will hold:

$$\mathbf{A}(\mathbf{A}.loc\langle i, 1\rangle) = \mathbf{A}.loc(i, 1)$$

The minimum and maximum global indices on a particular $P_{ID}$ are thus given by $\mathbf{A}.loc_p\langle 1\rangle$ and $\mathbf{A}.loc_p\langle end\rangle$.

### Algorithm 11.1.  Serial LU.
The algorithm factors a matrix $\mathbf{A}$ into lower $\mathbf{L}$ and upper $\mathbf{U}$ triangular matrices. The algorithm uses partial pivoting and stores the pivots in the vector $\mathbf{v}$. Line 3 finds the location of the largest value in column $i$. Line 4 swaps the current row with the pivot row. Lines 5 and 6 update the matrix. Lines 7 and 8 extract the upper and lower triangular matrices from $\mathbf{A}$.

$\mathbf{L}, \mathbf{U} : \mathbb{R}^{N \times N}, \mathbf{v} : \mathbb{Z}^N = \text{SERIALLU}(\mathbf{A} : \mathbb{R}^{N \times N})$
1   **for** $i = 1 : N - 1$
2       **do**
3           $\mathbf{v}(i) = \text{ARGMAX}(|\mathbf{A}(i + 1 : N, i)|) + i - 1$
4           $\mathbf{A} = \text{SWAP}(\mathbf{A}, i, \mathbf{v}(i))$
5           $\mathbf{A}(i + 1 : N, i) = \mathbf{A}(i + 1 : N, i)/\mathbf{A}(i, i)$
6           $\mathbf{A}(i + 1 : N, i + 1 : N) = \mathbf{A}(i + 1 : N, i + 1 : N)$
                $-\mathbf{A}(i + 1 : N, i) * \mathbf{A}(i, i + 1 : N)$
7   $\mathbf{L} = \text{LOWER}(\mathbf{A}) + \mathbf{I}$
8   $\mathbf{U} = \text{UPPER}(\mathbf{A})$

The goal of HPL is to measure the ability of the computer to perform floating-point operations. Performance is measured in gigaflops and is computed via

$$\text{Gigaflops}: \quad ((2/3)N^3 + (3/)N^2)/t_{run}/10^9$$

Validation is a critical part of any benchmark program. If $\mathbf{A}$ and $\mathbf{b}$ are initialized to random values, then a number of tests can be performed to determine if the correct answer has been computed. First, the residuals are computed

$$\mathbf{r} = \mathbf{b} - \mathbf{A}\mathbf{x}$$

and the infinity norm is taken $r_\infty = \|\mathbf{r}\|_\infty$. In addition, the following additional norms are computed:

$$r_1 = \frac{r_\infty}{\epsilon \|\mathbf{r}\|_1 N}$$
$$r_2 = \frac{r_\infty}{\epsilon \|\mathbf{r}\|_1 \|\mathbf{x}\|_1}$$
$$r_3 = \frac{r_\infty}{\epsilon \|\mathbf{r}\|_\infty \|\mathbf{x}\|_\infty}$$

where $\epsilon$ is the machine precision. The verification passes if the following inequality holds:

$$\max(r_1, r_2, r_3) < 16$$

Serial HPL and LU are simple to define and are representative of a wide variety of linear algebra operations. Parallel HPL and parallel LU are more complex and provide an opportunity to show how a hybrid programming model can be used to implement parallel linear algebraic operations.

### 11.2.1   Parallel LU

LU factorization captures important features of many linear algebra operations. Specifically, the algorithm works from the first to the last column, performing operations whereby the results of the next column depend upon the results of the previous column. This process poses certain difficulties in making a parallel algorithm, in particular, how to keep all the $P_{ID}$s busy when at any given time one column is being worked on.

The HPL benchmark is normally run on a scaled problem such that $N^2 \propto N_P$. The first step in making a parallel LU is to distribute the matrix $\mathbf{A}$ so that it can fit in the memory of the system. Typically, $\mathbf{A}$ is distributed so that each $P_{ID}$ has a block of columns. This distribution is denoted $\mathbf{A} : \mathbb{R}^{N \times P(N)}$.

The parallel LU algorithm proceeds by iterating from $p = 0$ to $p = N_P - 1$. When $p = P_{ID}$, that $P_{ID}$ performs serial LU on its $\mathbf{A}.loc$ and returns a local $\mathbf{L}_p$, $\mathbf{U}_p$ and pivots $\mathbf{v}_p$. $\mathbf{L}_p$ and $\mathbf{v}_p$ are then broadcast to all the $P_{ID}$s higher than $p$ for them to apply to their $\mathbf{A}.loc$. This algorithm is shown in Algorithm 11.2 (see caption for details). Because the communication between the $P_{ID}$s changes as the algorithm progresses, a hybrid distributed array and message passing approach is one effective model for programming this benchmark. The hybrid approach uses a distributed array to distribute $\mathbf{A}$ combined with message passing to send the results of the local LU to the different $P_{ID}$s.

**Algorithm 11.2. Parallel LU.**
The algorithm factors a column distributed matrix **A** into lower **L** and
upper **U** triangular matrices. Lines 1 and 2 compute the global column
indices of **A**.*loc*. Line 3 initializes the pivot vector **v**. Line 4 loops over
a block of columns. Lines 6 and 7 compute the global column indices
of **A**.*loc$_p$*. Line 8 initializes the message tags. Lines 9–16 compute the
LU factors on **A**.*loc* and send these to the other $P_{ID}$s. Lines 17 and 18
receive the messages from sent $P_{ID}$. Line 19 updates the pivots. Line
20 applies the pivots. Lines 21–25 apply **L**$_p$ to **A**.*loc*. Lines 26–28 insert
the results into the distributed arrays **L** and **U**.

$\mathbf{L}, \mathbf{U} : \mathbb{R}^{N \times P(N)}, \mathbf{v} : \mathbb{Z}^N = \text{PARALLELLU}(\mathbf{A} : \mathbb{R}^{N \times P(N)})$

1   $\mathbf{i} = \mathbf{A}.loc\langle 1, 1 : end\rangle, \qquad N_{loc} = \text{SIZE}(\mathbf{i})$
2   $i^1 = \mathbf{i}(1), \qquad i^2 = \mathbf{i}(N_{loc})$
3   $\mathbf{v} = 1 : N$
4   **for** $p = 0 : N_P - 1$
5       **do**
6           $\mathbf{i}_p = \mathbf{A}.loc_p\langle 1, 1 : end\rangle \qquad N_{loc}^p = \text{SIZE}(\mathbf{i}_p)$
7           $i_p^1 = \mathbf{i}_p(1), \qquad i_p^2 = \mathbf{i}_p(N_{loc}^p)$
8           $tag_{hi} = 2 * p + 1 \mod 32, \qquad tag_{lo} = 2 * p \mod 32$
9           **if** $p = P_{ID}$
10              **do**
11                  $\mathbf{L}_p, \mathbf{U}_p, \mathbf{v}_p = \text{SERIALLU}(\mathbf{A}.loc(i_1 : N, :))$
12                  $\mathbf{v}_p = \mathbf{v}_p + i_1 - 1$
13                  $\text{SENDMSG}((p+1) : (N_P - 1), tag_{hi}, \mathbf{L}_p, \mathbf{v}_p)$
14                  $\text{SENDMSG}(0 : (p-1), tag_{lo}, \mathbf{v}_p)$
15                  $\mathbf{L}_p(1 : N_{loc}, :) = \mathbf{L}_p(1 : N_{loc}, :) + \mathbf{U}_p - \mathbf{I}$
16                  $\mathbf{A}.loc(i_1 : N, :) = \mathbf{L}_p$
17          **if** $p < P_{ID} \qquad \mathbf{L}_p, \mathbf{v}_p = \text{RECVMSG}(p, tag_{hi})$
18          **if** $p > P_{ID} \qquad \mathbf{v}_p = \text{RECVMSG}(p, tag_{lo})$
19          $\mathbf{v}(i_p^1 : N) = \mathbf{v}(\mathbf{v}_p)$
20          **if** $p \neq P_{ID} \qquad \mathbf{A}.loc(\mathbf{i}_p, :) = \mathbf{A}.loc(\mathbf{v}_p, :)$
21          **if** $p > P_{ID}$
22              **do**
23                  $\mathbf{i}_L = (N_{loc}^p + 1) : \text{SIZE}(\mathbf{L}_p, 1), \qquad \mathbf{i}_A = (i_p^2 + 1) : N$
24                  $\mathbf{A}.loc(\mathbf{i}_p, :) = \mathbf{L}_p(1 : N_{loc}^p, :) \setminus \mathbf{A}.loc(\mathbf{i}_p, :)$
25                  $\mathbf{A}.loc(\mathbf{i}_A, :) = \mathbf{A}.loc(\mathbf{i}_A, :) - \mathbf{L}_p(\mathbf{i}_L, :) * \mathbf{A}.loc(\mathbf{i}_p, :)$
26  $\mathbf{L}.loc = \text{LOWER}(\mathbf{A}.loc, -i^1)$
27  $\mathbf{L}.loc(\mathbf{i}, :) = \mathbf{L}.loc(\mathbf{i}, :) + \mathbf{I}$
28  $\mathbf{U}.loc = \text{UPPER}(\mathbf{A}.loc, 1 - i^1)$

Algorithm 11.2 shows how distributed arrays and message passing can be
used together. Specifically, the distributed array **A** is used to split data across the
$P_{ID}$s. The information in **A** is also used to determine the global indices **i** owned by
each $P_{ID}$ as well as the global indices of $\mathbf{i}_p$ (the current columns being factored).
Notationally, lines 1 and 6 use the angle bracket notation to retrieve these global

indices. Recall that referencing a particular index in the local part is done in the usual way: $\mathbf{A}.loc(i,j)$. In general, the global index $\mathbf{A}(i,j)$ is a different element in the array from the local index $\mathbf{A}.loc(i,j)$. If the local part from a particular $P_{ID}$ is desired, then this can be further denoted $\mathbf{A}.loc_p$. When the global index of a particular local value is needed, this is denoted using $\mathbf{A}.loc\langle i,j\rangle$. Obviously, $i = \mathbf{A}\langle i,1\rangle$. More generally, the following identity will hold:

$$\mathbf{A}(\mathbf{A}.loc\langle i,1\rangle) = \mathbf{A}.loc(i,1)$$

The minimum and maximum global indices on a particular $P_{ID}$ are thus given by $\mathbf{A}.loc_p\langle 1\rangle$ and $\mathbf{A}.loc_p\langle end\rangle$.

These submatrices of $\mathbf{A}$ are depicted in Figure 11.1 for $N_P = 4$ and the current value of $p = 1$. First, on $P_{ID} = p$, the submatrix $\mathbf{A}.loc(i_p^1 : N,:)$ or $\mathbf{A}(i_p^1 : N, \mathbf{i}_p)$ will be factored into $\mathbf{L}_p$ and $\mathbf{U}_p$. $\mathbf{L}_p$ and its associated pivots $\mathbf{v}_p$ are then sent to all $P_{ID} > p$, where it is then applied to local submatrix $\mathbf{A}.loc(i^1 : N,:)$ or $\mathbf{A}(i^1 : N, \mathbf{i})$.

## 11.2.2   Critical path analysis

The block parallel LU algorithm is the simplest parallel LU algorithm but can potentially suffer from a number of performance bottlenecks. Specifically, there will be a load imbalance since not all $P_{ID}$s are working all the time. In addition, there will be time associated with communication $\mathbf{L}_p$ to all $P_{ID} > p$. The parallel LU contains many steps, and analyzing the performance of all of these steps is complex. Another approach is to examine the "critical path" of the algorithm, which consists of those steps that must be completed before the next steps can proceed. The critical path of Algorithm 11.2 consists of lines 11, 13, 24, and 25 executing on $P_{ID} = p$. If these lines complete, the algorithm is finished (see Figure 11.2). The other lines are important but are not on the critical path, and the time of execution of these lines will not delay other $P_{ID}$s from getting their work done.

To begin the analysis, the computation time for an ideal $N \times N$ LU factorization on $N_P$ processors is approximated as

$$T_{comp} = \frac{2}{3}N^3 t_{comp}/N_P$$

where $t_{comp}$ is the time to execute a single operation. Let the problem size scale with the $N_P$ by setting $N = rN_P$. Typically, $r$ will be constrained so that $r^2 N_P = c$, resulting in $\mathbf{A}.loc : \mathbb{R}^{N \times r}$, which has fixed total memory $c$ per $P_{ID}$. The computation time is then

$$T_{comp} = \frac{2}{3}N_P^2 r^3 t_{comp}$$

Now consider the time to perform a parallel LU factorization using a one-dimensional block distribution. The algorithm consists of $p = 0, \ldots, N_P - 1$ steps, and at each step, three operations must be completed before the next step can begin. First, a local LU factorization of an $(N - pr) \times r$ submatrix is performed on $P_{ID} = p$ with a computation time of

$$\left(N_p - p - \frac{5}{3}\right) r^3 t_{comp}$$

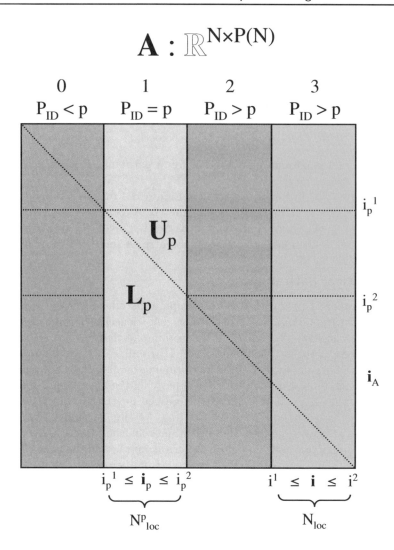

**Figure 11.1. Parallel LU design.**
Submatrices used in the parallel LU algorithm for $N_P = 4$. The algorithm is run from $p = 0$ to $p = 3$. Submatrices are shown at the stage when $p = 1$. $\mathbf{i}_p$ represents the global indices for $P_{ID} = p$. $\mathbf{i}$ represents the global indices for $P_{ID} \neq p$ and is shown for $P_{ID} = 3$.

Second, the result of this local LU factorization is broadcast to $P_{ID} > p$. However, only the communication from $P_{ID} = p$ to $P_{ID} = p + 1$ is on the critical path, with a communication time of

$$(N_P - p)r^2 t_{comm}$$

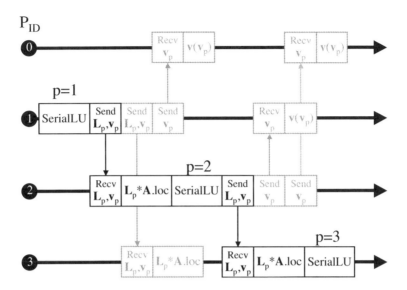

**Figure 11.2. Parallel LU critical path.**
Parallel LU algorithm for $N_P = 4$ starting with $p = 1$ and going to
$p = 3$. Steps on the critical path are shown in black. Steps not on the
critical path are shown in gray.

where $t_{comm}$ is the average time to send an 8-byte data element between two $P_{IDS}$
(assuming large messages). The third and final step is to apply the local LU factorization to the local part of the matrix stored on the processor using a lower triangle
update and a matrix-matrix multiply operation

$$r^3 t_{comp}(1 + N_P - p)$$

From this point forward, the formulas for the first and third steps are combined
since they differ only by a constant.

Summing the above steps from $p = 0$ to $p = N_P - 1$ yields the total time
required to compute the local LU factors, the lower triangle update, and the matrix
multiplies

$$2r^3 t_{comp} \sum_{p=0}^{N_P-1} \left( N_p - p - \frac{1}{3} \right)$$

$$= 2r^3 t_{comp} \sum_{p'=1}^{N_P} \left( p' - \frac{1}{3} \right)$$

$$= \frac{1}{3} N_P^2 r^3 t_{comp}(3 + N_P^{-1})$$

Similarly, the communication time is given by

$$r^2 t_{comm} \sum_{p=0}^{N_P-1} (N_P - p)$$

$$= r^2 t_{comm} \sum_{p'=1}^{N_P} p'$$

$$= \frac{1}{2} r^2 t_{comm} N_P^2 (1 + N_P^{-1})$$

Combining the computation and communication terms gives

$$N_P^2 r^3 \left[ t_{comp} \frac{1}{3}(3 + N_P^{-1}) + t_{comm} \frac{1}{2r}(1 + N_P^{-1}) \right]$$

Dividing the above time estimate by the ideal speedup gives the relative time of the one-dimensional parallel LU algorithm to the ideal case

$$\frac{1}{2}(3 + N_P^{-1}) + \frac{3}{4r} \frac{t_{comm}}{t_{comp}} (1 + N_P^{-1})$$

Consider the case where $10 < N_P < 1000$: then the $N_P^{-1}$ terms become small. For many parallel computing systems, the communication-to-computation ratio is typically $100 < t_{comm}/t_{comm} < 1000$ and $r = \sqrt{(c/N_P)} > 1000$ for a typical memory per node $c > 10^9$. Therefore, the second communication term will typically be $< 0.1$ and the overall performance relative to the ideal case is $\approx 1.5$. In many circumstances, this performance reduction is an acceptable trade for an algorithm that is simpler to implement.

## 11.3   Code

The next step is to write the HPL program. The implementation consists of two main parts. First is the control part of the code that sets the parameters, initializes **A** and **b**, executes the parallel LU, and then uses the result to solve for **x**. Second is the parallel LU algorithm, which is shown in Code Listing 11.1 (see `Examples/HPL/pLUfactor.m` for a complete listing). Keep in mind that this same code is run by every MATLAB instance. The only difference between these instances is that each has a unique $P_{ID}$ (i.e., `Pid`) that is used to determine which parts of a distributed array belong to each MATLAB instance (i.e., **A**.*loc*). In the parallel LU program,

   **Line 1** declares the function inputs and outputs. This function will work on either distributed or nondistributed square matrices. The maps of the output **L** and **U** will be the same as the input **A**. If **A** is distributed, only the one-dimensional block distribution is supported **A** : $\mathbb{R}^{N \times P(N)}$.

   **Lines 2–4** extract the local part of **A** and get the relevant sizes.

**Line 5** returns the global indices of **A** owned by each **P$_{\text{ID}}$**.

**Line 6** returns the global index ranges for all the $P_{ID}$s. This information is used to compute the global indices at each iteration $p$.

**Lines 9–10** compute the global indices owned by $P_{ID} = p$.

**Lines 11–12** set the message tags that $P_{ID} = p$ will use to send data to the other $P_{ID}$s.

**Lines 13–20** are executed only on $P_{ID} = p$. These lines perform an LU factor on **A**.*loc* and send the resulting **L**$_p$ and **v**$_p$ to $P_{ID} > p$. Only **v**$_p$ is sent to $P_{ID} < p$.

**Line 22** receives **L**$_p$ and **v**$_p$. This line is executed only on $P_{ID} > p$.

**Line 24** receives **v**$_p$. This line is executed only on $P_{ID} < p$.

**Lines 26–29** update the pivots everywhere and pivot the rows of **A**.*loc* on $P_{ID} \neq p$.

**Lines 30–35** apply **L**$_p$ to **A**.*loc* for all $P_{ID} > p$.

**Lines 37–41** use **A**.*loc* to fill in **L**.*loc* and **U**.*loc*.

The code below is a good example of how the distributed array programming environment can be combined with message passing to implement a program in which different $P_{ID}$s are performing different calculations. Specifically, operations like `global_ind` and `global_block_ranges` can be very useful for determining which rows and columns of the **A** to work on at each iteration $p$.

The most complicated part of the parallel LU code is the five different sets of processors: all $P_{ID}$, $P_{ID} = p$, $P_{ID} > p$, $P_{ID} < p$, and $P_{ID} \neq p$. Each set of processors will perform a different functionality throughout the course of the algorithm. This functionality is enforced explicitly using `if` statements.

**Code Listing 11.1.  Parallel LU MATLAB program.**

```
1  function [L,U,v] = pLUfactor(A)
2    N = size(A,2);                      % A size.
3    Aloc = local(A);                    % Local A.
4    Nloc = size(Aloc,2);                % Aloc size.
5    i = global_ind(A,2);                % Local columns.
6    allJ = global_block_ranges(A,2);    % All ranges.
7    v = (1:N)';                         % Init pivots.
8    for p = 0:Np-1                      % Loop over each Pid.
9      ip = allJ(p+1,3):allJ(p+1,2);     % p columns.
10     Nlocp = length(ip);               % p Aloc size.
11     tagHigh = mod(2*p+1,32);          % Pid>p message tags.
12     tagLow = mod(2*p,32);             % Pid<p message tags.
13     if Pid == p
14       [Lp Up vp] = lu(Aloc(ip,:),'vector');   % LU factor.
15       vp = vp+ip(1)-1;                % Update pivots.
16       pHigh = (p+1):Np-1; pLow = 0:(p-1);     % Higher Pids.
17       SendMsg(pHigh,tagHigh,Lp,vp);% Send Lp, vp to Pid>p.
18       SendMsg(pLow,tagLow, vp);      % Send vp to Pid<p.
19       Lp(1:Nlocp,:)  = Lp(1:Nlocp,:)+(Up-eye(Nlocp,Nlocp));
20       Aloc(ip(1):N,:)  = Lp;         % Copy to Aloc.
21     elseif Pid > p
22       [Lp vp] = RecvMsg(p,tagHigh);% Receive Lp and vp.
23     elseif Pid < p
24       vp = RecvMsg(p,tagLow);        % Receive vp.
25     end
26     v(ip(1):N) = v(vp);              % Update pivots.
27     if not(p = Pid)
28       Aloc(ip(1):N,:)  = Aloc(vp,:); % Pivot rows.
29     end
30     if Pid > p
31       iL = (ip(1)+1):size(Lp,1);     % Lower rows of Lp.
32       iA = (ip(end)+1):N;            % Lower rows of Aloc.
33       Aloc(ip,:)  = Lp(1:Nlocp,:)\Aloc(ip,:); % Solve.
34       Aloc(iA,:)  = Aloc(iA,:)-Lp(iL,:)*Aloc(ip,:); % Update.
35     end
36   end
37   Lloc = tril(Aloc,-i(1));          % Get lower triangle.
38   Lloc(i,:)  = Lloc(i,:)+eye(Nloc,Nloc);   % Add identity.
39   L = put_local(A,Lloc);            % Put into distributed L.
40   Uloc = triu(Aloc,-(i(1)-1));      % Get upper triangle.
41   U = put_local(A,Uloc);            % Put into distributed U.
42  end
```

There are a number of properties of the map-based approach that can be observed in this code example:

- Code Impact. Converting the program from a serial to a parallel program using a hybrid approach results in a code that is significantly larger than the serial code. However, the hybrid code is significantly smaller than a pure message passing approach because all the array indexing information is provided by the distributed arrays.

- Serial code is preserved. This code will work without change in both serial and parallel.

- Modest parallel library footprint. In addition to the usual distributed array functions Np and Pid, the program uses the distributed array index functions global_ind and global_block_ranges, as well as the core message passing functions SendMsg and RecvMsg. Six parallel library functions are used in all, which is a slightly higher number than used in a pure distributed array program.

- Scalable. The code can be run on any problem size $N$ and for any values of $N_P$.

- Bounded communication. Because local variables and direct message passing are used, there is strict control of when communication takes place. In addition, the hybrid approach allows communication patterns that are far more complex than can be typically supported using only distributed arrays.

- Map dependence. A byproduct of the hybrid approach is that the code will run only using a block distributed map.

- Serial performance guarantee. Because the serial linear algebra operations are applied to local variables that are regular MATLAB numeric arrays, there is a guarantee that there is no hidden performance penalty when running these lines of code.

## 11.4  Debug

As mentioned earlier, parallel debugging brings up many challenges. The primary benefit of the map-based approach is that it lends itself to a well-defined code-debug-test process (see Table 2.2). A hybrid coding approach requires that this process be modified.

Step 1 runs the program in serial on the local machine with the matrix A constructed as an ordinary array (i.e., PARALLEL=0). This step ensures that the basic serial code is still correct. For this serial code to work, additional steps need to be taken beyond those that would be used with a pure distributed array code. First, all the array indexing functions need to provide valid results on nondistributed arrays. Second, all messaging code is written such that for $N_P = 1$ it will not be executed. In Code Listing 11.1, the variables pHigh and pLow are constructed so that they will be empty if $N_P = 1$, so their corresponding messages will not be executed.

Step 2 runs the program in serial on the local machine with A as a distributed array (i.e., PARALLEL=1) and ensures the program works properly with distributed arrays as inputs. As in step 1, the code must be written so that no messaging is invoked when $N_P = 1$.

Step 3 runs the program in parallel on the local machine. This step will detect if the parallel maps that generate A and Aloc are correct. More importantly, this step will be the first time the messaging code is exercised. Of all the steps, this is the most important since message passing can easily produce many errors. In parallel LU, the most common errors are due to managing which operations are performed on which of the five sets of processors. Implementing these multiple processor sets with if statements can easily result in the wrong code being run on the wrong processor set. Unfortunately, the only way to debug this kind of code is by looking at the output from all the $P_{ID}$s to verify that the correct code is being run.

Step 4 runs the program in parallel on the remote machine.

Step 5 runs the program in parallel on the remote machine but with a problem size of interest. Up to this point, all the testing should have been done on a small problem size. This step allows the performance on a real problem to be measured.

These steps essentially mirror those that were done during the "getting started" section, and each step tests something very specific about the parallel code. In addition to functionally debugging the program, the above process also can be used to optimize the performance of the code (see next section). The HPL benchmark uses some additional coding practices to assist with debugging beyond the above steps.

The HPL program prints the program parameters that describe the size of the problem $N$, the number of bytes required, and the number of updates performed. This step is done on every $P_{ID}$ of the program. Comparing these values by looking at the different output files from each $P_{ID}$ (i.e., MatMPI/*.out) is a powerful way to catch bugs.

HPL also displays the allocation time and launch time for every $P_{ID}$. These times describe how long it takes before the program starts running. A signal that something is wrong early in the program is these values differing significantly across $P_{ID}$s.

Because HPL is a benchmark, the performance of the execution is measured and reported in terms that relate back to the processor. If the performance values differ significantly across $P_{ID}$s, it can be an indication of a deeper problem in the program (e.g., very different array sizes being created).

Finally, the HPL program has a correctness check that ensures the program is giving the proper results. In a real application, this check is usually not possible, but more approximate checks can be performed and these are very useful. For example, often the sign of the values in an array can be checked or the sum of the values in an array can be checked. Again, displaying these from every $P_{ID}$ is useful because it can highlight errors that are dependent on the $P_{ID}$.

## 11.5  Test

As will become apparent, HPL is a good example of a program whose performance does increase with increasing $N_P$. In fact, HPL is designed to highlight the peak computational performance on a wide range of computing architectures. For these reasons, HPL is worthwhile to study. HPL illustrates a complex parallel program that can perform very well when run in parallel because of its inherently high computation-to-communication ratio. Competitive implementations of HPL all use complex two-dimensional block-cyclic distributions. In this chapter, a simpler one-dimensional block distribution was chosen because it results in a simpler parallel LU algorithm. HPL is an ideal program for exploring the trade-off between performance and code complexity.

### 11.5.1  Multicore performance

Testing a parallel program—assuming that it has been debugged and is giving the right answers—mainly involves looking at how long it took to run and seeing if it is performing as expected. Most of the performance data necessary to conduct this analysis was collected in the "getting started" section. Table 11.1 shows the multicore performance of HPL on an eight-core system.

**Table 11.1. Multicore HPL performance.**
Relative allocation time, absolute launch time, relative execution, and relative performance of the HPL benchmark using the one-dimensional block algorithm for a scaled problem size ($N^2 \propto N_P$) on an eight-core processor. All values are normalized to column 2 in which $N_P = 1$ with the distributed arrays turned off (`PARALLEL=0`). Columns 3–6 are the values with distributed arrays turned on (`PARALLEL=1`). The notation 1*8 means that $N_P = 8$, and all $P_{IDS}$ were run on the same processing node with the same shared memory.

| Multicore processors: | 1 | 1*1 | 1*2 | 1*4 | 1*8 |
|---|---|---|---|---|---|
| Relative allocation time | 1 | 1.0 | 1.33 | 1.92 | 3.13 |
| Launch time (sec) | 0 | 0 | 1.13 | 1.88 | 1.61 |
| Relative execution time | 1 | 1.0 | 1.30 | 1.83 | 2.89 |
| Relative Gigaflops | 1 | 1.0 | 2.18 | 4.41 | 7.85 |

The first test is to compare the performance of running the program using $N_P = 1$ with distributed arrays turned off (`PARALLEL=0`) and distributed arrays turned on (`PARALLEL=1`). Columns 2 and 3 in Table 11.1 provide this data. In this case, the performance differences are negligible and indicate that distributed arrays do not incur a performance penalty. If using distributed arrays with $N_P = 1$ slows things down significantly, then this must be addressed. It is very difficult to get any benefit with $N_P > 1$ if the $N_P = 1$ case is slower than the base serial code. Working only on the local parts of distributed arrays almost guarantees the performance will be the same as for the case in which distributed arrays are not being used.

Columns 3–5 of Table 11.1 show the parallel performance of the code on a multicore system. The relative allocation time rows show that allocation generally increases with increasing $N_P$ because each $P_{ID}$ is allocated the same amount of data along with some additional data structures that are held within the distributed array. Typically, allocation time will not be a large fraction of the overall computation. However, in cases in which $N_P$ is large, these overheads can become important; so, it is always good to measure allocation time and make sure it is reasonable.

The launch time row shows a generally increasing launch time with $N_P$. Ideally, it would be a constant value that is independent of $N_P$. However, depending upon the underlying launch mechanism, this time can be an increasing function of $N_P$. Typically, launch time will not be a large fraction of the overall computation, but it can easily become significant when $N_P$ is large. For example, suppose launch time was proportional to $N_P$ and each additional $P_{ID}$ added 1 second. If $N_P = 100$, then the launch time would be 100 seconds. If this is the Amdahl fraction of the program, then the program will need to run for at least $N_P^2$ seconds in order to achieve a 50x speedup over the serial case.

The most interesting rows are the relative execution time and relative gigaflops rows. Since $N^2 \propto N_P$, the execution time increases with $N_P$ even though the performance is also increasing with $N_P$. As expected, near-linear speedup is seen on HPL even using the simplified parallel LU algorithm.

## 11.5.2   Multinode performance

The results for running both the spray and tree algorithms on a multinode system are shown in Table 11.2.

### Table 11.2. Multinode HPL performance.

Relative allocation time, absolute launch time, relative execution time, and relative performance of the HPL benchmark using the one-dimensional block algorithm for a scaled problem size ($N^2 \propto N_P$) on a 16-node system. All values are normalized to column 2 in which $N_P = 1$ with the distributed arrays turned off (PARALLEL=0). Columns 3–7 are the values with distributed arrays turned on (PARALLEL=1). The notation 16*1 means that $N_P = 16$, and each $P_{ID}$ was run on a separate processing node with a separate memory.

| Multinode processors:     | 1 | 1*1 | 2*1  | 4*1  | 8*1  | 16*1 |
|---------------------------|---|-----|------|------|------|------|
| Relative allocation time  | 1 | 1.0 | 1.40 | 2.02 | 3.03 | 4.1  |
| Launch time (sec)         | 0 | 0   | 10.1 | 8.98 | 13.3 | 14.9 |
| Relative execution time   | 1 | 1.0 | 2.33 | 3.72 | 5.77 | 9.34 |
| Relative Gigaflops        | 1 | 1.0 | 1.20 | 2.14 | 3.91 | 6.83 |

The relative allocation time is similar for multicore and multinode systems. The launch time on a multinode system tends to increase with $N_P$ and shows a lot of variation. Furthermore, the launch time is much longer than in the multicore case because separate systems must be contacted over a network to start each $P_{ID}$.

The relative performance increases with $N_P$ for both multicore and multinode systems. The performance increase for the multicore is somewhat greater because the communication bandwidth between multicore processors is somewhat higher than between multinode processors. Bandwidth will most affect the performance of the parallel LU algorithm for small values of $N_P$. The critical path performance analysis of the algorithm indicates that as $N_P$ increases, bandwidth becomes less important, thus accounting for the increasing slope for the multinode performance curve (see Figure 11.3).

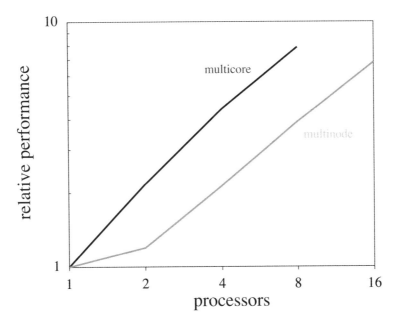

**Figure 11.3. Parallel HPL relative performance.**
Relative performance of the parallel HPL on multicore and multinode systems.

# References

[Bliss & Kepner 2007] N. Bliss and J. Kepner, pMATLAB parallel MATLAB library, Special Issue on High Productivity Programming Languages and Models, International Journal of High Performance Computing Applications, Vol. 21, No. 3, pp. 336–359, 2007.

[Demmel 2001] J. Demmel, Dense linear algebra, CS 267 Applications of Parallel Computers class notes, University of California Berkeley, 2001, available online at http://www.cs.berkeley.edu/~demmel.

[Dongarra and Luszczek 2005] J. Dongarra and P. Luszczek, Introduction to the
    HPC Challenge Benchmark Suite, Technical Report UT-CS-05-544, University
    of Tennessee, 2005.

# Appendix

# Notation for Hierarchical Parallel Multicore Algorithms

### Summary

The increasing complexity of parallel multicore processors necessitates the use of correspondingly complex parallel algorithms. These algorithms often exploit hierarchical data access patterns and pipeline execution patterns. To facilitate the discussion of these algorithms a mathematical notation based on distributed arrays is introduced. This notation extends existing distributed array notation to handle hierarchical arrays and allows algorithms to be constructed that have a high degree of data locality. In addition, pipeline constructs composed of "tasks" and "conduits" are presented.

## A.1   Introduction

Effectively using parallel multicore processors requires developing complex algorithms that maximize the locality of data and minimize communication. These algorithms often employ hierarchical descriptions of data and pipeline execution. Describing these algorithms is difficult and can be facilitated with the appropriate notation. Such notation is presented here for consideration.

Using the proposed notation it is possible to describe a wide range of parallel algorithms and data access patterns. From these algorithms it is then possible to derive the software requirements for supporting any particular class of algorithms. Many of these algorithms can be supported using existing technologies such as PVL, pMatlab, VSIPL++, pMatlabXVM, ROSA, and PVTOL. However, no one technology exists that supports all of the possible algorithms that can be represented with this notation.

A key initial step in developing a parallel algorithm is identifying sets of operations that can be done in parallel or concurrently. More specifically, concurrent operations are sets of operations that do not depend upon the order in which they are performed. Fortunately, identifying concurrency in a signal processing program is straightforward because most programs are based on arrays, which are naturally concurrent. Most operations on one or more arrays that results in a new array can be performed concurrently over all the elements in the output array. In fact, concurrency in most signal processing programs is ubiquitous; thus, writing programs that run in parallel is not difficult. The real challenge is writing parallel programs that run fast. The key step to writing these programs is identifying the concurrency in the program that will also result in a high degree of locality. Such a program is able to execute its concurrent operations with a minimal amount of data movement.

The distributed array programming model is unique among all the parallel programming models in that locality is usually addressed first by the simple act of creating a distributed array. The concurrency in the problem can then be derived from the locality, thus leading to a well-performing parallel program. In contrast, other parallel programming models usually have the programmer address the concurrency and then deal with the more difficult locality problem during implementation.

The introduction of the notation is presented in the context of a specific example. Section A.2 presents a basic serial algorithm example and a variety of data parallel algorithms. Section A.3 introduces pipeline parallel constructs.

## A.2   Data parallelism

Data parallelism involves creating a data array and having different processors execute the same code but on their "own" part of the array. This parallel execution scheme is often referred to as the Single-Program Multiple-Data (SPMD) model [Flynn 1972]. Likewise, this data handling policy is often referred to as the "owner computes" model.

The first subsection describes a simple serial 2D filtering algorithm. The second subsection introduces the basic distributed array notation that allows this algorithm to employ data parallelism. The third subsection describes a slightly more complex version of the algorithm that further blocks the data into specific chunks on the local processors. Subsection four goes a step further and describes the algorithm using a hierarchical distributed array. The final subsection combines blocking and hierarchy.

### A.2.1   Serial algorithm

The example algorithm is a basic 2D filtering algorithm commonly found in many signal processing contexts. The algorithm has two stages. The first stage filters the rows of an $N \times M$ complex valued matrix. The second stage filters the columns of the matrix. A serial description of the algorithm is given in Algorithm A.1.

**Algorithm A.1. Serial 2D filter.**
Stage 1 performs a frequency base filter of the rows of a matrix. Stage 2 performs an FFT of the rows.

$\mathbf{Y} : \mathbb{C}^{N \times M} = \text{FILTERSERIAL}(\mathbf{X} : \mathbb{C}^{N \times M})$

1  $\mathbf{c} : \mathbb{C}^M$
2  **for** $i = 1 : N$
3          **do**          ▷ Stage 1.
4                  $\mathbf{X}(i, :) = \text{IFFT}(\text{FFT}(\mathbf{X}(i, :)) \,.* \, \mathbf{c})$
5  $\mathbf{Y} = \mathbf{X}$          ▷ Copy data.
6  **for** $j = 1 : M$
7          **do**          ▷ Stage 2.
8                  $\mathbf{Y}(:, j) = \text{FFT}(\mathbf{Y}(j, :))$

The above algorithm is very similar to a wide range of useful computations. As written, stage 1 is identical to the HPEC (High Performance Embedded Computing) Challenge FDFIR (Frequency Domain Finite Impulse Response) benchmark (see http://www.ll.mit.edu/HPECchallenge). Removing the IFFT (Inverse Fast Fourier Transform) from stage 1 would transform the code into the HPC (High Performance Computing) Challenge FFT benchmark (see http://www.hpcchallenge.org). Removing both the IFFT and the multiplication by the coefficient vector $\mathbf{c}$ would result in a straightforward 2D FFT, which is widely used across many domains.

As mentioned earlier, understanding where an array lies in physical memory (its locality) is essential for achieving good performance. From a memory perspective, the physical location of the array can be depicted using a Kuck diagram (see Figure A.1).

## A.2.2   Parallel algorithm

Describing parallel algorithms requires some additional notation. In particular, the number of processors used by the computation will be given by $N_P$. When an algorithm is run in parallel, the same algorithm (or code) is run on every processor. This is referred to as the SPMD computation model [Flynn 1972]. To differentiate the $N_P$ programs, each program is assigned a unique processor ID denoted $P_{ID}$, which ranges from 0 to $N_P - 1$.

In distributed array programming, it is necessary to map the elements of an array onto a set of processors. This mapping process describes the indices of a distributed array each processor "owns." "P notation" provides a convenient shorthand for describing this mapping [Choy & Edelman 1999]. P notation takes a regular matrix and converts it into a parallel matrix by applying a map. A matrix that is mapped such that each processor has a block of rows can be denoted in this notation as

$$\mathbf{A} : \mathbb{R}^{P(N) \times N}$$

$$\mathbf{A} : \mathbb{R}^{\mathrm{N \times N}}$$

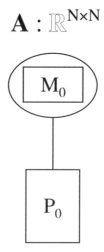

**Figure A.1. Single processor Kuck diagram.**
Kuck diagram for a serial array on a single processor system. Subscripts
denote the level of the memory hierarchy ($P_{ID}$ can be denoted with a
superscript when necessary). The figure depicts a single level proces-
sor/memory system. The (blue) box within the oval depicts that the
array $\mathbf{A}$ resides in the memory denoted by $M_0$.

The "map" in the above line is $P() \times$. Likewise, a matrix that is mapped such that
each processor has a block of columns is given by

$$\mathbf{A} : \mathbb{R}^{N \times P(N)}$$

The map in this line is $\times P()$. Decomposing along both rows and columns can be
written as

$$\mathbf{A} : \mathbb{R}^{P(N) \times P(N)} \quad \text{or} \quad \mathbf{A} : \mathbb{R}^{P(N \times N)}$$

These two maps are equivalent; in other words, $P() \times P() = P(\times)$. In this instance,
it may be also necessary to specify a processor grid (e.g., $N_P/4 \times 4$). These different
distributions are illustrated in Figure A.2.

Accessing a particular data element in a distributed array is given by the
usual subarray notation. If $\mathbf{A} : \mathbb{R}^{P(N) \times N}$, then $\mathbf{A}(i, j)$ will cause the processor that
owns the $i, j$ element of $\mathbf{A}$ to send this value to all the other processors. Similarly,
given two matrices with different mappings $\mathbf{A} : \mathbb{R}^{P(N) \times N}$ and $\mathbf{B} : \mathbb{R}^{N \times P(N)}$, the
statement

$$\mathbf{B} = \mathbf{A}$$

will cause the data to be remapped from $\mathbf{A}$ into the new mapping of $\mathbf{B}$.

Access to just the local part of a distributed array is denoted by the *.loc* ap-
pendage. For $\mathbf{A} : \mathbb{R}^{P(N) \times N}$ the local part is $\mathbf{A}.loc : \mathbb{R}^{(N/N_P) \times N}$. This notation
is very useful when specifying operations that are entirely local to each processor

block rows                    block columns         block
                                                    columns & rows

$\mathbf{A} : \mathbb{R}^{P(N) \times N}$    $\mathbf{A} : \mathbb{R}^{N \times P(N)}$    $\mathbf{A} : \mathbb{R}^{P(N \times N)}$

map              map              map
grid: 4x1        grid: 1x4        grid: 2x2

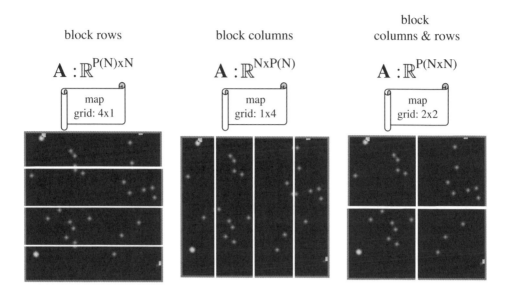

**Figure A.2. Parallel maps.**
A selection of maps that are typically supported in a distributed array
programming environment.

and require no communication. Using this notation, a simple data parallel implementation of the example 2D filtering algorithm can be written as shown in
Algorithm A.2.

**Algorithm A.2. Parallel 2D filter.**
Each stage of the application has been modified to operate only on the
data that is local to each processor.

$\mathbf{Y} : \mathbb{C}^{N \times P(M)} = \text{FILTERPARALLEL}(\mathbf{X} : \mathbb{C}^{P(N) \times M})$
1    $\mathbf{c} : \mathbb{C}^M$
2    **for** $i = 1 : \text{SIZE}(\mathbf{X}.loc, 1)$
3        **do**          $\triangleright$ Stage 1.
4            $\mathbf{X}.loc(i, :) = \text{IFFT}(\text{FFT}(\mathbf{X}.loc(i, :)) \, .* \, \mathbf{c})$
5    $\mathbf{Y} = \mathbf{X}$          $\triangleright$ Cornerturn data.
6    **for** $j = 1 : \text{SIZE}(\mathbf{Y}.loc, 2)$
7        **do**          $\triangleright$ Stage 2.
8            $\mathbf{Y}.loc(:, j) = \text{FFT}(\mathbf{Y}.loc(j, :))$

Referencing a particular index in the local part is done in the usual way: $\mathbf{A}.loc(i, j)$.
In general, the global index $\mathbf{A}(i, j)$ is a different element in the array than the local

index $\mathbf{A}.loc(i,j)$. If the local part from a particular processor is desired, then this can be further denoted $\mathbf{A}.loc_p$. Finally, it is often the case that the global index of particular local value is needed. This will be denoted using $\mathbf{A}.loc\langle i,j\rangle$. Obviously, $(i,j) = \mathbf{A}\langle i,j\rangle$. More generally, the following identity will hold:

$$\mathbf{A}(\mathbf{A}.loc\langle i,j\rangle) = \mathbf{A}.loc(i,j)$$

From a parallel memory perspective, the physical location of a distributed array can be depicted using the corresponding Kuck diagram (see Figure A.3).

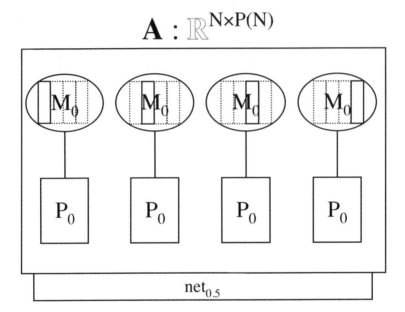

**Figure A.3. Parallel processor Kuck diagram.**
Kuck diagram for a distributed array on a parallel processor system. Subscripts denote the level of the memory hierarchy ($P_{ID}$ can be denoted with a superscript when necessary). $net_{0.5}$ denotes the network that connects the different memories at the 0th level. The dashed (blue) box within each oval depicts the entire array $\mathbf{A}$. The solid (blue) box within each oval shows the local portion of the array $\mathbf{A}.loc$ residing in the local memory of each processor.

## A.2.3  Block parallel algorithm

Implicit in the aforementioned $P()$ notation was the idea that the data is broken up into logically contiguous blocks of data. This can be stated explicitly by employing the $P_b()$ notation, which differentiates the block distribution from the cyclic distribution denoted by $P_c()$. In a cyclic distribution the data elements owned by a particular processor are given by

$$(i - 1 + P_{ID}) \mod N_P, \quad i = 1 : N$$

A generalization of this distribution is to deal out the elements in contiguous sub-blocks. This block-cyclic distribution is denoted by $P_{c(n)}()$, where $n$ is the size of the subblocks. Referencing the $k$th local subblock on a processor is denoted by $\mathbf{A}.loc.blk_k$. Cyclic distributions are often used to help with load balancing (i.e., to even out the work on multiple processors). Block-cyclic distributions are often used to optimize the performance of an algorithm for a memory hierarchy. By working on the algorithm in blocks, it is often possible to move the data into a processor, perform a number of operations on that block, and then move the data out of the processor. Using this notation, a simple block-cyclic data parallel implementation of the example 2D filtering algorithm can be written as shown in Algorithm A.3.

**Algorithm A.3. Block parallel 2D filter.**
Each stage of the application has been modified to operate on each block one at a time.

$\mathbf{Y} : \mathbb{C}^{N \times P_{c(n)}(M)} = \text{FILTERBLOCKPARALLEL}(\mathbf{X} : \mathbb{C}^{P_{c(n)}(N) \times M})$
1    $\mathbf{c} : \mathbb{C}^M$
2    **for** $k = 1 : \mathbf{X}.loc.N_{blk}$, $i = 1 : \text{SIZE}(\mathbf{X}.loc.blk_k, 1)$
3            **do**            $\triangleright$ Stage 1.
4                  $\mathbf{X}.loc.blk_k(i, :) = \text{IFFT}(\text{FFT}(\mathbf{X}.loc.blk_k(i, :)) \ . * \ \mathbf{c})$
5    $\mathbf{Y} = \mathbf{X}$            $\triangleright$ Cornerturn data.
6    **for** $k = 1 : \mathbf{Y}.loc.N_{blk}$, $k = 1 : \text{SIZE}(\mathbf{Y}.loc.blk_k, 2)$
7            **do**            $\triangleright$ Stage 2.
8                  $\mathbf{Y}.loc.blk_k(:, j) = \text{FFT}(\mathbf{Y}.loc.blk_k(:, j))$

## A.2.4    Hierarchical parallel algorithm

The previous subsections introduced notation for describing canonical "flat" distributed arrays. This notation can be used to describe any $N$-dimensional block cyclic distribution of data. Multicore processors, with their complex memory hierarchies, often require algorithms that go beyond what can be described using this notation. Consider the case where each $P_{ID}$ in the processor set $P$ is further responsible for a set of co-processors $\bar{P}$, each of which is identified with a corresponding $\bar{P}_{ID}$ that ranges from 0 to $N_{\bar{P}}$. Distributing an array across this hierarchical set of processors requires extending the notation as follows. A matrix that is mapped such that each $P_{ID}$ has a block of rows and in turn each $\bar{P}_{ID}$ has a block of rows is given by

$$\mathbf{A} : \mathbb{R}^{P(\bar{P}(N)) \times N}$$

The "map" in the above line is $P(\bar{P}())\times$. Likewise, a matrix that is mapped hierarchically in columns is is given by

$$\mathbf{A} : \mathbb{R}^{N \times P(\bar{P}(N))}$$

The map in the above expression is $\times P(\bar{P}())$. $P()$ and $\bar{P}()$ do not have to be applied to the same dimensions. A matrix that is mapped such that each $P_{ID}$ has a block of rows and in turn each $\bar{P}_{ID}$ has a block of columns within this block of rows is given by

$$\mathbf{A} : \mathbb{R}^{P(N) \times \bar{P}(N)}$$

Again, the "map" in the above expression is $P() \times \bar{P}()$.

Referencing the $\bar{p}$th local subblock on a processor is denoted by $\mathbf{A}.loc.blk_{\bar{p}}$. Operations on a hierarchical array are implicitly done with the processors at the lowest level in the hierarchy (in this case the $\bar{P}$ processors). If this requires communication into a different address space, this is implicit. The first access $\mathbf{X}.loc.loc$ will cause that data to be loaded into the memory of the $\bar{P}$ processors. This can also be made explicit in the code if so desired. Using this notation the 2D filtering algorithm can be written hierarchically as shown in Algorithm A.4.

**Algorithm A.4. Hierarchical parallel 2D filter.**
Distributes arrays over two levels of processors $P$ and $\bar{P}$.

$\mathbf{Y} : \mathbb{C}^{N \times P(\bar{P}_{c(n)}(M))} = \text{FILTERHIERPARALLEL}(\mathbf{X} : \mathbb{C}^{P(\bar{P}_{c(n)}(N)) \times M})$

1   $\mathbf{c} : \mathbb{C}^M$
2   **for** $i = 1 : \text{SIZE}(\mathbf{X}.loc.loc, 1)$
3       **do**        $\triangleright$ Stage 1.
4           $\mathbf{X}.loc.loc(i, :) = \text{IFFT}(\text{FFT}(\mathbf{X}.loc.loc(i, :)) . * \mathbf{c})$
5   $\mathbf{Y} = \mathbf{X}$        $\triangleright$ Cornerturn data.
6   **for** $j = 1 : \text{SIZE}(\mathbf{Y}.loc.loc, 2)$
7       **do**        $\triangleright$ Stage 2.
8           $\mathbf{Y}.loc.loc(:, j) = \text{FFT}(\mathbf{Y}.loc.loc(:, j))$

From a memory perspective, the physical location of a hierarchical distributed array can be depicted using the corresponding Kuck diagram (see Figure A.4).

## A.2.5   Hierarchical block parallel algorithm

Hierarchy and blocking are often combined to better manage memory hierarchy constraints. Specifically, when the $\bar{P}$ processor local memories are small and cannot hold all of $\mathbf{A}.loc.loc$, then the $\bar{P}$ can be further decomposed into blocks. This is denoted

$$\mathbf{A} : \mathbb{R}^{P(\bar{P}_{b(n)}(N)) \times N}$$

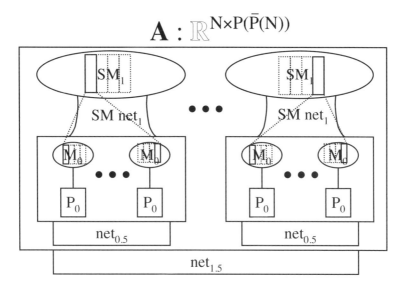

**Figure A.4. Hierarchical parallel processor Kuck diagram.**
Kuck diagram for a hierarchical distributed array on a hierarchical parallel processor system. Subscripts denote the level of the memory hierarchy ($P_{ID}$ can be denoted with a superscript when necessary). $net_{0.5}$
denotes the network that connects the different memories at level 0.
$SM$ $net_1$ denotes the network that connects the processors at level 0
with the shared memory at level 1. $net_{1.5}$ connects the memories at
level 1 together. The **A**, **A**.*loc*, and **A**.*loc.loc* are depicted with corresponding solid and dashed (blue) boxes within the oval.

The $k$th block on subprocessor $\bar{p}$ on processor $p$ is then denoted by $\mathbf{A}.loc_p.loc_{\bar{p}}.blk_k$.
This allows the data to be moved into the $\bar{P}$ memory in a block size that will
fit. Using this notation, the 2D filtering algorithm can be rewritten as shown in
Algorithm A.5.

If necessary, an array can be declared read-only via the declaration

$$\mathbf{A} : {}_{\Rightarrow}\mathbb{R}^{N \times M}$$

or write-only using

$$\mathbf{A} : \mathbb{R}^{N \times M}_{\Rightarrow}$$

The first access to a block causes the data to be loaded into $\bar{P}$ memory. Normally,
reading the next block would cause the previous block to be written back to memory.
However, if it is a read-only array, the current block will be discarded. Likewise,
if the array is write-only, accessing the next block does not read in the block but
writes out the current block.

**Algorithm A.5. Hierarchical block parallel 2D filter.**
Distributed array is further decomposed into blocks that will fit into the memory available on each $\bar{P}_{ID}$.

$\mathbf{Y} : \mathbb{C}^{N \times P(\bar{P}_{b(n)}(M))} = \text{FILTERHIERBLOCKPARALLEL}(\mathbf{X} : \mathbb{C}^{P(\bar{P}_{b(n)}(N)) \times M})$

1   $\mathbf{c} : \mathbb{C}^M$
2   **for** $k = 1 : \mathbf{X}.loc.N_{blk}$, $i = 1 : \text{SIZE}(\mathbf{X}.loc.loc, 1)$
3          **do**          ▷ Stage 1.
4                 $\mathbf{X}.loc.loc.blk_k(i,:) = \text{IFFT}(\text{FFT}(\mathbf{X}.loc.loc.blk_k(i,:)) .* \mathbf{c}$
5   $\mathbf{Y} = \mathbf{X}$          ▷ Cornerturn data.
6   **for** $k = 1 : \mathbf{Y}.loc.N_{blk}$, $j = 1 : \text{SIZE}(\mathbf{Y}.loc.loc, 2)$
7          **do**          ▷ Stage 2.
8                 $\mathbf{Y}.loc.loc.blk_k(:,j) = \text{FFT}(\mathbf{Y}..loc.loc.blk_k(:,j))$

## A.3   Pipeline parallelism

Pipeline parallelism is often used in multistage algorithms with multiple input data sets. This allows one set of processors to perform one stage of the algorithm and then send the data to the next set of processors to perform the next stage of the algorithm. Thus, at any given time the different sets of processors are working on different instances of the data. The SPMD model is generally followed within each set of processors working on a specific algorithm stage. The primary benefit of pipeline algorithms is when data movement is required between stages (e.g., a corner turn). In this situation, it can be possible to hide this communication time by overlapping computation and communication.

The first subsection describes a parallel pipeline implementation of the 2D filtering algorithm using an implicit approach by mapping arrays to different sets of processors. The second subsection introduces the concepts of "tasks" and "conduits," which explicitly support pipelining. The third subsection describes using pipelining at a finer level of granularity. Subsection four illustrates how pipeline constructs can be used to enable the generic execution of computation kernels on hierarchical distributed arrays.

### A.3.1   Implicit pipeline parallel

Parallel pipelines can be set up implicitly by creating a distributed array with a processor set

$$\mathbf{A} : \mathbb{R}^{P^{S1}(N) \times N}$$

where $S1$ is a set of $P_{ID}$. For example, to map $\mathbf{A}$ onto the first half of the processors in $P$, $S1$ would be given by $S1 = \{0, \ldots, \lfloor N_P/2 \rfloor\}$. In this case, $\mathbf{A}$ exists on all processors but stores only data on the processors in $S1$, i.e., $\mathbf{A}.loc_{p \notin S1} = \emptyset$. Using the owner computes rule, any processor that doesn't own any data in the array would skip this operation and proceed to the next statement in the algorithm.

Mapping an array onto the second half of $P$ is given by

$$\mathbf{B} : \mathbb{R}^{N \times P^{S2}(N)}$$

where $S2 = \{\lfloor N_P/2 \rfloor, \ldots, N_P\}$. In an assignment statement from one set of processors to another set of processors

$$\mathbf{B} = \mathbf{A}$$

the $S1$ processors will send their data to appropriate processors in $S2$ and then proceed. Likewise, the $S2$ processors will wait until they have received their data from $S1$ before proceeding. Using processor sets it is possible to turn the 2D filter algorithm into a parallel pipeline algorithm (see Algorithm A.6).

**Algorithm A.6. Implicit pipeline 2D filter.**
Pipelining occurs when distributed arrays are assigned to different sets of processors.

$\mathbf{Y} : \mathbb{C}^{N \times P^{S2}(M)} = \text{FILTERIMPLICITPIPE}(\mathbf{X} : \mathbb{C}^{P^{S1}(N) \times M})$

1  $\mathbf{c} : \mathbb{C}^M$
2  **for** $i = 1 : \text{SIZE}(\mathbf{X}.loc, 1)$
3      **do**          $\triangleright$ Stage 1 on processor set 1.
4          $\mathbf{X}.loc(i, :) = \text{IFFT}(\text{FFT}(\mathbf{X}.loc(i, :)) .* \mathbf{c})$
5  $\mathbf{Y} = \mathbf{X}$          $\triangleright$ Send from set 1 to set 2.
6  **for** $j = 1 : \text{SIZE}(\mathbf{Y}.loc, 2)$
7      **do**          $\triangleright$ Stage 2 on processor set 2.
8          $\mathbf{Y}.loc(:, j) = \text{FFT}(\mathbf{Y}.loc(j, :))$

## A.3.2  Task pipeline parallel

Processor sets can be used to implicitly set up simple parallel pipelines. However, there are often circumstances where far more complex pipelines are desired (e.g., round-robin processing stages, multibuffered pipelines, etc.). "Tasks" and "conduits" are introduced to specify these more complex situations. In their simplest terms, tasks are just the "boxes" in a signal flow graph, while conduits specify the "arrows." More specifically, a task creates a SPMD subprogram mapped to specific sets of processors. Within this program, all further maps are relative to the parent set of processors.

Figure A.5 illustrates the basic task and conduit notation and its implications on the program flow. A task is denoted by giving a function a superscript with a set of processors that the function is to be run on, such as $\text{TASK1}^{S1}()$, where $S1 = \{0, 1, 2, 3\}$. A conduit is created between two tasks by first designating one task as a writer to the conduit using the construct

$$\tilde{\mathbf{A}} = (\mathbf{A} \stackrel{Topic12}{\underset{n}{\Longrightarrow}} )$$

where $\mathbf{A}$ is a distributed array defining the size, type, and map of the input to the conduit, "Topic12" is the conduit identifier, $n$ denotes the number of write buffers, and $\tilde{\mathbf{A}}$ is the first available write buffer from the conduit. A conduit reader is declared using the corresponding construct

$$\tilde{\mathbf{B}} = ( \quad \overset{Topic12}{\Longrightarrow}_m \quad \mathbf{B})$$

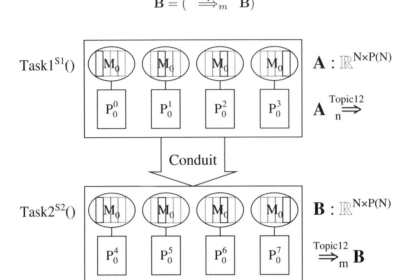

**Figure A.5. Two tasks connected by a conduit.**
Task1 is mapped over processor set $S1 = \{0, 1, 2, 3\}$ and contains a distributed array $\mathbf{A}$. Task2 is mapped over processor set $S2 = \{4, 5, 6, 7\}$ and contains a distributed array $\mathbf{B}$. The data in $\mathbf{A}$ is passed to be $\mathbf{B}$ via a conduit denoted by "Topic12."

Algorithm A.7 is the 2D filter algorithm rewritten using tasks and conduits. It is broken up into two separate functions FILTERSTAGE1 and FILTERSTAGE2. The functions are turned into tasks by running them on a specific processor set via the notation $\text{FILTERSTAGE1}^{S1}()$ and $\text{FILTERSTAGE2}^{S2}()$. Inside these functions, all mapping is done relative to these processor sets. After these functions have been called, these tasks are now outside of each other's SPMD scope. That is, neither FILTERSTAGE1 nor FILTERSTAGE2 has any knowledge of what is occurring inside the other function.

Passing data between tasks is done via the conduit construct $\Longrightarrow$. To use a conduit a task must first subscribe to the conduit "topic." A task can either write to or read from a conduit. To connect a writer and reader, a third broker process must exist that keeps track of all the topics and sets up all the detailed point-to-point data movements that are required to redistribute data. After subscribing to a conduit, a task that is writing to a conduit will "borrow" the next available write buffer from that conduit. It can then fill this buffer with data and send it to the reader. Likewise, a task that is reading from a conduit will initially receive an invalid buffer. It can then wait on this buffer until it has filled and become valid.

**Algorithm A.7. Task parallel 2D filter.**
Superscripts of processor sets indicate a function should be run on just that set of processors.

1  $\textsc{FilterStage1}^{S1}()$ $\triangleright$ Stage 1 on processor set 1.
2  $\textsc{FilterStage2}^{S2}()$ $\triangleright$ Stage 2 on processor set 2.

$\textsc{FilterStage1}()$
1  $\mathbf{X} : \mathbb{C}^{P(N) \times M})$ $\qquad$ $\mathbf{c} : \mathbb{C}^{M}$
2  $\tilde{\mathbf{X}} = (\mathbf{X} \overset{Topic12}{\underset{n}{\Longrightarrow}})$ $\triangleright$ Init conduit.
3  **for** $i = 1 : \textsc{Size}(\mathbf{X}.loc, 1)$
4  $\qquad$ **do** $\qquad$ $\triangleright$ Stage 1 on processor set 1.
5  $\qquad\qquad$ $\tilde{\mathbf{X}}.loc(i, :) = \text{IFFT}(\text{FFT}(\mathbf{X}.loc(i, :)) . * \mathbf{c})$
6  $\tilde{\mathbf{X}} \Rightarrow$ $\qquad\qquad$ $\triangleright$ Write to conduit.

$\textsc{FilterStage2}()$
1  $\mathbf{Y} : \mathbb{C}^{N \times P(M)}$
2  $\tilde{\mathbf{Y}} = (\overset{Topic12}{\underset{m}{\Longrightarrow}} \mathbf{Y})$ $\triangleright$ Init conduit.
3  $\Rightarrow \tilde{\mathbf{Y}}$ $\qquad$ $\triangleright$ Read from conduit.
4  **for** $j = 1 : \textsc{Size}(\mathbf{Y}.loc, 2)$
5  $\qquad$ **do** $\qquad$ $\triangleright$ Stage 2 on processor set 2.
6  $\qquad\qquad$ $\mathbf{Y}.loc(:, j) = \text{FFT}(\tilde{\mathbf{Y}}.loc(j, :))$

The writer side of the conduit is initialized and used as follows. In Algorithm A.7, line 2 of $\textsc{FilterStage1}$ initializes the writer side of the conduit. The conduit topic is "Topic12." The type, size, and distribution of the data to be written to the conduit is given by the distributed array $\mathbf{X}$. The number of write buffers is given by the subscript $n$ in front of $\Longrightarrow$. The first available buffer is returned in the form of the distributed array $\tilde{\mathbf{X}}$. This buffer is filled with data in line 5. Line 6 writes this buffer to the conduit and then borrows the next available write buffer.

The reader side of the conduit is initialized and used as follows. In Algorithm A.7, line 2 of $\textsc{FilterStage2}$ initializes the writer side of the conduit. The conduit topic is "Topic12." The type, size, and distribution of the data to be written to the conduit is given by the distributed array $\mathbf{Y}$. The number of write buffers is given by the subscript $m$ after $\Longrightarrow$. An invalid buffer is returned in the form of the distributed array $\tilde{\mathbf{Y}}$. This buffer is filled with data in line 3. Line 6 uses this buffer to perform the calculation.

## A.3.3    Fine-grained task pipeline parallel

Tasks and conduits are typically used to manage coarse grain parallelism, but they can also be used to manage parallelism at a finer granularity. For example, suppose in the 2D filter algorithm the first stage processes each row of data as it is read in and then immediately sends the results to the next stage. This functionality can be implemented with tasks and conduits but requires adding the concept of a replicated task (see Figure A.6). A replicated task denoted $\text{TASK1}_R^{S1}()$ creates $R$ replicas of the tasks, with each replica containing $N_{S1}/R$ processors. A conduit coming from a replicated task will round-robin the output of the conduit to the subsequent tasks.

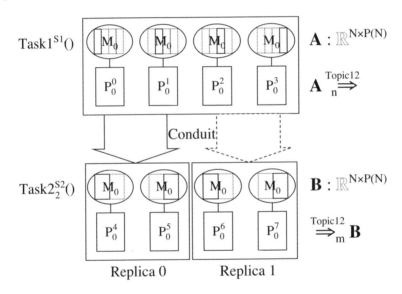

**Figure A.6. Replicated task connected by an unreplicated task.**
Task1 is mapped over processor set $S1 = \{0, 1, 2, 3\}$ and contains two replicas. Replica 0 is on processor set $\{0, 1\}$ and replica 1 is on processors set $\{2, 3\}$. Each contains the distributed array $\mathbf{A}$. Task2 is mapped over processor set $S2 = \{4, 5, 6, 7\}$ and contains a distributed array $\mathbf{B}$. The data in $\mathbf{A}$ is passed to be $\mathbf{B}$ via a conduit denoted by "Topic12." Task2 alternates between receiving data from replicas 0 and 1.

Algorithm A.8 is the 2D filter algorithm rewritten using fine-grained tasks and conduits. The functions are turned into tasks by running them on a specific processor set via the notation $\text{FILTERSTAGE1}_{N_{S1}}^{S1}()$ and $\text{FILTERSTAGE2}^{S2}()$. The first stage is run with a replication factor $N_{S1}$ such that each task replica is running on just one processor. Inside of $\text{FILTERSTAGE1}$ all the operations are performed on the vector $\mathbf{x}$. The second stage collects the output vectors of all the results into the matrix $\mathbf{Y}$ and then performs the second stage.

**Algorithm A.8. Fine-grained task parallel 2D filter.**
Tasks and conduits used to move the rows of a matrix.

1    $\text{FILTERFINE1}_{N_{S1}}^{S1}()$ $\triangleright$ Replicated Stage 1 on processor set 1.

2    $\text{FILTERFINE2}^{S2}()$ $\triangleright$ Stage 2 on processor set 2.

$\text{FILTERFINE1}()$

1    $\mathbf{x} : \mathbb{C}^M)$      $\mathbf{c} : \mathbb{C}^M$

2    $\tilde{\mathbf{x}}_0 = (\;\overset{Topic01}{\underset{m}{\Longrightarrow}}\; \mathbf{x}) \triangleright$ Init input conduit.

3    $\tilde{\mathbf{x}}_1 = (\mathbf{x} \;\overset{Topic12}{\underset{n}{\Longrightarrow}}\;\;) \triangleright$ Init output conduit.

4    $\Rightarrow \tilde{\mathbf{x}}_0$          $\triangleright$ Read from input conduit.

5    **while** $\tilde{\mathbf{x}}_0$

6        **do**        $\triangleright$ Stage 1 on processor set 1.

7           $\tilde{\mathbf{x}}_1 = \text{IFFT}(\text{FFT}(\tilde{\mathbf{x}}_0 \;.*\; \mathbf{c})$

8           $\tilde{\mathbf{x}}_1 \Rightarrow$       $\triangleright$ Write to output conduit.

$\text{FILTERFINE2}()$

1    $\mathbf{Y} : \mathbb{C}^{N \times P^{S2}(M)},$      $\mathbf{y} : \mathbb{C}^{P(M)}$

2    $\tilde{\mathbf{y}} = (\;\overset{Topic12}{\underset{m}{\Longrightarrow}}\; \mathbf{y}) \triangleright$ Init conduit.

3    **for** $i = 1 : N$

4        **do**        $\triangleright$ Stage 2 on processor set 2.

5           $\Rightarrow \tilde{\mathbf{y}}$        $\triangleright$ Read from conduit.

6           $\mathbf{Y}.loc(i,:) = \tilde{\mathbf{y}}.loc$

7    **for** $j = 1 : \text{SIZE}(\mathbf{Y}.loc, 2)$

8        **do**        $\triangleright$ Stage 2 on processor set 2.

9           $\mathbf{Y}.loc(:,j) = \text{FFT}(\tilde{\mathbf{Y}}.loc(j,:))$

## A.3.4   Generic hierarchical block parallel algorithm

Defining the exact parallel operation for every function can be tedious, especially when certain data movement patterns are common across a variety of functions. For example, a common operation is to run some "kernel" function on a hierarchical distributed array. A typical execution pattern would be to simply have every $\bar{P}_{ID}$ execute the kernel on the data that is mapped to it. Doing this implicitly was depicted in Algorithm A.5. However, it is often the case that each $\bar{P}_{ID}$ can process one block of its data at a time. In this situation it is desirable to set up conduits that stream the data into each $\bar{P}_{ID}$, process the data, and stream the data out. Algorithm A.9 illustrates this approach using the generic helper functions shown in Algorithm A.10. For a given processor architecture, the optimal way to apply this kernel function may be common for many algorithms.

**Algorithm A.9.  Generic hierarchical block parallel 2D filter.**
Helper functions are used to run specific kernels on hierarchical distributed arrays.

$\mathbf{Y} : \mathbb{C}^{N \times P(M)} = \text{FILTEREXPHIERBLOCKPARALLEL}(\mathbf{X} : \mathbb{C}^{P(\bar{P}(N)) \times M})$

1   HIERRUN(KERNEL1, $\mathbf{X}$)
2   $\mathbf{Y} = \mathbf{X}$              $\triangleright$ Cornerturn data.
3   HIERRUN(KERNEL2, $\mathbf{Y}$)


$\mathbf{X}_1 : \mathbb{C}^{n \times N)} = \text{KERNEL1}(\mathbf{X}_0 : \mathbb{C}^{n \times M})$

1   $\mathbf{c} : \mathbb{C}^M$
2   **for** $i = 1 : \text{SIZE}(\mathbf{X}_0, 1)$
3       **do**
4           $\mathbf{X}_1(i, :) = \text{IFFT}(\text{FFT}(\mathbf{X}_0(i, :)) \ .* \ \mathbf{c})$


$\mathbf{Y}_1 : \mathbb{C}^{N \times n)} = \text{KERNEL2}(\mathbf{Y}_0 : \mathbb{C}^{N \times n})$

1   **for** $j = 1 : \text{SIZE}(\mathbf{Y}_0, 2)$
2       **do**
3           $\mathbf{Y}_1(:, j) = \text{FFT}(\mathbf{Y}_0(:, j))$


The HIERRUN function uses the KERNELTASK function to launch a kernel as a set of independent tasks on $\bar{P}$. In addition, both HIERRUN and KERNELTASK set up the necessary conduits to and from the kernel to allow the data to be streamed in and out. The result is that the user need only write the high-level program and the low-level kernel functions. The data flow is derived from the map of the hierarchical distributed array and automatically performed via the helper functions.

**Algorithm A.10. Hierarchical helper functions.**
Run and task functions for composing hierarchical programs.

$\text{HIERRUN}(\text{KERNEL}, \mathbf{X})$

1  $\tilde{\mathbf{X}}_0 = (\mathbf{X}.loc.loc.blk \overset{Topic01}{\Longrightarrow} )\ \triangleright$ Init input conduit.
2  $\tilde{\mathbf{X}}_1 = ( \overset{Topic12}{\Longrightarrow} \mathbf{X}loc.loc.blk)\ \triangleright$ Init output conduit.
3  $\text{KERNELTASK}^{\bar{P}}_{N_{\bar{P}}}(\text{KERNEL}, \mathbf{X})$
4  $\Rightarrow \tilde{\mathbf{X}}_0 \qquad\qquad \triangleright$ Read from input conduit.
5  **for** $k = 1 : \mathbf{X}.loc.N_{blk}$
6     **do**
7        **for** $\bar{p} = 1 : N_{\bar{P}}$
8           **do** $\qquad \triangleright$ Stage 1.
9              $\tilde{X}_0 = \mathbf{X}.loc.loc_{\bar{p}}.blk_k$
10             $\tilde{X}_0 \Rightarrow$
11       **for** $\bar{p} = 1 : N_{\bar{P}}$
12          **do** $\qquad \triangleright$ Stage 1.
13             $\Rightarrow \tilde{X}_1$
14             $\mathbf{X}.loc.loc_{\bar{p}}.blk_k = \tilde{X}_1$

$\text{KERNELTASK}^{\bar{P}}_{N_{\bar{P}}}(\text{KERNEL}), \mathbf{X})$

1  $\tilde{\mathbf{X}}_0 = ( \overset{Topic01}{\Longrightarrow} \mathbf{X}.loc.loc.blk)\ \triangleright$ Init input conduit.
2  $\tilde{\mathbf{X}}_1 = (\mathbf{X}loc.loc.blk \overset{Topic12}{\Longrightarrow} )\ \triangleright$ Init output conduit.
3  **while** $\tilde{\mathbf{X}}_0$
4     **do**
5        $\Rightarrow \tilde{X}_0$
6        $\tilde{\mathbf{X}}_1 = Kernel(\tilde{\mathbf{X}}_0)$
7        $\tilde{X}_1 \Rightarrow$

# References

[Choy & Edelman 1999] Ron Choy and Alan Edelman, Parallel MATLAB: Doing it right, Proceedings of the IEEE (Feb. 2005) Vol. 93, No. 2, pp. 331–341.

[Flynn 1972] Michael Flynn, Some computer organizations and their effectiveness, IEEE Trans. Comput., Vol. C-21, p. 948, 1972.

# Index